A MARMAC GUIDE TO
PHILADELPHIA

By
Janet Ruth Falon

PELICAN PUBLISHING COMPANY
GRETNA 1988

Information in this guidebook is based on authoritative data available at the time of printing. Prices and hours of operation of businesses listed are subject to change without notice. Readers are asked to take this into account when consulting this guide.

Manufactured in the United States of America
Published by Pelican Publishing Company, Inc.
1101 Monroe Street, Gretna, Louisiana 70053

CONTENTS

MAPS

KEY TO LETTER CODE

E	Expensive	CH	Entrance Charge
M	Moderately Expensive	NCH	No Charge
I	Inexpensive		

The Marmac Guidebook series was created and is directed by Marge McDonald of Atlanta, Georgia. As owner of a convention and sightseeing service in Atlanta for fourteen years, she learned from visitors and those relocating to Atlanta what information was important to them. She also served as president and CEO of the Georgia Hospitality and Travel Association for four years and in 1978 was named Woman of the Year in Travel by the Travel Industry Association of America. She is president of Marmac Publishing Company.

FOREWORD

The Marmac guidebooks are designed for the traveler and new resident who seek comprehensive information in an easy-to-use format and who have a zest for the best in each city and area mentioned in this national series.

We have chosen to include only what we can recommend to you on the basis of our own research, experience, and judgment. Our inclusions are our reputation.

We first escort you into the city or area introducing you to a new or perhaps former acquaintance and we relate the history and folklore that is indigenous to this particular locale. Secondly, we assist you in *learning the ropes*—the essentials of the community, necessary matters of fact, transportation systems, lodging and restaurants, nightlife, and theater. Section three will point you toward available activities—sightseeing, museums and galleries, shopping, sports, and excursions into the heart of the city and its environs. And lastly we salute the special needs of special people—the resident, the international visitor, students and children, senior citizens, and the handicapped person.

The key area maps are placed at the opening of each book, always at your fingertips for quick reference. Subsidiary maps include a downtown street map, intown and out-of-town touring maps, and special interest maps.

The Marmac guide serves as your scout in a new territory among new people or as a new friend among local residents. We are committed to a clear, bold, graphic format from our cover design to our contents, and through every chapter of the book. We will inform, advise, and be your companion in the exciting adventure of travel in the United States.

Please write to us with your comments and suggestions at Marmac Publishing Co. Inc., 5775 Peachtree Dunwoody Road, Building E, Suite 200, Atlanta, GA 30342. We will always be glad to hear from you.

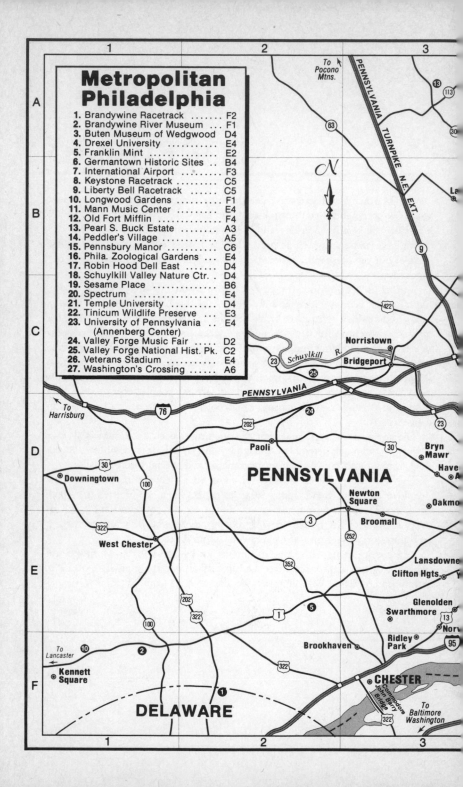

Metropolitan Philadelphia

1. Brandywine Racetrack F2
2. Brandywine River Museum ... F1
3. Buten Museum of Wedgwood D4
4. Drexel University E4
5. Franklin Mint E2
6. Germantown Historic Sites .. B4
7. International Airport F3
8. Keystone Racetrack C5
9. Liberty Bell Racetrack C5
10. Longwood Gardens F1
11. Mann Music Center E4
12. Old Fort Mifflin F4
13. Pearl S. Buck Estate A3
14. Peddler's Village A5
15. Pennsbury Manor C6
16. Phila. Zoological Gardens ... E4
17. Robin Hood Dell East D4
18. Schuylkill Valley Nature Ctr.. D4
19. Sesame Place B6
20. Spectrum E4
21. Temple University D4
22. Tinicum Wildlife Preserve ... E3
23. University of Pennsylvania .. E4
    (Annenberg Center)
24. Valley Forge Music Fair D2
25. Valley Forge National Hist. Pk. C2
26. Veterans Stadium E4
27. Washington's Crossing A6

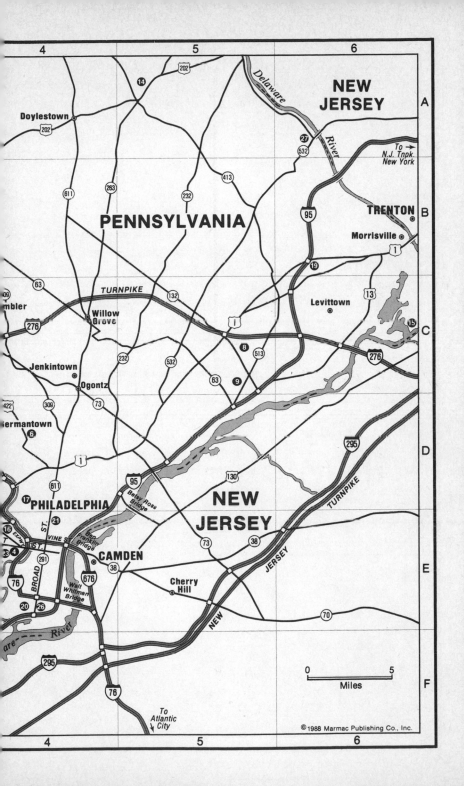

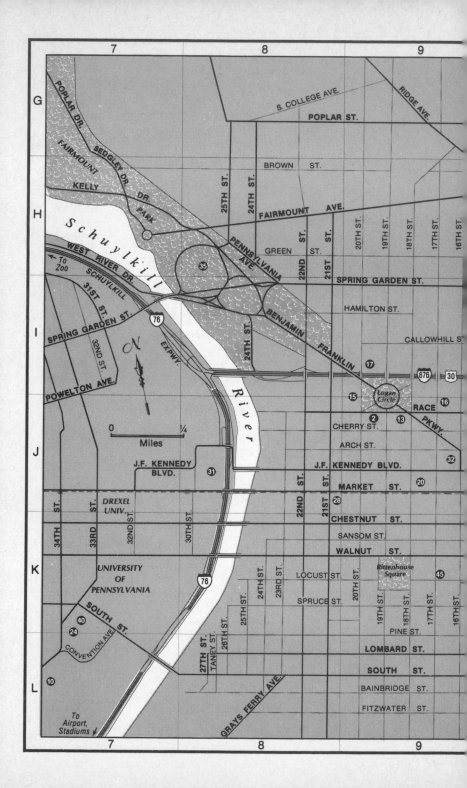

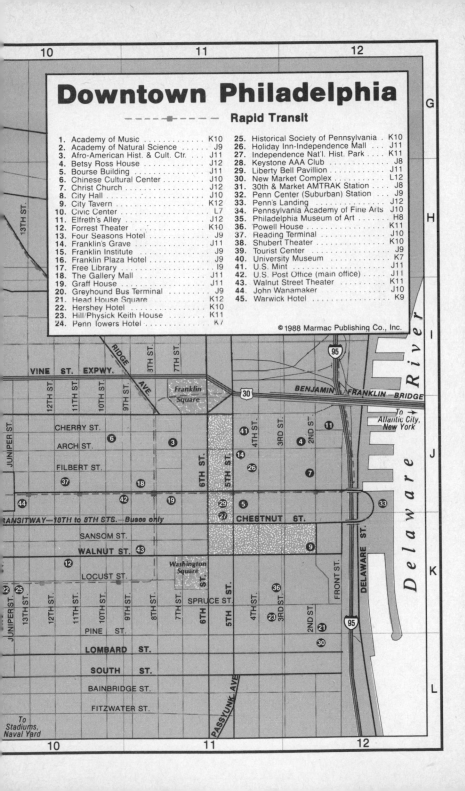

Downtown Philadelphia

Rapid Transit

1. Academy of Music K10
2. Academy of Natural Science J9
3. Afro-American Hist. & Cult. Ctr. . . . J11
4. Betsy Ross House J12
5. Bourse Building J11
6. Chinese Cultural Center J10
7. Christ Church J12
8. City Hall J10
9. City Tavern K12
10. Civic Center L7
11. Elfreth's Alley J12
12. Forrest Theater K10
13. Four Seasons Hotel J9
14. Franklin's Grave J11
15. Franklin Institute J9
16. Franklin Plaza Hotel J9
17. Free Library I9
18. The Gallery Mall J11
19. Graff House J11
20. Greyhound Bus Terminal J9
21. Head House Square K12
22. Hershey Hotel K10
23. Hill/Physick Keith House K11
24. Penn Towers Hotel K7

25. Historical Society of Pennsylvania . K10
26. Holiday Inn-Independence Mall . . . J11
27. Independence Nat'l. Hist. Park K11
28. Keystone AAA Club J8
29. Liberty Bell Pavillion J11
30. New Market Complex L12
31. 30th & Market AMTRAK Station . . . J8
32. Penn Center (Suburban) Station . . . J9
33. Penn's Landing J12
34. Pennsylvania Academy of Fine Arts J10
35. Philadelphia Museum of Art H8
36. Powell House K11
37. Reading Terminal J10
38. Shubert Theater K10
39. Tourist Center J9
40. University Museum K7
41. U.S. Mint J11
42. U.S. Post Office (main office) J11
43. Walnut Street Theater K11
44. John Wanamaker J10
45. Warwick Hotel K9

© 1988 Marmac Publishing Co., Inc.

The Liberty Bell   City of Philadelphia

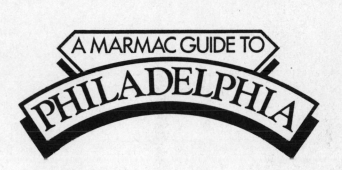

A MARMAC GUIDE TO

PHILADELPHIA

PHILADELPHIA PAST

Indian Origins

Four hundred years ago, The City of Brotherly Love was inhabited by a tribe of Indians known as the Lenni Lenape (The Original People), a trusting, sharing tribe that saw no threat in the arrival of the first British and Dutch seamen in the early 1600s. With the area's lush and game-filled forests, its rivers and streams teeming with fish, the Lenni Lenape believed that there was plenty for everyone. By 1640, they had helped the Swedish settlers establish a tiny colony along the Delaware River.

Eventually the newcomers from Europe began fighting for control of the area. The Lenni Lenape, the first Americans, were also the first casualties. Today, this Indian heritage remains in the Philadelphia area in the nomenclature of such towns and creeks as Tacony—"the empty place," Passyunk—"the level place," Wissinoming—"the place of fear," and Wissahickon—"the catfish stream."

William Penn

Before they disappeared forever, the Lenni Lenape made a lasting friendship with a man they called "the white truth-teller." He insisted upon buying land from them instead of taking it. In admiration and respect, the tribe gave this man a belt of wampum, its beads depicting a clasp of hands, one red, the other white.

The man's name was William Penn. Raised in the British aristocracy, Penn became a believer of religious freedom at an early age. In 1667 he shunned the Church of England to join the highly persecuted Society of Friends, the Quakers. He was imprisoned three times for his writing and preaching.

Fortunately, the crown owed Penn's late father a debt of some $80,000. In 1681 Penn persuaded King Charles II to repay the debt with land in the New World, and the following year he sailed across the Atlantic to breathe reality into his dream that men could co-exist in freedom and peace regardless of their religious beliefs.

A "Holy Experiment" is what Penn called his plan. It was to unfold in a city called Philadelphia, Greek for "brotherly love," and in a colony known as Pennsylvania or "Penn's woods," in memory of his father. Many of the principles that Penn wrote into his Frame of Government after his arrival in October of 1682 were the same principles that the colonists would go to war for less than a century later.

Because his beliefs had been widely publicized in Europe, Penn was followed to his "greene Countrie Towne" by thousands of people suffering from religious persecution. As a result, Philadelphia quickly became known not only as a city of religious freedom, but also as one of economic opportunity. Its location on the Delaware River made the city a hub of shipping and trade in the colonies.

The Revolutionary War

Among the many people that Philadelphia attracted was a 17-year-old printer from Boston named Benjamin Franklin. Though he arrived with little more than the shirt on his back, Franklin was soon running the colonies' most successful newspaper, and in 1731 he published his first issue of *Poor Richard's Almanac*. As a burgeoning inventor, author, and philosopher, he also became Philadelphia's top civic leader, as well as one of the colonies' most influential statesmen.

Freedom of thought and expression was so important in Philadelphia that after the British imposed unpopular trade policies and taxes in the mid-1700s, the city became the logical choice as a convention site to formalize the rights of the colonies. In July of 1774 the First Continental Congress convened in Carpenter's Hall; less than a year later, following the initial salvos of the Revolutionary War, the Second Continental Congress met in the Pennsylvania State House, now Independence Hall. It was there that the Declaration of Independence was adopted on July 4, 1776.

On that same day, more than 30,000 British troops arrived in New York Harbor and immediately began marching south. As they burned and looted their way through New Jersey in the ensuing months, George Washington, the general of the Continental Army wrote, "I tremble for Philadelphia."

A year later on September 26, 1777, the British finally captured Philadelphia with their victory at the Battle of Brandywine. A week after that, Washington tried to regain the city in a surprise attack on Germantown. After being turned back, he took his army to Valley Forge and settled in for the winter.

On February 5, 1778, France officially joined the colonists' war effort and, though the winter months had been hard ones, Washington's army emerged from Valley Forge in the spring as a unified fighting force. In June, the British pulled out of Philadelphia to avoid being trapped by the French fleet.

In July, Congress again met in Philadelphia and continued to do so until 1783. Four years later, the Constitution of the United States was signed in Independence Hall, and from 1790 to 1800 Philadelphia served as the capital of the new nation.

The Pennsylvania Dutch ——————————————

In 1793, Philadelphia was struck by a severe epidemic of yellow fever that claimed 5000 lives and drove thousands further inland. Among those forced to move were waves of Moravian Germans who settled in the rich farmland of Lancaster, Berks, York, and other interior counties. Though none were actually from the Netherlands, these people became known as the Pennsylvania Dutch because the word "Deutsch," which means "German," had been misinterpreted. Their genius for farming turned the region into a veritable garden spot, and today they still honor centuries-old habits of work and dress. Also among these settlers were the Amish and the Mennonites who still refuse to use such necessities of modern life as cars and tractors.

The City Flourishes ——————————————

Freed of British trade restrictions as a result of the successful war for independence, Philadelphia continued to grow and prosper. Coal mines flourished to the west, railroads were built, and new canals were dug. Individual fortunes were amassed in iron, shipping, machinery, and textiles.

By the late 1700s, Philadelphia had become the site of the first life insurance company, the first commercially-chartered bank, the first bank partly-owned by the government, the first stock exchange, the first mint, and the first building and loan society. Through the efforts of financier Robert Morris, who with Haym Salomon had raised huge sums of money to finance the Continental Army during the war, Philadelphia became known as "the cradle of finance."

Waves of Immigration and the Civil War ——

In the early 1800s, thousands of Irish Catholics arrived in Philadelphia, followed in mid-century by Germans and Italians. Although the first blacks were slaves, many more came later as freemen as a result of the Quakers' anti-slavery movement.

During the Civil War, Philadelphia, already one of the busiest manufacturing centers in the country, continued to flourish. The wealthy built mansions in Rittenhouse Square and along what became known as "the Main Line." In an inspired bit of foresight 20 years earlier, the city had bought many of the estates along the Schuylkill River and produced Fairmount Park, the largest city park in the world. It was there in 1876 on the 100th anniversary of the birth of the nation that the first World's Fair in the Western Hemisphere was staged.

At the turn of the century, still more Europeans flocked to Philadelphia; from 1880 to 1920, the city's population swelled from 850,000 to 1,800,000.

Turn of the Century

Not everyone in Philadelphia was making fortunes, however, for by the turn of the century slums had begun to appear in the city's core. Those who could afford to move left the city to build homes, mansions, and estates in outlying areas. A substantial part of the city's tax base left with these people, and the only major municipal project to be approved around the turn of the century was construction of the Benjamin Franklin Parkway. Over the next 40 years, many of the city's homes, buildings, streets, and historical sites lapsed into decay.

By the end of World War II, Philadelphians were appalled at the status of their once-proud city. More than 400,000 attended the Better Philadelphia Exposition in 1947, and the vast majority of those polled said that they would pay higher taxes to see the designs of the exposition reach fruition. The federal government shared their desires, declaring the Independence Hall area a national park and providing partial funds for restoration.

Urban Revitalization

A new city charter was quick to follow in 1951, along with the rise to power of Democratic party reformers Joseph S. Clark and Richardson Dilworth in City Hall. A year later, the Chinese Wall, a mass of elevated railroad tracks on Market Street that had prevented Center City redevelopment, was torn down. Replacing it was the commercial complex known as Penn Center.

Elsewhere, the old Dock Street produce markets were razed, clearing the way for the revitalization of Old Philadelphia and the construction of Society Hill Towers. Rittenhouse Square was given a facelift and a host of new shops and restaurants arose around it. With city government and private enterprises working hand-in-hand, Philadelphia embarked upon an era of restoration and new construction that lasted into the mid-1960s.

The city then began gearing up for the Bicentennial. The year 1976, however, proved to be a disappointment. The federal government provided only half the money Philadelphia had expected. The Tall Ships, a primary attraction, headed instead for New York. The summer also brought the tragedy of Legionnaires' disease. By the end of the year, 7 million tourists had visited Philadelphia when 20 million had been expected.

Century IV to the Present

Six years later, the city celebrated its 300th birthday with a year-long party called Century IV, an event which proved that more than a few lessons had been learned from the Bicentennial experience. For a fraction of the money that had been spent in 1976, Philadelphia offered, along with a host of special events, attractions that truly accented the past, present, and future of the city. Among these was the internationally-famous Flower Show featuring 300 years of gardening, an outdoor Restaurant Festival on Benjamin Franklin Parkway, and a Neighborhoods Festival in which some 50 of the city's "small towns" opened their arms to welcome thousands of visitors.

This time, not only did the Tall Ships come in splendor, but the world's mightiest ocean liner, the Queen Elizabeth II, also breezed in, having sailed the identical course that William Penn followed when he crossed the Atlantic Ocean 300 years before.

Century IV's impact on Philadelphia was by all accounts a glorious success. Urban celebration and national publicity caught onto the soaring Philadelphia spirit.

A truly restored "City of Brotherly Love," Philadelphia was the site of the nation's celebration of the U.S. Constitutional Convention's 200th anniversary during the summer of 1987. The successful celebration drew millions of visitors for parades, special exhibits, lectures, and appearances by a variety of dignitaries. "A Promise of Permanency," an interactive computer exhibit on the Constitution, continues through 1992 at the Independence National Historical Park Visitor's Center. "Born Out of Time," a multi-media sound-and-light show that illustrates Ben Franklin's many contributions to the modern world, is now a permanent exhibit at the Franklin Institute Science Museum.

PHILADELPHIA TODAY

The "greene Countrie Towne" that William Penn envisioned 300 years ago is today a vibrant, exciting, and almost undiscovered city whose heritage remains remarkably apparent as 18th-century homes play neighbor to gleaming 20th-century skyscrapers. The home of America's independence, this burgeoning metropolis and fifth largest city in the United States is composed of many individual neighborhoods and small towns, each with its own ethnic character, flavor, and traditions. The result is a city so uniquely diverse that even Philadelphia's natives have difficulty defining it.

Founded on a stretch of land between the Delaware and Schuylkill Rivers, as Philadelphia grew, so did its boundaries. As a result, many old memories of the past were spared from the wrecking crew. It is this permanence that lends such a strong feeling of nostalgia and history to Philadelphia. Society Hill, a model of urban restoration with Federal-style townhouses, cobblestone streets, Franklin lamps, and a wealth of museums, boutiques, and restaurants, is just one of the city's fascinating landmarks. The historic splendor of Independence Mall and Old City, the waterfront area of Penn's Landing, the beauty of Fairmount Park, the heritage of Germantown, and the flag-draped vistas of "America's Champs-Elysees," Benjamin Franklin Parkway, all contribute to make Philadelphia a city unlike any other.

Beyond the historic, Philadelphia offers even more through its people, their accomplishments, and their offerings. The huge Victorian train stations that workers labored to erect a century ago still stand. Freighters move silently along the Delaware, a reminder of the city's ever-busy port. Philadelphia offers the best in elegant and unusual shopping. The city is also a grab bag of ethnic culinary wonders, right down to Philly's own soft pretzels and cheese steaks. The sleek office buildings and hotels of Center City are evidence of Philadelphia's status as an international city. Beneath the grit of raucous sports crowds lie proud hearts that truly care about their hometown teams. Mario Lanza, Eddie Fisher, Frankie Avalon, Eugene Ormandy, and the late Princess Grace of Monaco have all called Philadelphia home. In addition to its world-famous Philadelphia Orchestra, Philadelphia's quiet excellence in education, medicine, art, and culture will astound you.

Separated from both New York and Washington, D.C. by short train rides, Philadelphia is also within easy reach of a revitalized Atlantic City to the east and the Pocono Mountains to the north. Visitors have always enjoyed this historic city; since the Bicentennial and the 200th birthday of the

Constitution, however, tourists and residents alike have continued in growing numbers to discover Philadelphia. There can be no greater joy in doing this than by exploring the city on foot and intermingling with its people. What one finds is a large city with a small-town friendliness, in the words of painter and native Philadelphian William Wharton, "a blend of tradition and change, immutability and progress."

Cultural and Educational Center

Without question, Philadelphia is one of the most prolific cultural and educational cities in the world. It is the site of the Walnut Street Theater, which, having presented its first play in 1809, is the oldest active theater in the nation. The magnificent Academy of Music, circa 1857, is the oldest opera house in the United States and has been home of the famed Philadelphia Orchestra since it was founded in 1900. The Benjamin Franklin Parkway has more museums than any other boulevard in the world, including the Philadelphia Museum of Art, the Rodin Museum, the Academy of Natural Sciences (founded in 1812, the oldest natural science museum in the country), and the Franklin Institute (founded in 1824, the nation's first museum of science and technology).

The Pennsylvania Academy of Fine Arts operates the nations's oldest art museum, circa 1805, while the Historical Society of Pennsylvania offers a host of paintings about the history of the state and the nation. Established by Benjamin Franklin in 1731, the Library Company of Philadelphia was the first U.S. lending library and still contains volumes that once belonged to William Penn, George Washington, and Thomas Jefferson. The Free Library has its main location on the parkway and 48 branches throughout the five-county area.

With 20 colleges and universities within its boundaries, including the University of Pennsylvania, Temple, LaSalle, Drexel, and St. Joseph's, and another 30 colleges and universities nearby, Philadelphia and its counties provide an atmosphere of intellectual stimulation, Among Philadelphia's educational "firsts" are the Pennsylvania Academy of Fine Arts, the oldest art school in the country, and the Moore College of Art which opened in 1844, the oldest art school for women in the nation.

Boom Town?

Philadelphia may well be *the* American city of the 1980s and 1990s. It has been transformed from a center of heavy manufacturing into a center for service industries, including finance, insurance, real estate, communications, management investment, and electronics. Philadelphia has always been one of the nation's foremost centers of medical training, research, and treatment, with numerous medical colleges, teaching hospitals, pharmaceutical companies, and bio-technical facilities. The city has six medical schools and over 100 general and specialized hospitals within or near its boundaries.

Revitalization of Center City ———————

Philadelphia "offers a complete range of settings, scenery, facilities, transport, prices, sports, and savvy . . . Philadelphia is the biggest rebirth of a metropolis since Toronto." At the heart of this rebirth is Center City in downtown Philadelphia, a sleek and exciting collection of shopping malls, terrific restaurants, hotels, condominiums, and office buildings. Motivated by federal aid and attractive real-estate opportunities, private developers have invested millions of dollars into this area.

Philadelphia has been the scene of a "restaurant renaissance," with over 400 new eateries opening since the early 1970s. Center City is just one of the sections in Philadelphia that has gained from this culinary explosion. Add to this the wealth of diversified shopping opportunities, as well as the number of businesses located here, and you will find that Center City is an exciting, sophisticated, and beautiful area surrounded and enhanced by the parks, ethnic neighborhoods, and historic sites of Philadelphia.

The city's revival is the product of its maturing urban renewal programs and its emergence as a regional service center. The outlook for further growth and expansion continues because land for development in the area is available at prices generally more reasonable than elsewhere in the country.

One of the most tangible signs that Philadelphia is moving into a new era is the construction of Liberty Place in Center City. After much debate, this elegant skyscraper was allowed to be built higher than the statue of William Penn atop City Hall, traditionally the "ceiling" on Philadelphia's skyscrapers. The new skyline has a very modern look.

And as the city is building "up," so is it building out, revitalizing its waterfront along the Delaware River in a manner similar to the waterfront development in Boston in the 1970s. The waterfront already bustles with marinas, new luxury apartments and tennis piers, and many more projects are in the works.

International Network ———————

With its history of international diplomacy, world trade, and cultural and educational exchange, Philadelphia ranks among the nation's leading cities in its response to both corporate and public participation in the international scene. A few years ago, local corporate and community leaders embarked on a plan to make Philadelphia a truly "international city" that would serve as a home for internationally-oriented industries and organizations, with the social, cultural, and educational atmosphere to sustain such business.

Leading Philadelphia's efforts in this endeavor are four major international organizations, all of them non-profit, and each featuring a specialized array of services.

The Council for International Visitors introduces leading foreign visitors, tour groups, and international conference participants to the economic, cultural, and academic atmosphere of Philadelphia, as well as to its historic contributions to the nation as a whole. International House of Philadelphia, a residence and cultural center, promotes international and intercultural understanding. International Business Forum, Inc. advances and increases the effectiveness of international companies in Pennsylvania, Delaware, and New Jersey. World Affairs Council of Philadelphia provides lectures, seminars, debates, and conferences on international events and issues, and assists business leaders in developing an awareness of international issues among their employees.

A Port of Prominence

When the Queen Elizabeth II sailed up the Delaware River to dock in Philadelphia during the 1982 Century IV celebration, it appeared that every boat in Pennsylvania, Delaware, and southern New Jersey had turned out to greet her, and with good reason. Since William Penn decided to place his city "where most ships may best ride," Philadelphia has become one of the largest ports for waterborne commerce in the nation.

Only 90 miles up the Delaware River from the sea, the Port of Philadelphia trades with more than 300 ports in over 100 countries and handles 76 million tons of international cargo annually. Most of this tonnage is comprised of bulk ores and petroleum products. Philadelphia is the largest oil-refining center on the east coast, along with millions of tons of steel, steel products, and chemicals.

In all, the port has nearly 300 piers, with dockworkers loading and unloading 5000 ships per year; it is this kind of activity, combined with the network of rail, air, and highway routes through the city, that makes Philadelphia the same major hub of transportation that it was during colonial times.

Philadelphia has been one of the world's leading shipbuilding centers since the Revolutionary War, and in 1982, when the aircraft carrier Saratoga was refitted on schedule, the Philadelphia Naval Yard was assured of refitting more carriers and ships.

Philadelphia and its Counties

Embracing Philadelphia County, which is the city's limits, are four more counties—Bucks, Montgomery, Delaware, and Chester—that enhance the entire Philadelphia area. Large areas of the four counties have developed into surging business centers in recent years; still, historical roots run deep, rolling hills and stands of trees grace the countryside, and the region is packed with numerous outposts of charm and interest.

A number of buildings and former homes have been restored and transformed into restaurants, as have some of the old taverns along former Conestoga wagon and stagecoach trails. Some of these taverns have been in continuous operation for 200 years. Inside is still to be found good food, drink, and when the weather is the least bit nippy outside, a crackling fireplace. Also to be found in the surrounding counties are old covered bridges (Pennsylvania leads the nation with 390 of them) and "the great stone barns" of brown, white, and green in Bucks and Chester counties.

Each county has special attractions that draw thousands of Philadelphia-area inhabitants and tourists every year. Bucks County has New Hope, a cluster of antique and craft shops where William Lathrup founded the nation's first art colony in 1900. History buffs will head for Pennsbury, the faithful reconstruction of William Penn's manor on the Delaware. Montgomery County has the Peter Wentz Farmstead, a restored colonial farmhouse used by Washington before and after the Battle of Germantown. Delaware County is the site of the Brandywine Battlefields, the Franklin Mint museum, and the nation's first fox hunt club, the Rose Tree Club. Chester County, the largest and least populated of the counties, is currently the fastest-growing county in the state; within its borders are Swiss Pines, Longwood Gardens, and Valley Forge. Chester County is also the mushroom capital of America, producing 125 million pounds of mushrooms per year. It's fox-hunting country, too, with numerous events that include the prestigious Pennsylvania Hunt Cup Race in November.

Climate and Dress

With the Atlantic Ocean to its east and the Appalachian mountains to its west, Philadelphia benefits from a moderate climate. Conditions change rapidly, and periods of extreme temperature or high humidity rarely last for more than a few days. Philadelphians enjoy four distinct and dramatic seasons, highlighted by dazzling autumns and sparkling springs. Two or three substantial snowfalls can be expected each winter. Rainfall is fairly evenly distributed, with the heaviest precipitation in fast-moving thunderstorms in late July and August. Because of fast-changing conditions, it is recommended that you dress in layers of clothing that may be adjusted according to the weather, particularly during fall and winter.

Philadelphia is as fashionable as many of its sites are old-fashioned. In the downtown business district you will find formality in dress during both working hours and in the evening. A more casual approach is in evidence in the suburban areas, particularly at night.

The City's People

Philadelphia displays its heritage not only though its historical landmarks, but also through its people. In a country as young as the United States, a city as old as Philadelphia holds a special place in the hearts of its residents, symbolizing as it does so much of the richness of background and tradition that has made this country what it is today.

This sense of the past allows a unique melding of the old with the new. Surrounded by modern business and shopping complexes, natives of this city still cling to their "hometown" ethnic neighborhoods. From these people come the wealth of food, events, and sites that bestow on Philadelphia the honor of being "one of the best kept secrets in the world."

Philadelphians may be happy to keep their marvelous city a secret, but that is no longer possible as Philadelphia claims its rights as a city as rich in the arts and academe as New York or Washington, D.C. With an enthusiasm that would have made William Penn proud, this city's natives have opened their arms to people the world over who wish to share in the special attractions that Philadelphia has to offer.

MATTERS OF FACT

AAA—Keystone Motor Club; 569-4321.

Ambulance—Graduate Hospital; 893-2000.

Area Code—215.

Babysitter—Check with your hotel's front desk.

Calendar of Events—Friday supplements to *The Philadelphia Inquirer* ("Weekend" section) and *The Philadelphia Daily News* ("Friday" section); Sunday editions of *The Philadelphia Inquirer,* and *Philadelphia Magazine.*

Climate—Annual averages
Rainfall: 41.18 inches.
Snowfall: 20.3 inches (30 inches in northwest suburbs).
Sunny days: Average 91.
Partly sunny days: Average 100.
Days above 90 degrees: Average 19.
Days below 32 degrees: Average 19.
Driest month: October.
Rainiest month: August.
Coldest month: January.
Warmest month: July.
Wind: West-southwest prevailing.

Dentist—American Dental Association; 925-6050 from 9 am–5 pm weekdays; evenings and weekends, referral tape.

Doctor—Medical Association of Philadelphia; 563-5343 from 9 am–5 pm weekdays; evenings and weekends, contact hotel doctor or visit nearest hospital (see below).

Emergency Counseling—686-4420.

Emergency Room—448-7963. (Hahnemann Medical Hospital).

Fire—911 (emergency) or 563-6700.

Hospitals—

Graduate Hospital, 19th and Lombard Sts.; 893-2000.

Hahnemann Medical Hospital, 230 N. Broad St.; 448-7000.

Hospital of the University of Pennsylvania, 3400 Spruce St.; 662-4000.

Lankenau Hospital, Lancaster and City Line Aves.; 645-2000.

Thomas Jefferson University Hospital, 11th and Walnut Sts.; 928-6000.

Law—Dial Law; 238-1131 (taped answers to common legal questions).

Lawyer—Lawyer Reference Service; 238-1701.

Legal Aid—Community Legal Services; 893-5300.

Library, Public—Central branch, Free Library of Philadelphia, Logan Sq.; 686-5322.

Liquor Laws—Legal drinking age, 21. All alcoholic beverages in Pennsylvania, except beer, sold in state-owned liquor stores; special beverage stores sell beer. Bars close at 2 am; no liquor sales until 1 pm on Sunday.

Newspapers—*The Philadelphia Inquirer, The Philadelphia Daily News,* and numerous suburban newspapers.

Pets—Humane Society of Pennsylvania; 426-6300; and The Women's SPCA of Pennsylvania; 225-4500.

Police—911 (emergency) or 231-3131.

Population—1,688,000.

Port of Philadelphia—As the No. 1 port of foreign waterborne commerce in the United States, it trades with 300 ports in 100 countries and handles 76 million tons of international cargo annually, producing $328 million in U.S. Customs receipts.

Post Office—Main Office, 30th and Market Sts.; 596-5577.

Radio Stations—

AM—

WFIL (560) Country.

WIP (610) Adult, contemporary music; Eagles football, Flyers hockey.

WVCH (740) Talk.

WDVT (900) Talk.

WPEN (950) Oldies.

WZZD (990) Talk.

KYW (1060) All news.

WCAU (1210) Talk; specials; Phillies baseball.

WHAT (1340) Black-oriented talk, music.

WPGR (1540) Oldies.

FM—

WHYY (90.9) National Public Radio; music, drama, and commentary.

WMMR (93.3) Rock music.

WYSP (94.1) Rock.

WFLN (95.7) Classical music.

WWDB (96.5) Talk.

WCAU (98.1) Top 40s music.

WUSL (98.9) Black music.

EAZY (101.1) Easy listening.

WIOQ (102.1) Rock/pop.

Senior Citizens—Senior Citizens Assistance and Referral Agency; 496-0535.

Social Services—United Way of Southeastern Pennsylvania; 665-2500.

Southeastern Pennsylvania Transportation Authority (SEPTA Bus and Rail)—6 am–1 am daily, altered service on weekends and holidays; 574-7800.

State Patrol—560-6200.

Tickets—Ticketron, 885-2515; Central City Ticket Office, 735-1350; Wanamaker's Ticket Office, 568-7100.

Time—846-1212.

Time Zone—Eastern Standard Time. Daylight Savings, April to October.

Tourist Information— Philadelphia Convention and Visitors Bureau, 1525 JFK Blvd.; 568-7255.

Traffic Laws, State—Right turn allowed on red light, except where posted otherwise.

Traveler's Aid—546-0571.

TV Stations—

Channel 3 (NBC) KYW.

Channel 6 (ABC) WPVI.

Channel 10 (CBS) WCAU.

Channel 12 (PBS) WHYY.

Channel 17 WPHL.

Channel 29 WTAF. Fox Broadcasting.

Channel 57 WGBS. Grant Broadcasting.

Weather—936-1212.

TRANSPORTATION

Philadelphia is in the heart of the busy "northeast corridor" of the United States, with Boston to the northeast, Washington to the south, and New York City only 90 miles away. The following information will help you travel to Philadelphia via air, rail, car, or bus, and enable you to move about the metropolitan area as well.

TO PHILADELPHIA

Air

Philadelphia International Airport

The airport has undergone a $200 million facelift in recent years and is the site of more than 1000 departures and arrivals daily. The Overseas Terminal is host to flights from Europe, Canada, and Mexico, and is also a departure and receiving point for connecting flights to the Orient. The airport is served by a number of commuter airlines that take passengers to and from New York, Washington, Atlantic City, and the Pocono Mountains.

Located on Route 291, Philadelphia International Airport is 8 miles southwest of Center City (or 20 minutes by cab), and is accessible from all directions by major highways.

Airlines serving Philadelphia International, including their reservations and information telephone numbers, are:

Domestic

American Airlines	365-4000	Ozark Airlines	922-7350
Braniff Airlines	800-272-6433	Pan American Airlines	800-221-1111
Continental Airlines	592-8005	Piedmont Airlines	568-3805
Delta Air Lines	928-1700	Republic Airlines	800-441-1414
Eastern Airlines	923-3500	Trans World Airlines	800-221-2000
Midway Airlines	800-621-5700	United Airlines	568-2800
Northwest Airlines	563-7501	US Air	563-8055

Commuter

Air Virginia	492-2154	Ransome Airlines	934-6360
Allegheny Commuter	800-428-4253	Republic Airlines	800-441-1414
Atlantic Air	800-243-9830	US Air	563-8055
Precision	800-451-4221	Wings Airways	800-572-1448

International

Air Jamaica	265-1001	Mexicana Airlines	800-531-7921
British Airways	492-2460	Trans World Airlines	800-221-2000
Lufthansa Airlines	800-645-3880		

Ground Service To and From the Airport

Private charters only; prices vary according to distance traveled—351-9500, 831-7656.

SEPTA (Southeastern Pennsylvania Transportation Authority) Airport Express Service; 574-7800. SEPTA runs a train between Center City and the airport, running every half hour from 6 am to midnight. Center City stops include 11th and Market Streets, Suburban Station, and 30th Street Station. Travel time is approximately 26 minutes. Price $4 (one way.)

Taxi service has improved markedly in the recent years, in both the number of cabs available and companies from which to choose. Cabs should be waiting outside your arrival terminal; the approximate fare to Center City, including tip, is between $16 and $21.

Animals—Ground Services To and From the Airport

The transportation of animals is handled by the individual airlines. However, women of the Philadelphia SPCA are at the airport daily, making sure the departure and arrival of your animal at Philadelphia International Airport is a safe one. For further information, contact the SPCA; 225-4500.

Aircraft Rental and Charter

Atlantic Aviation, at Philadelphia International Airport; 800-AJC-JETS.

Executive Jet Aviation, Columbus, Ohio; 614-239-5500.

Aero Taxi, Philadelphia International Airport; 365-6553.

C.D.S. Enterprises of Philadelphia; 566-5635.

Automobile

The Philadelphia area is embraced by a network of major highways. Principal access routes from the north and south are the New Jersey Turnpike and I-95, and from east and west, the Pennsylvania Turnpike, via the Schuylkill Expressway.

Bus

Greyhound and Trailways have a major terminal in Center City. **Greyhound,** 17th and Market Sts.; 568-4800. **Trailways;** 569-3100.

Rail

AMTRAK service is so comprehensive that some Philadelphians commute to and from jobs in New York City and various stops in-between. Many of the trains operating between Boston and Washington are Metroliners traveling in excess of 100 miles per hour, and virtually all of them stop at the 30th Street Station. Tickets are available at the 30th Street Station, at a few suburban stations in the area, and through a travel agent. Call AMTRAK; 824-1600.

Package Tours

Package tours are growing in popularity nationwide, but have always been a hot item in the Philadelphia area. They include weekends or several days at special prices, and can include hotel room, attraction tickets, meals, and chauffeured limousines. Many major hotels, especially those in Atlantic City, offer attractive packages. For further information, call **Rosenbluth Travel Service;** 563-1070.

AROUND PHILADELPHIA

Auto Rental

Rental cars are available by the day, week, or longer. Rental locations include the airport and various locations throughout the city, including major hotels. Major credit cards expedite the procedure, and be sure to have your driver's license. Prices vary greatly, so it is wise to check with various companies for rates and specials that suit your particular needs.

Auto Rentals

American International
Rent-A-Car 492-1750
Avis Rent-A-Car 492-9220
Budget Rent-A-Car. 492-3900

Dollar Rent-A-Car 492-2164
Hertz Rent-A-Car 972-0422
National Rent-A-Car. . . . 492-2750

Chauffeured Limousine Service

Ace Transportation 386-5555

Chauffeured Limousine
Service. 236-0300

Private Car

Thanks to the grid plan designed by William Penn in 1682, Philadelphia streets run north-south and east-west between the Delaware and Schuylkill Rivers. Going west from Front Street on the Delaware River, north-south streets are numbered (2nd, 3rd, 4th, etc.) except for Broad Street, which would have been 14th. Elsewhere, streets, roads, and state routes can meander and be much less predictable, so consult maps.

Major access arteries are I-95, which runs parallel to the Delaware River from northeast to southwest, and the Schuylkill Expressway, I-76, which links Center City with King of Prussia, Valley Forge, and the northwestern suburbs. During the morning and evening rush hours, however, it is wise to avoid these two routes—especially the Schuylkill, which offers only two lanes in each direction.

Linking the northwest with the northeastern portions of the metropolitan area is the Pennsylvania Turnpike, US 276. Numerous garages and lots provide ample parking for central Philadelphia. Rates are 75¢ per hour on parking meters.

In case of emergency or when in need of assistance, call:

Philadelphia Police 231-3131
Pennsylvania State Police 560-6200

Public Transportation

SEPTA, Southeastern Pennsylvania Transportation Authority, is Philadelphia's public transportation system. It operates 2500 public buses, trolleys, subways, elevated trains, and commuter trains in the region.

A $325 million Center City Commuter Terminal, running from Penn Center to a portal north of Spring Garden Street between 8th and 9th Streets, joins the six former Reading commuter rail lines with the six former Penn Central lines.

SEPTA's transit stops are indicated at mid-block or on street-corner locations. For schedules and maps of SEPTA routes, visit the Customer Service office in the underground concourse office at 15th and Market Streets, or call 574-7800. SEPTA charges $1.25 per ride on buses and subways; exact change is required. A transfer is 25¢ extra. Trans passes for SEPTA buses are $12 weekly and $45 monthly. A package of 10 tokens costs $8.50. Two downtown loop bus lines, Mid-City Loop and the Penn's Loop, make getting around Center City easier. The loop bus fare is only 60¢ and the lines operate from 7:30 am–7:50 pm weeknights, and to 10:20 pm on Fridays and Saturdays. Train schedules vary greatly, so be sure to consult SEPTA for times and schedules.

Patco High Speed Line, Port Authority Transit Corp.; 922-4600. A high-speed commuter rail line that whisks you between Philadelphia and New Jersey. It begins at 16th and Locust Streets, and stops at 13th, 10th, 9th and Locust, and 8th and Market. As it crosses the Benjamin Franklin Bridge, you'll get a magnificent view of the Delaware River.

Taxis

With 725 new operating certificates issued in the last year, more and better cab service is available in Philadelphia than ever before. Rates are $2.90 for the first mile and $1.40 per mile thereafter. Some suggested cab companies:

United	854-0750	**Quaker City**	728-8000
Yellow	922-8400	**Liberty**	365-8414
	(senior citizens, 627-5100)	**Victory**	224-9400

Tours

Several companies offer daily sightseeing tours of the city and attractions in nearby areas. Call for times and tours or check at your hotel.

Centipede, Inc.; 735-3123.
Culture Tours; 947-8991.
Gray Line Tours of Philadelphia; 569-3666.

Unique Ways to See Philadelphia

Fairmount Park Trolley Tours, Memorial Hall, Fairmount Park. Philadelphia's most popular Bicentennial feature, the Fairmount Park Trolley was custom-made to capture the flavor of the old trolley that once operated in the park. The new trolley-bus travels a scenic 90-minute loop, stopping at many cultural, historic, and recreational treasures along the way. Several special tours are offered, among them the "Town and Country Tour," which highlights the urban and country living in Old City areas, and the "Wonders of the Wissahickon Tour," featuring sections of the park that are legendary in Philadelphia. For schedules and further information, call 879-4044.

SEPTA's trolleys offers a rather refreshing experience, too. There are almost a dozen trolley lines that cover the city, and three that reach into the suburbs. For schedules and information, call 574-7800.

Carriage Rides are a delightful way to ride through historic areas of Philadelphia. Three companies are at your service. Standard pickup points are Independence Hall and Head House Squares.

Ben Franklin Carriages; 634-0545.
Philadelphia Carriage; 922-6840.
'76 Carriage; 923-8516.

To see Philadelphia the way William Penn saw it, we recommend a cruise up the Delaware River. This is available periodically. Check newspaper listings or consult Tourist Center.

Audio Walk and Tour lets you see Philadelphia's historic sites at your own pace. You rent a tour cassette, map, and tape player at the Norman Rockwell Museum at 6th and Sansom Streets. It is $8 for one person, $12 for two, and $16 for three to eight. 925-1234.

Driving Tour of Philadelphia Movie Sites takes you past locations shot in "Blow Out," "Witness," "Birdy," "Trading Places," "Mannequin," etc. Approximate driving time is two hours. Call for copy, 686-2668.

Walking ――――――――――――――――――――

The new breed of walker who enjoys a few hours seeing the city will be delighted with the compact nature of Center City Philadelphia. We recommend the daylight hours for walking and taxi service during the evening. An excellent spot to start is the **Tourist Center,** 1525 John F. Kennedy Blvd., where maps, brochures, and expert advice are available. Hours are 9 am–5 pm every day except Christmas; 636-1666. (see SELF-GUIDED CITY TOURS, The Downtown Walking Tour).

LODGING

Philadelphia has recently increased its number of hotel rooms in its goal to compete as a major convention city in the United States. With the opening of some new hotels and the elegant renovation of many others, accommodations in and near Center City have been greatly increased and enhanced. Elsewhere in the northeast, the Valley Forge area, West Philadelphia, and near the airport, lodging is equal to the demand, with hotels and motels to suit every mood, taste, and budget. In an effort to generate more tourism, Philadelphia approved a 3 percent tax on hotel room bills with the funds earmarked for promotion of the city's many attractions and historical sites. This tax also applies in Delaware and Montgomery counties.

Below we have listed hotels, motels, inns, resorts, and campgrounds that are anxious to make your visit to Philadelphia a most pleasant and enjoyable one.

The following key is used at the end of each listing.

D	Discounts offered.
FP	Family plans offered.
MAP	Modified American plan.
PA	Pets allowed.
PAC	Packages available.

We will abbreviate the following recipients:

AP	Airline personnel.
C	Clergy.
CR	Commercial rates for corporate business.
F	Faculty.
G	Government/Military.
SC	Senior citizens.
ST	Students.
TA	Travel agents.

Remember that although all lodgings have rates that will be categorized as expensive, moderate, or inexpensive, they may offer discounts or weekend specials that may reduce these rates. Some rates may fluctuate according to the season of the year. Call for information.

E	Expensive, $90 and up for a double room;
M	Moderate, $60—90 for a double room;
I	Inexpensive, less than $60 for a double room.

LODGING BY AREA

BUCKS COUNTY

Black Bass Hotel, M.
Colonial Woods Family
    Campground, I.
Holiday Inn–New Hope, M.
Logan Inn, Country Inn, M.
Tohickon Family Campground, I.
The Warrington, I.

CENTER CITY

The Barclay, E.
Comfort Inn at Penn's Landing, M.
Franklin Plaza, E.
Hershey Philadelphia Hotel, E.
Holiday Inn–Center City, E.
Holiday Inn–Independence Mall,
    E.
Holiday Inn–Midtown, M-E.
Latham Hotel, E.
Philadelphia Centre Hotel, E.
Quality Inn Chinatown Suites, M.
Warwick, E.

CENTER CITY–PARKWAY

Four Seasons Hotel, E.
The Palace, E.
The Quality Inn, I.

CHESTER COUNTY

Coventry Forge Inn, I.
Guest Quarters Hotel, M.
Hidden Acres, I.
Holiday Inn–Lionville, M.
Howard Johnson's Airport South, I.
Quality Inn Brandywine Hotel &
    Resort, M.
Tabas Hotel, M.
West Chester Inn, I-M.
West Chester KOA, I.

CITY AVENUE

Adams Mark Hotel, E.
Holiday Inn–City Line, M.

DELAWARE COUNTY

Alpine Inn Motor Lodge, I.
Fairways Inn, I.
Ramada Inn Chadds Ford, M.
St. David's Inn, E.
The Wayne Hotel, E.

LANCASTER COUNTY

All Seasons Resort, I-E.
Holiday Inn–Resort, M-E.
Howard Johnson's Lancaster-
    Reading, I-M.
Mill Bridge Village Campground, I.
Sheraton Lancaster Resort, M.
Treadway Resort Inn, M.
Willow Valley Farms Inn, M.

MONTGOMERY COUNTY

Fiesta Motor Inn, I.
George Washington Lodge, M.
Holiday Inn–Fort Washington, M.
Holiday Inn–Valley Forge, M-E.
Howard Johnson's Valley Forge, M.
Ramada Inn Fort Washington, M.
Sheraton Executive Tower, M.
Sheraton Valley Forge, E.
Stouffer's Valley Forge, E.
Valley Forge Hilton, E.

NORTHEAST PHILADELPHIA

George Washington Lodge, M.
Holiday Inn–Northeast, M.
Howard Johnson's North, I-M.
Sheraton Inn Northeast, M.
Treadway Mohawk Inn, M.
The Trevose Hilton, E.

NORTHWEST PHILADELPHIA

Chestnut Hill Hotel, M-E.

OLD CITY–SOCIETY HILL

Society Hill Hotel, M-E.

SOUTH PHILADELPHIA

Guest Quarters Hotel, M.
Holiday Inn Airport, M.
Philadelphia Airport Hilton Inn, E.
Philadelphia Marriott Hotel
    Airport, E.

Quality Inn Airport, M.
Ramada Inn Airport, M.

UNIVERSITY CITY

Penn Towers, E.
Sheraton University City, E.

HOTELS AND MOTELS

ADAM'S MARK HOTEL, City Ave. and Monument Rd., Philadelphia, PA 19131; 581-5000, 800-231-5858. *E.* Less than six years old, this sleek new hotel has brought 515 deluxe rooms to the bustling Golden Mile. Located only ten minutes from Center City and 20 minutes from Philadelphia International Airport, the Adam's Mark has a wide range of facilities for meetings, banquets, and exhibits. Its *Marker Restaurant* features excellent American and continental cuisine, and its three cocktail lounges, *Pierre's*, *Players*, and *Quincy's* are already among the more popular night spots in town. Another dining room, *Appleby's*, is priced for the entire family. Fine shopping is within walking distance. For relaxation, the hotel features two racquetball courts, indoor and outdoor swimming pools, and a health club with Nautilus exercise equipment, a whirlpool, sauna, and steam rooms. Free parking. Scheduled limousine to and from the airport. PA (small lap dogs) and PAC.

AIRPORT RAMADA INN (see Ramada listing).

ALPINE INN MOTOR LODGE, 650 Baltimore Pike, Springfield, PA 19064; 544-4700. *I.* This motel offers 140 rooms, meeting facilities, and next door at the *Alpine Inn*, a gourmet dining room with a huge salad bar and a cocktail lounge with entertainment nightly.

THE BARCLAY, 237 S. 18th St., Philadelphia, PA 19103; 545-0300. *E.* Built in 1929 on fashionable Rittenhouse Square, this has long been one of Philadelphia's most elegant hotels. Many of the city's most notable visitors stay here, and the $2 million renovation in 1981 greatly enhanced its Old World atmosphere of marble floors, Oriental rugs, and crystal chandeliers. *Le Beau Lieu* is one of the city's most opulent restaurants, and the piano bar off the lobby is a truly unique spot to enjoy a cocktail. PA (on leash) and PAC.

BLACK BASS HOTEL, Lumberville, PA 18933; 297-5770. *M.* Located on the Delaware River, this 18th-century hotel is the perfect place to really unwind. Seven rooms and suites are decorated in truly historic style, and the restaurant is known for its outstanding American dishes.

THE CHESTNUT HILL HOTEL, 822 Germantown Ave., Philadelphia, PA 19118; 242-5905. *M–E.* This stately hotel has been totally renovated and patterned after a European bed-and-breakfast spot. Its 28 rooms include three suites and five deluxe rooms, but all are beautifully decorated with early 19th-century reproduction furniture. A fine place to stay, with fine dining available in the *Chautauqua* and *J. B. Winberie*, and quaint shops nearby.

COMFORT INN AT PENN'S LANDING, 100 N. Delaware Ave., Philadelphia, PA 19106; 724-4000, 800-228-5150. M. Open since October 1987, this hotel offers 185 rooms and nine suites with in-room hot tubs. Within walking distance of 50 restaurants, there are no in-house eateries, but rates include a full continental breakfast. There's a lobby lounge, fitness room and free parking.

COVENTRY FORGE INN, Route 23, Coventryville, PA 19464; 469-6222. I. Nestled in the rolling hills of Chester County, this lovely 1717 inn offers five tastefully furnished rooms, continental breakfast on the porch, and fine French dishes in the dining room.

FAIRWAYS INN, 351 E. Township Line Rd. (Route 1), Upper Darby, PA 19082; 449-5577. I. The Inn offers a panoramic view of the golf course and a resort atmosphere with recently redecorated guest rooms. The Fairways is convenient to the Main Line, only six miles from Center City. There is also an outdoor pool. Short-term rental apartments have a two-month minimum. FP.

FIESTA MOTOR INN, Route 611, Exit 27 on the Pennsylvania Turnpike, Willow Grove, PA 19090; 659-9300. I. Fiesta has 160 rooms, the *C.S. Murphy's* restaurant and cocktail lounge, as well as a recreation room with sauna, meeting and banquet facilities, and airport limousine service. Military and commercial discounts available. D, CR.

FOUR SEASONS HOTEL, One Logan Sq., Philadelphia, PA 19103; 963-1500, 800-828-1188. E. As another of Philadelphia's newest deluxe downtown hotels, the $44 million Four Seasons is link number 19 in the award-winning Four Seasons chain. Overlooking Benjamin Franklin Parkway, it shares a 2½-acre site with a soaring office tower; between the two is a landscaped courtyard accessible from a lobby highlighted by panelled wood, marble, and a fountain. The 371 rooms are large and magnificently appointed, and offer sweeping views of Logan Square, the Art Museum, and Center City. The *Fountain Restaurant*, also, has a striking view of the Parkway, while the adjacent *Swann Lounge* offers more casual dining and nightly entertainment. Five "boardrooms," one on each of the five guest-room floors, are especially designed for business meetings. The health club features a swimming pool, whirlpool, saunas, and massage rooms. D, FP (18 and under).

FRANKLIN PLAZA, 17th and Race Sts., Philadelphia, PA 19103; 448-2000, 800-828-7447. E. With its initial venture in the U.S., the Canadian Pacific chain spearheaded new hotel construction in Philadelphia and has scored handsomely with the Franklin Plaza. Now owned by Wyndham Hotels

*The Fountain Restaurant at
the Four Seasons Hotel*

The Four Seasons Hotel

and conveniently located near the city's business, cultural, and historical activity, it offers a near-resort atmosphere of beauty, fine restaurants and lounges, 800 luxuriously appointed rooms, and full banquet and meeting facilities. *Between Friends* features French tableside service, while *The Terrace* is a lovely spot to dine just off an airy lobby beneath a 70-foot glass roof. *Clark's Uptown*, the health club, is one of the city's finest, with an indoor swimming pool, racquetball and squash courts, outdoor handball courts, and an outdoor tennis court surrounded by a jogging track. FP (14 and under), PA, PAC.

GEORGE WASHINGTON LODGE. There are four of these lodges, each located near various points of interest in the Philadelphia suburbs. Discounts and Family Plan are standard in all.

George Washington Lodge, Route 202, King of Prussia, PA 19406; 265-6100. M. With convenient access to Valley Forge National Historic Park and the huge King of Prussia Mall, this lodge has 335 rooms, free parking, indoor and outdoor pools, and lots of dining and socializing next door at *Sportster's*.

George Washington Lodge, Route 422 and Plymouth Rd., Norristown, PA 19462; 825-1980. M. This 215-room facility has an outdoor pool, a restaurant and lounge, and convenient access to Plymouth Meeting Mall.

George Washington Lodge, Route 1 and Exit 28 on the Pennsylvania Turnpike, Trevose, PA 19020; 357-9100. M. The 161 rooms have been renovated with convenient access to Keystone and Liberty Bell Race Tracks and Sesame Place. Also, an indoor-outdoor pool, ballroom, and meeting facilities.

George Washington Lodge, Route 611, Willow Grove, PA 19090; 659-7200. M. Expect convenient shopping at Willow Grove Mall. Also, convention and banquet services in this 230-room hotel.

GUEST QUARTERS HOTEL, 888 Chesterbrook Blvd., Wayne, PA 19087; 647-6700. M. Located near the booming Great Valley Corporate Center, this 230-suite hotel features *The Grill at Chesterbrook* restaurant and the *Atrium Lounge*. There's an indoor pool and exercise room, too.

GUEST QUARTERS HOTEL, 1 Gateway Center, 4101 Island Ave., Philadelphia, PA 19153; 365-6600. M. This hotel features 251 suites, conveniently located near the Philadelphia airport. There's the *Atrium Cafe and Lounge*, an indoor pool, fitness club, and meeting space.

HERSHEY PHILADELPHIA HOTEL, Broad and Locust Sts., Philadelphia, PA 19107; 893-1600, 800-533-3131. E. Built in 1982 at a cost of $45 million, the 25-story Hershey is the first hotel to rise in the midst of Philadelphia's central business district in 35 years. The four-story atrium lobby, a tasteful montage of burgundy and emerald accented by dozens of green plants is the entranceway to 431 spacious rooms and suites, all with the most modern conveniences. The *Main Line Club* on the top floor offers select luxurious accommodations, private check-in, concierge, and a VIP lounge. The

Cafe Academie has light food from breakfast through late-night snacks with a beautiful view of the Academy of Music, while elegant lunches and dinners are served in the art deco atmosphere of *Sarah's*. The *Bar*, which features live entertainment, is one of three tastefully appointed lounges. Led by the huge Ormandy Ballroom, the Hershey offers the full range of meeting and banquet facilities, while its health club includes an indoor pool, sauna, racquetball courts, game room, tanning salon, and an outdoor jogging track and sundeck. D, FP, and PAC.

HILTON HOTELS.

Philadelphia Airport Hilton Inn, 10th St. and Packer Ave., Philadelphia, PA 19148; 755-9500. *E.* Located almost adjacent to Veterans Stadium and the Spectrum, this Hilton offers 238 rooms, meeting and banquet facilities, and free parking. Its *Cahoots* lounge is a popular spot, especially following sports events, and the *Cinnamons Restaurant* has a leisurely atmosphere for breakfast, lunch, and dinner. D (M, G, TA, CR, AP), FP, PA.

The Trevose Hilton, 2400 Old Lincoln Hwy., Trevose, PA 19047; 638-8300. *E.* Ideally located near the variety of things to do in Bucks County, this hotel has 300 rooms, *The Atrium*, *The Seasons*, and *Rumors Lounge*. A health club and outdoor pools are also available. The nearby Neshaminy and Oxford Valley malls feature more than 200 stores and shops. D (G, TA, AP), PAC.

Valley Forge Hilton, 251 W. DeKalb Pike, King of Prussia, PA 19406; 337-1200. *E.* Here you will find luxurious surroundings and 347 rooms near Valley Forge National Historic Park, the Valley Forge Music Fair, the King of Prussia shopping mall, and Chester County. Its three fine restaurants are the *Kobe Steak House* (Japanese hibachi cooking), *Alexander Cafe & Lounge* (glass-enclosed on a poolside patio), and the *Rain Forest*. Its lounge, *Touché*, features live entertainment nightly. D, CR and PAC.

HOLIDAY INN. The star shines throughout the Philadelphia area as a symbol of fine accommodations, food and relaxation facilities. Most offer the same range of services and amenities. Call toll-free 800-238-8000.

Holiday Inn-Airport, 45 Industrial Hwy., Essington, PA 19029; 521-2400. *M.* Offers 307 rooms, restaurant, swimming pool, free parking, free airport transportation, and meeting and banquet facilities. D (GR), FP, PA, and PAC.

Holiday Inn-Center City, 18th and Market Sts., Philadelphia, PA 19103; 561-7500. *E.* Completely refurbished from top to bottom, here you will find 449 rooms in the heart of Philadelphia's business and shopping activity. There's also a pool and two restaurants, the newest of which, *Reflections*, offers energetic nightly entertainment. Full banquet and meeting services are available. D, FP, PAC.

Holiday Inn-City Line, City Ave. at the Schuylkill Expressway, Philadelphia, PA 19131; 477-0200, 800-HOLIDAY. *M.* This modern high-rise hotel on the Golden Mile has 350 rooms and one restaurant on the premises. *The Glass Tree* offers American family-style dining and buffet-style breakfast seven days a week. There is also a cocktail lounge, *Remy's*, meeting and banquet facilities, a glass-domed, solar-heated swimming pool, and whirlpool. Fine shopping is within walking distance. Free parking. D (G, CR) FP, PA, PAC (long-term).

Holiday Inn-Independence Mall, 4th and Arch Sts., Philadelphia, PA 19106; 923-8660. E. Located in the heart of historical downtown Philadelphia, this Holiday Inn has 364 rooms decorated in a colonial motif and featuring free Showtime television. Fine cuisine is served in *Benjamin's*, quick meals at *Cafe Plain and Fancy*, and live entertainment in *Wings*.

Holiday Inn-Fort Washington, 432 Pennsylvania Ave., Fort Washington, PA 19034; 643-3000. M.

Holiday Inn-Lionville, Route 100, Lionville, PA 19353; 363-1100. M.

Holiday Inn-Midtown, 1305-11 Walnut St., Philadelphia, PA 19107; 735-9300. E.

Holiday Inn-New Hope, Route 202, New Hope, PA 18938; 862-5221. M.

Holiday Inn-Northeast 3499 Street Rd., Bensalem, PA 19020; 638-1500. M.

Holiday Inn-Resort, Route 30 and Hempstead Rd., Lancaster, PA 17601; 717-299-2551. M–E.

Holiday Inn-Valley Forge, 260 Goddard Blvd., King of Prussia, PA 19406; 265-7500. E.

HOWARD JOHNSON'S MOTOR LODGES. For travelling Americans, this pioneer of the motor-lodge concept offers dependable accommodations and dining.

Howard Johnson's Airport South, 1300 Providence Rd., Chester, PA 19013; 876-7211. I. D (SC-AARP cardholders), FP.

Howard Johnson's Lancaster-Reading, Route 272, Exit 21 on the Pennsylvania Turnpike; Lancaster, PA 17517; 267-7563. I–M. D (SC-AARP cardholders), FP (18 and under), PAC.

Howard Johnson's North, 11580 Roosevelt Blvd. (U.S. 1), three miles south of Exit 28 on the Pennsylvania Turnpike; Philadelphia, PA 19116; 464-9500. I–M. D (SC-AARP cardholders), FP (18 and under).

Howard Johnson's Valley Forge, Route 202, Exit 24 on the Pennsylvania Turnpike; Philadelphia, PA 19406; 265-4500. M. D (SC-AARP cardholders).

LATHAM HOTEL, Walnut and 17th Sts., Philadelphia, PA 19103; 563-7474. E. The Latham is a small hotel accented by the finest traditions of Europe. An apartment house until 18 years ago, it hosts no conventions and assures the ultimate in personal service. Its 110 rooms are exquisite chambers decorated in burgundy or green. From the doorman in his English riding boots to the crystal chandelier in the lobby to the bedtime "sleep well"

Godiva mints on your pillow at night, the Latham is a delight. Liquor, soft drinks, and ice are available in each room. The cocktail lounge, *Not Quite Crickett*, is one of Philadelphia's finest, as is *Bogart's*, the Casablanca-style restaurant. Free parking in the nearby garage. PAC.

THE LOGAN INN, Main and Ferry, New Hope, PA 18938; 862-5134. M. Located in the heart of historic New Hope, this 1727 inn is believed to be one of the oldest in the area. In any of the ten rooms, you will find beautiful antiques, brass beds, and fine paintings. Excellent dining is available in the Victorian Red Room, and, during the warm months, in the glass-enclosed conservatory.

MARRIOTT HOTELS. Both hotels in the Philadelphia area adhere to the quality in service and fine dining that have forged an excellent reputation for the Marriott chain throughout the world.

Philadelphia Marriott Hotel, City Ave. and Monument Rd., Philadelphia, PA 19131; 667-0200. E. Offers a relaxed, resort-style atmosphere on the Golden Mile with seven lounges and restaurants, including the *Kona Kai*, and 560 rooms, suites, and parlors. A mini-shopping arcade features gift shop, barber and beauty shops, realtor, ticket mart, travel agency, antique store, and cosmetic boutique. There's an indoor pool, two outdoor, and also a hydrotherapy pool. Also, platform tennis courts, with racquetball and tennis courts, are less than a mile away. A 1¼-mile jogging course is on the premises. Full banquet and meeting facilities; free HBO in rooms. D, FP, PAC.

Philadelphia Marriott Hotel Airport, 4509 Island Ave., Philadelphia, PA 19153; 365-4150. E. This hotel, within minutes of Philadelphia International Airport, has been completely renovated including all 331 rooms, its two restaurants, and lounge. It now offers an indoor pool. health spa with saunas, and free HBO in the rooms. Turn-of-the-century artifacts highlight the *Harper's* restaurant, where the specialty is Philadelphia snapper soup. *Chardonnay's*, serving dinner only, specializes in continental food. *Sigi's*, the lounge, offers 13-ounce drinks and a nightly DJ. Free parking; free airport van service. Full meeting and banquet facilities. D, FP, PAC.

THE PALACE, Benjamin Franklin Pkwy. at 18th St., Philadelphia, PA 19103; 963-2222, 800-223-5672. E. This deluxe hotel is located in the midst of some of Philadelphia's most noted cultural institutions. Nearby are fashionable shops, boutiques, and several excellent restaurants. The 28-story circular building offers a commanding view from many of its 298 rooms, most of which are parlors with one bedroom and include wet bar, refrigerator, and a private terrace. The Palace also has a terrace-level swimming pool, one of the city's most elegant French/continental restaurants, *Cafe Royal*, and meeting facilities that can accommodate up to 100 people. Underground parking. PAC.

PENN TOWERS, 34th St. and Civic Center Blvd, Philadelphia, PA 19104; 387-8333. E. This beautiful, 21-story high-rise is located next to the campuses of the University of Pennsylvania and Drexel University. It offers 229 rooms including 10 suites with refrigerators and wet bars. The *Terrace Coffee House* serves American dishes from early morning to late evening. D (CR, AP), PAC.

PHILADELPHIA CENTRE HOTEL, 1725 John F. Kennedy Blvd., Philadelphia, PA 19103; 568-3300, 800-523-4033. *E.* Located atop the Suburban Train Station, minutes from the AMTRAK station and across the street from the Greyhound Bus Terminal, there are 850 recently renovated rooms only a few minutes' walk from a large slice of the city's cultural area, fine shopping, and restaurants. A recent multimillion dollar facelift has included a new facade, and complete redesign of the lobby and restaurants. *Amelia's,* the new lobby lounge, is a popular place. Full banquet and meeting facilities accommodate up to 2400 people. Limo service to and from the airport. D (CR), PAC.

THE QUALITY INN, 22nd St. and Benjamin Franklin Parkway, Philadelphia, PA 19130; 568-8300. *I.* Formerly the Franklin Motor Inn, this newly-renovated budget motor lodge offers 289 rooms and convenient access to some of the city's most famous historical sites. There's free parking, a restaurant and lounge called *The Hemingway,* an outdoor cafe, and an outdoor pool. D, FP, and PAC.

QUALITY INN AIRPORT, 20th and Penrose Sts., Philadelphia, PA 19145; 755-6500. *M.* Voted one of the top Quality Inns in the nation by members of its chain, this is close to the sports complex, ethnic South Philadelphia, the airport, and offers 240 rooms as well as a heated outdoor pool. meeting and banquet facilities, and free limousine service to and from the airport. Its restaurant, *Café West,* is one of Philadelphia's most popular night spots, featuring live music straight out of the 1930s and 1940s on Saturday nights. Its *Press Box* restaurant is a favorite for hearty sandwiches, soups, salads, and drinks before and after games at the Vet and the Spectrum. D (AP,CR,G,SC,ST), FP, PA, PAC.

QUALITY INN BRANDYWINE HOTEL & RESORT, Route 30, Downingtown, PA 19335; 269-2000. *M.* Here is a mini-resort on the way to Lancaster County, with many of the sights of Chester County within convenient driving distance. In addition to an 18-hole PGA championship golf course, miniature golf, and shuffleboard, the "Sports Palace" includes tennis, indoor and outdoor pools, racquetball, bowling, archery, and a shooting range. There's also a health spa with whirlpools, steam room, sauna, and massage rooms, restaurant, lounge, and a dinner theater that features top-notch talent in some of Pennsylvania's finest productions. Full banquet and meeting facilities. D (AP, CR, GR, SC), PAC (theme weekends).

QUALITY INN CHINATOWN SUITES, 1010 Race St., Philadelphia, PA 19107; 922-1730, 800-228-5151. *M.* This brand-new hotel, right in the heart of Chinatown, offers 96 suites and the *Silver Palace Restaurant*, featuring a Chinese menu and limited American cuisine. There's a fitness center, meeting and conference space, and limited free parking.

RAMADA INNS. This fine lodging chain has three distinctive inns in the Philadelphia area. Call toll-free 800-228-2826.

Ramada Inn Airport, 76 Industrial Hwy., Essington, PA 19029; 521-9600. M. A modern high-rise with 305 rooms within minutes of Philadelphia International Airport. In addition to its delightful *Butterflies Are Free* restaurant and lounge, there is an Olympic-sized heated outdoor pool, 24-hour coffee shop, barber shop, game room, exercise room, and nearby tennis courts. Full banquet and meeting facilities, highlighted by the Meadows Ballroom (the largest in Delaware County), can accommodate up to 1300 people. D (AP, CR, TA) and PAC.

Ramada Inn Chadds Ford, Routes 1 and 202, Glen Mills, PA 19342; 358-1700. M. Located near the historic Brandywine Battlefields, this Ramada features 96 rooms, an outdoor pool, and ballroom that seats up to 250 for banquets and meetings. When the current expansion is completed, 50 more rooms will be available. The *Mark IV* restaurant offers American cuisine, salad bar, and Sunday brunch, while the *Rumors* lounge has nightly dancing to the music of a DJ and live bands. D (GR, SC).

Ramada Inn Fort Washington, Route 309 and Exit 26 on the Pennsylvania Turnpike, Fort Washington, PA 19034; 542-7930. M. Features 106 luxury guest rooms and suites near the splendid shops of Chestnut Hill, with all the fun of New Hope not far away. Its *Coach Inn* is a novel restaurant comprised of three Victorian era railroad cars, each refurbished and decorated as authentic dining cars. The latest addition was "Delaware No. 90," which was President Eisenhower's railroad car during his years in the White House. The *La Gare* disco has a superior sound system. Outdoor pool, full banquet and meeting facilities. D (CR, SC), FP.

SHERATON HOTELS. These hotels have an international reputation for service and special amenities. Call toll-free 800-325-3535.

Sheraton Executive Tower, 530 Pennsylvania Ave., Fort Washington, PA 19034; 643-1111. M. Offers 135 rooms, with more on the way, one restaurant, a lounge, and a delicatessen, all near historic Chestnut Hill. Entertainment nightly in the lounge. Full banquet and meeting facilities. D (CR, G, SC, ST, TA).

Sheraton Lancaster Resort, 222 N. Oregon Pike, Lancaster, PA 17604; 717-656-2101. M. Nestled in the quiet of Lancaster County are 132 rooms with sunken tubs and in-room steam baths. Tropical courtyard, indoor swimming pool, sauna, tennis courts, and miniature golf. Fireside dining in the restaurant and entertainment nightly in the *Yankee Doodle Tavern.* D (SC-AARP cardholders, CR, TA), FP. Full banquet and meeting facilities.

Sheraton Inn Northeast, Roosevelt Blvd. and Grant Ave., Philadelphia, PA 19152; 671-9600. M. Located next to North Philadelphia Airport, the racetracks and Sesame Place, this Sheraton has 200 deluxe rooms and suites, a domed swimming pool, a restaurant and lounge, and excellent meeting and conference facilities for up to 600 people. Guest passes to nearby racquetball club. D (AP, CR, SC), FP (under 18).

Sheraton University City, 36th and Chestnut Sts., Philadelphia PA 19104; 387-8000. E. Adjacent to the University of Pennsylvania campus and within walking distance of the Civic Center, this 20-story hotel offers 377 deluxe rooms and 13 special executive suites, the ever-popular *Smart Alex* restaurant and lounge, a heated indoor pool on the sixth floor, and indoor parking. The *Dalmaire Ballroom* can accommodate up to 735 people. D (GR, SC, ST), FP, PA, and PAC.

Sheraton Valley Forge, 1st Ave. and North Gulph Rd., King of Prussia, PA 19406; 337-2000. E. Located next to Valley Forge and the King of Prussia shopping mall, this circular tower on 37 acres is one of the most exciting spots to stay in the area. In addition to 240 deluxe rooms, there are superb facilities for swimming, volleyball, basketball, handball, squash, racquetball, steam, sauna, and massage. An 18-hole golf course and twin cinemas are nearby. Gourmet dining in the elegant *Chumley's* and matchless Las Vegas revues at *Lily Langtry's.* The plush *Scintillations* nightclub is worth an evening, too. A new conference center, the Sheraton Towers, houses 160 more guest rooms, 55 theme suites, and a sports complex. D (CR, G, TA), FP.

SOCIETY HILL HOTEL, 3rd and Chestnut Sts., Philadelphia, PA 19106; 925-1394. M–E. Built in 1832, this lodging served as temporary housing for longshoremen before it became Philadelphia's first bed-and-breakfast hotel. Still the city's smallest hotel (12 rooms), Society Hill Hotel is nestled within Old City and Society Hill, two blocks from Independence Hall. A charming place in the European tradition, it offers personal touches such as fresh squeezed juice, coffee and tea, and warm rolls with sweet butter in each room in the morning. The rooms themselves have brass double beds with canopies and are always graced by freshly cut flowers. With its stained glass greenery and jazz the *Society Hill Bar and Restaurant* is an absolute delight and features a spectacular light menu as well as an outstanding Sunday brunch. Indoor parking nearby.

ST. DAVID'S INN, 591 E. Lancaster Ave., Philadelphia, PA 19087; 688-5800. E. Located on seven landscaped acres in the heart of Philadelphia's Main Line, the St. David's Inn is surrounded by large homes and estates, excellent shopping, eight colleges and universities, and the world headquarters of seven Fortune 500 companies. Its 170 rooms have been beautifully redone, as has the cocktail lounge, which has entertainment nightly except Sunday. Restaurant and full banquet and meeting facilities. The Valley Forge Golf Club and indoor-outdoor tennis courts are only minutes away, and the inn has a fleet of limousines available. Free parking. D (CR).

STOUFFER'S VALLEY FORGE, 480 N. Gulph Rd., King of Prussia, PA 19406; 337-1800. E. Located next to historic Valley Forge, the vibrant

King of Prussia shopping mall, the Valley Forge Music Fair, and other attractions, Stouffer's has 300 rooms, each with a terrace. There's an outdoor pool, a cocktail terrace where drinks and light food can be enjoyed in warm weather, and golf is available on several nearby courses. The restaurant features fine American cuisine dining, and *Justin's* lounge has dancing at night. The special Concierge Floor offers additional services. D (CR, G, TA), FP, and PAC.

TABAS HOTEL, Lancaster Ave., Downingtown, PA 19335; 269-6000. *E.* Co-owned by actor Mickey Rooney, the Tabas offers a resort atmosphere that features indoor-outdoor swimming, tennis, golf, and roller skating. In the winter, enjoy skiing at nearby Chadds Peak. The health spa includes gym facilities and a sauna. You'll find elegant dining in the restaurant, and the nightclub is highlighted by the entertainment of top stars. There's also Hollywood movies, and one dinner theater is nearby. D (AP, C, CR, GR, TA), and PAC.

TREADWAY INN. This moderately-priced chain offers fine accommodations in the Philadelphia area.

Treadway Mohawk Inn, 4200 Roosevelt Blvd., Philadelphia, PA 19124; 289-9200. M. The Mohawk Inn has 116 rooms, a pool, and free parking. Historical and cultural attractions are nearby. Full banquet and meeting facilities. FP (under 17), PAC.

Treadway Resort, 222 Eden Rd., Lancaster, PA 17601; 569-6444. M. With easy access to all Pennsylvania Dutch attractions, this Treadway offers 247 rooms, indoor and outdoor pools, a health club, restaurant, and nightly entertainment in the cocktail lounge. D (AP, GR, SC, TA), PAC.

THE WARRINGTON MOTOR LODGE, Route 611, Warrington, PA 18976; 343-0373. *I.* Located in a secluded, wooded area, this excellent motor lodge has been operated by the same family for generations. It has 75 lovely rooms and executive suites, new banquet facilities, and a restaurant that specializes in fine American and Italian cuisine. This may be one of the few hotels in the world with a chapel on the premises. Only 20 minutes from New Hope. Outdoor pool, baby-sitting service, car rental, air taxi or limo to Philadelphia International Airport. Banquet and meeting facilities can accommodate up to 400 people. FP (under 12), PA.

WARWICK HOTEL, 17th and Locust Sts., Philadelphia, PA 19103; 735-6000, 800-223-1900. *E.* Opened in 1929, this English Renaissance building just off Rittenhouse Square has become a Philadelphia landmark. Through the years, such luminaries as President Eisenhower, Jack Benny, and Bob Hope have stayed here, and now after a $17 million facelift in the late 1970s, it is the ultimate in European style and taste. The Warwick's 180 rooms and suites are beautifully furnished and decorated, and the lobby features a barber shop, apothecary, and fashionable boutiques. The banquet and meeting facilities, led by the Grand Ballroom, can accommodate up to 500 people. Its *Maxwell's* restaurant is open until 2 am, and the club, *Polo Bay*, offers excellent continental cuisine, dancing at night, and an outstanding champagne brunch on Sunday. The concierge is happy to arrange for such amenities as baby-sitting, flowers, and limos. D (CR), FP (14 and under).

THE WAYNE HOTEL, 139 E. Lancaster Ave., Wayne, PA 19087; 687-5000. E. This charming Victorian hotel was built in 1906 and over the years was converted to many uses. Around 1985 it was restored as a hotel with 37 rooms, all furnished in Victorian reproductions. A porch typical of the period wraps around the building and the lobby rooms exude charm. Excellent restaurant serves complimentary continental breakfast to weekend guests.

WEST CHESTER INN, 943 S. High St., off Route 202, West Chester, PA 19380; 692-1900. M. This motel offers 102 rooms, free HBO, outdoor swimming pool, and *Cyrano's*, a restaurant/lounge that features fine food and outstanding entertainment including jazz and comedy. Their Saturday night seafood buffet is a winner. Host to the Philadelphia Eagles during training camp. D (CR, GR, SC, TA), PA, and PAC.

WILLOW VALLEY INN, 2416 Willow St. Pike, Lancaster, PA 17602; 717-464-2711, out of state, 800-233-0093; in state, 800-732-0047. M. These 185 acres of rolling hills in the midst of Amish Country offer fun for the whole family. There's an indoor and an outdoor pool, a jacuzzi, game room, nine-hole golf course, lighted tennis courts, skating in the winter, a special playground for children, and even a bike rental. Tours to Pennsylvania Dutch Country. The restaurant is noted for its all-you-can-eat smorgasbord, and in the *Bake Shoppe*, you can watch delicacies being made. D (C, CR, TA), FP, MAP.

Hotel Safety Rules

As a public-safety service we include in this chapter the following guidance in case of a hotel fire. All information is taken from a publication of the National Safety Council.

Preliminary precautions start after you check into your hotel. Check the exits and fire alarms on your floor, count the doorways between your room and the exit, keep your key close to your bed and take it with you if you leave your room in case you need to return. In case smoke blocks your exit, check the window latches and any adjoining buildings or decks for low level escape.

In case of fire, take your key and crawl to the door. Don't stand; smoke and deadly gases arise. If the doorknob is hot—do not open—stay in your room. Then open the window, phone for help, hang a sheet from the window to signal for help, turn on the bathroom fan, fill the tub with water, wet towels and sheets to put around doors if smoke seeps in and make a tent over your head with a blanket at a partially opened window to get fresh air.

If the doorknob is not hot, leave, close the door to your room, proceed to the exit, counting doorways in the dark, and walk down to the ground level. If blocked at lower levels, turn around, walk up to the roof and keep the roof door open to vent stairwell. Wait for help on the roof.

Do not use elevator. Remember to lie low to avoid smoke and gases.

ALTERNATIVE LODGING

Bed-and-Breakfast ─────────────────────

Bed-&-Breakfast of Philadelphia, P.O. Box 630, Chester Springs, PA 19425; 884-1084. The British tradition of bed-and-breakfast has become very popular in Philadelphia and its surrounding counties. More than 100 townhouses, high-rises, duplexes, and historic homes offer a private guest room with bath and continental breakfast for a moderate fee. Single from $20–70 per night; double from $35–70.

Campgrounds ─────────────────────

The Philadelphia area has a number of campgrounds with facilities ranging from basic water and electrical hook-ups to complete community services.

All-Seasons Resort, Route 10, five miles south of Route 30, Honeybrook, PA 19344; 273-9323. *I-E.* This 149-acre membership campground, with wooded sites on a lake, offers everything from putting up your own tent to renting a trailer on the site. Fishing, basketball, volleyball, self-guided tours to Amish Country and Philadelphia, two playgrounds, game room, and miniature golf. PA.

Colonial Woods Family Campground, Lonely Cottage Dr., Upper Black Eddy, PA 18972; 847-5808. *I.* Open all year, features boating, hay rides, hiking, playground, swimming, tennis, and a recreation hall. Shopping in nearby New Hope. Pets allowed on leash.

Hidden Acres, off Route 340, Coatesville, PA 19320; 857-3990. *I.* Located on the highest ground in Lancaster, Chester, and Delaware counties, this site boasts a new swimming pool, children's fishing, playground, recreation room, and a pavilion. Near Amish Country. Pets welcome if kept under control.

Mill Bridge Village Campground, one-half mile south of Route 30, east on Ronks Rd., Lancaster, PA 17579; 717-687-8181. *I.* Located in the heart of Lancaster County and on the same site as the quaint Mill Bridge Village, this campground offers fishing, boating, hiking, a country store, and entertainment every weekend from Memorial Day through late October. Pets allowed.

West Chester KOA, Route 162, seven miles west of West Chester, West Chester, PA 19375; 486-0447. *I.* Nineteen acres along the Brandywine River feature canoeing, swimming. Also, game room, TV lounge, and van routes to Philadelphia. Pets on a leash.

RESORTS

The Philadelphia area is one of those rare places in which the natural wonders of an ocean and a mountain range are so nearby. Only an hour's drive from Center City is the revitalized Atlantic City with its Boardwalk on the sandy beaches of the Atlantic, and, of course, casino gambling. The entire Jersey Shore is a haven for countless Philadelphians and visitors during the summer, with Cape May as one of the most historic resort areas to be found anywhere in the country. In another direction, about a two-hour drive to the northwest, are the beautiful Pocono Mountains, a year-round resort area highlighted by skiing in the winter and a wealth of other activities in the spring, summer, and fall.

Atlantic City

How to Get There

Atlantic City is about an hour's drive from Center City Philadelphia on the Atlantic City Expressway. Regular bus service is available, some of it provided by the hotel casinos themselves; and air service is provided between Philadelphia International Airport and two airports in the Atlantic City area, Bader Field and Atlantic City International Air Terminal.

Atlantic City Past

A century ago, Atlantic City was *the* resort on the East Coast. In 1870, the city opened the first boardwalk in the world; two years later, it spun the first ferris wheel. In 1876, it hosted the world's first Easter Parade; in 1893, it produced the first picture postcards (of Atlantic City, of course).

Although Atlantic City had become famous for its Boardwalk, salt-water taffy, and the Miss America Pageant (circa 1921), the town began to settle into a slow decline that hit rock bottom in the 1950s. This continued until the late 1970s, when the city rolled the dice on its future with casino gambling.

The Casino Scene

Now, with countless millions of dollars invested in hotel-casinos, Atlantic City is once again alive with visitors and poised to surpass Las Vegas as the gambling capital of the world. Already called "the Las Vegas of the East," the city draws hordes of tourists who find it an ideal stopover before or after visits to New York, Washington, and Philadelphia.

Although gambling and the top entertainers that accompanied it provided the impetus for rebirth, Atlantic City also has a host of activities for those whose interests lie outside the casinos. The Boardwalk itself is vibrant once more, with its piers offering a variety of amusements for youngsters and hundreds of young artists displaying and selling their work from June to September. Cycling is a must, and bicycles are for rent at convenient locations.

Recreation and Attractions

For sunworshipers, Atlantic City offers a free beach. For anglers, there is excellent deep sea fishing in the Atlantic and in the bays. Boats for fishing and sightseeing can be chartered from the inlet docks. Golf is available on six nearby courses, tennis abounds on numerous indoor and outdoor courts, and there is hiking and canoeing in the nearby Pine Barrens.

In addition to the Miss America Pageant, the Convention Center hosts a boat show, a dog show, an antique collectors' show, and midget auto races among its many special events. It also has huge convention exhibits and one of the world's largest pipe organs. You'll also find thoroughbred horse racing at Atlantic City Race Course, stock-car racing in nearby Pleasantville, and professional boxing in casino hotel auditoriums.

Shopping For Fun

With crowds flocking to the hotel casinos and other attractions, Atlantic City offers a wide range of quality shopping opportunities. One of the newest attractions on the Boardwalk is Ocean One, a pier resembling a docked ocean liner replete with portholes, masts, flags, and deck chairs—but actually a shopping mall with 120 stores and shops, ten restaurants, and 30 fast-food eateries.

Eating Out

Atlantic City runs the dining gamut from sidewalk hot dog stands to haute cuisine. Each hotel casino has a top-flight restaurant and various other eateries, but only a block or two away you're sure to find other fine restaurants, usually less expensive, that feature everything from seafood and Italian specialties to Chinese and Mexican food.

Getting Around

Should you drive to Atlantic City expect to pay a premium price for parking. The casino parking charges fluctuate from no charge to $8 depending upon the season. Independent lots, though plentiful, are competitive.

Jitneys, those little buggies that seat up to 13 people, are a traditional and inexpensive mode of transportation in Atlantic City; you can cover the full length of the city for 75¢. The Boardwalk trams are a fun way to ride the Great Wooden Way; tram charge—adults $1, children and senior citizens, 75¢.

Where to Stay

There are many smaller hotels and motels in Atlantic City that are less expensive than the $75-to-$120 per night charged in the hotel casinos. Regarding your specific requirements, we suggest you write or call the Atlantic City Visitor's Bureau, Convention Hall, Atlantic City, NJ 08401; 609-348-7044. Remember, Atlantic City's peak season is the summer; reservations should be made well in advance and rates are the highest. Also, the casinos themselves are required to be closed between 4 am and 10 am on weekdays, and from 6 am to 10 am Saturdays, Sundays, and holidays.

Listed below are the twelve hotel casinos currently in operation:

Atlantis Hotel and Casino, Florida Ave. and the Boardwalk, Atlantic City, NJ 08401; 609-344-4000. The Atlantis has 500 rooms, four restaurants, three lounges, a health club and pool, exercise room, racquetball courts, and arcade game room.

Bally's Park Place, Park Pl. and the Boardwalk, Atlantic City, NJ 08401; 609-340-2000. Bally's has 512 rooms, eight restaurants, one lounge, a video game room, pool, and health spa. Its *Park Cabaret* seats 550.

Caesar's Boardwalk Regency, Arkansas Ave. and the Boardwalk; Atlantic City, NJ 08401; 609-348-4411. Caesar's has 509 rooms, five restaurants, three lounges, an amusement arcade, beach club with volleyball courts, domed pool, rooftop garden with tennis courts, and free use of bicycles on the Boardwalk. *Caesar's Cabaret Theater* seats 500.

The Claridge Hotel and Casino, Indiana Ave. and the Boardwalk, Atlantic City, NJ 08401; 609-340-3400. The Claridge has 504 rooms, five restaurants, two lounges, a health club with glass-enclosed pool, HBO and cable TV in all rooms. The *Hi-Ho Palace* seats 550.

Golden Nugget, Boston Ave. and the Boardwalk, Atlantic City, NJ 08401; 609-347-7111. The Golden Nugget has 504 rooms, four restaurants, two lounges, a health club with a Victorian-style indoor pool, and arcade. The *Opera House* seats 524.

Harrah's Marina Hotel Casino, Brigantine Blvd., Atlantic City, NJ 08401; 609-441-5000. Harrah's has 506 rooms, five restaurants, five lounges, enclosed pool, nautilus room, deck tennis and shuffleboard, an arcade, and supervised nursery. *Broadway by the Sea* theater seats 850.

Resorts International Hotel Casino, North Carolina Ave. and the Boardwalk, Atlantic City, NJ 08401; 609-344-6000. This, the first casino in Atlantic City, has 721 rooms, seven restaurants, six lounges, a beauty parlor, health club, and glass-domed pool, sundeck, rooftop Jacuzzi, and a shopping arcade. *Superstar Theater* seats 1650.

The Sands Hotel and Casino, Indiana Ave. and Brighton Park, Atlantic City, NJ 08401; 609-441-4000. As Atlantic City's fourth casino, the Sands has 504 rooms, three restaurants, one lounge, health club with racquetball courts and Nautilus, and use of Greate Bay Country Club in Somers Point for registered guests. The *Sands Copa Room* seats 853.

Showboat Hotel and Casino, Delaware Ave. and the Boardwalk, Atlantic City, NJ 08401; 609-343-4000. The Showboat has 560 rooms, 11 restaurants, five lounges, miniature golf, a pool, a bowling center, and a video arcade.

The Tropicana, Iowa Ave. and the Boardwalk, Atlantic City, NJ 08401; 609-340-4000. As Atlantic City's ninth casino, the Tropicana has 521 rooms, six restaurants, three lounges, weekly boxing matches, glass enclosed elevators, a mall of shops, and indoor pool. The *Royal Swan Ballroom* seats 1100.

Trump Castle Hotel and Casino, Huron Ave. and Brigantine Blvd., Atlantic City, NJ 08401; 609-441-2000. The Castle has 606 rooms and suites, seven restaurants, three lounges, a health club, jogging track, marina, outdoor pool, and the *King's Court Show Room*.

Trump Plaza Hotel and Casino, Mississippi Ave. and the Boardwalk, Atlantic City, NJ 08401; 609-441-6000. This hotel has 586 rooms, eight restaurants, six lounges, a health club, pool, and tennis courts.

Cape May

How To Get There

Regularly scheduled bus service is available from Philadelphia and Atlantic City. If you're driving, follow the Atlantic City Expressway to Atlantic City and head south on Ocean Drive, a total drive of about 40 miles from Atlantic City.

An Overview

Located at the southernmost tip of the New Jersey peninsula, Cape May is a reminder of a century ago when it was one of the most renowned resort areas in the nation and America's oldest seaside resort. If one takes into account the "vacations" of the Lenni Lenape Indians who visited what is now Cape May County to fish and relax in the 15th and 16th centuries, the resort actually pre-dates the nation itself.

Cape May is now a blend of the best of both the 19th and 20th centuries. Quiet and classic, rooted in solid residential stock, the entire city of Cape May has been designated a National Historic Landmark, and its almost Southern ambiance stands in bold relief to the more hectic atmosphere of some other New Jersey resort areas. With its Victorian architecture of more than 600 authentic 19th-century buildings and homes, its small boardwalk and picture-postcard beach, Cape May is a place for relaxation, strolling or biking through its tree-shaded streets, shopping, sunning, and dining in fine restaurants.

The Atlantic is filled with an overwhelming variety of fish, including bluefish, marlin, fluke, and sea trout. The inland waterways and Delaware Bay to the west offer a variety of different kinds of fishing. Excursion boats and charters operate daily. Crabbing is excellent, too.

Golf, tennis, horseback riding, roller skating, and miniature golf are just a few of the other recreational attractions nearby. You'll also find parks, playgrounds, shuffleboard courts, band concerts, antique car shows, parades, and regattas.

In addition to fine modern and historic lodging in the city itself, Cape May County includes penthouse motel and condo suites, apartments, cottages, bungalows, motels, and efficiency apartments. There are more than 42 privately-owned campgrounds with thickly wooded sites for small tents to lakeside trailers and recreational sites with complete hookups.

Prices at Cape May can be high. Rooms in the bed and breakfast inns run from $50 to $75 per night. Each house tour costs between $2 and $3.50, and prices at superior restaurants can add up, too.

For specific information, we recommend you write to Cape May City Hall's publicity department, Box A-83, Cape May, NJ 08204.

Pocono Mountains

Little more than an hour's drive northwest of Philadelphia will take you to the breathtaking Pocono Mountains, 2400 square miles of beautiful scenery with an abundance of recreational activities year-round. For details, see ONE-DAY EXCURSIONS.

DINING

Philadelphia's "restaurant renaissance," which began in the mid-1970s, continues today. Food connoisseurs emerging from the city's restaurants have applauded Philadelphia with kudos generally reserved for the dining establishments of New York and San Francisco.

The wealth and variety of ethnic food available, from Thai food to a range of pastas to mouth-watering French delicacies, make Philadelphia dining a special treat not to be found in many other large cities. The close proximity to the Atlantic Ocean assures one of fresh and inventive seafood dishes in a number of tempting restaurants. An unusual number of historic buildings now housing eateries add charm and beauty to restaurants of all descriptions throughout this famous old city. And don't forget Philadelphia's own brand of America's favorite food, soft pretzels and cheese steak sandwiches.

There are too many experiences available in and around Philadelphia now, too much excellence, service, variety, and competition for the mediocre to survive. From the elegant to the casual, from old inns to sidewalk and garden cafes, from haute cuisine to neighborhood ethnic, you are assured of satisfying your every dining mood in grand Philadelphia.

Our cost categories based on appetizer, entree, and dessert are:

E—Expensive, over $20 per person.

M—Moderate, $10–$20 per person.

I—Inexpensive, under $10 per person.

RESTAURANTS BY AREA

BERKS COUNTY

The Inn at Oley, French, M.
La Petite Auberge, French, M.
Moslem Springs Inn, American/
Pennsylvania Dutch, I–M.

BUCKS COUNTY

Black Bass Hotel, American, M.
Blue Ram, Continental, M–E.
Chez Odette, French, M.

Conti Cross Keys Inn, Continental, M.
El Sombrero, Mexican, I.
Golden Pheasant, International, E.
The Hacienda, International, M.
Hotel du Village, French, M.
Jenny's, Continental, M.
Misbehavin' Mama's, International, M.
Mother's Restaurant, International, I–M.
Plumbsteadville Inn, Continental, M.

Sign of the Sorrel Horse, French, M.
Upper Black Eddy Inn, Continental, M.
Walking Treaty Inn, Continental, M.

CENTER CITY

The Abbott Cafe in the Abbott Building, International, I–M.
Annie's Place, Eastern European, I.
Apropos, American, M.
Arline, Continental, M.
Arturo's American, M.
Astral Plane, International, M.
Bogart's, Latham Hotel, Continental, M–E.
Bookbinder's Seafood House, Seafood, M–E.
Borscht and Tears, Russian, M.
The Cafe Borrelli, Italian, M–E.
Carolina's, Continental, M–E.
Cavanaugh's, American, I–M.
Chameleon, Etcetera, I.
China Castle Restaurant, Chinese, I.
China Gate Restaurant, Chinese, I.
Chocho Japanese Restaurant, Japanese, I.
Chun Hing Restaurant, Chinese, I.
The Commissary, International, I–M.
Corned Beef Academy, Etcetera, I.
The Cypress Restaurant, Continental, M–E.
Dante and Luigi's, Italian, M–E.
Deja Vu, French, E.
Deux Cheminees, French, M–E.
DiLullo Centro, Italian, M–E.
Diner on the Square, Etcetera, I.
The Dockside Fish Company, Seafood, M.
Ecco, Continental, M–E.
Eden, Cafeteria, I.
European Dairy Restaurant, Eastern European, I.
The Fish Market, Seafood, M.
Flynn's Landing, American, I.
The Fountain, International, E.
Frankie's Trattoria, Italian, M.
Fratelli, Italian, M.

Friday, Saturday, Sunday, Continental, M.
Gaetano, Italian, E.
The Garden, Continental, M.
Harry's Bar and Grill, Continental, M.
H. A. Winston, American, I–M.
Hoffman House, German, M.
Horizons, Continental, M–E.
Ho Sai Gai, Chinese, I.
Houlihan's Old Place, American, Brunches, I–M.
Hu-Nan, Chinese, M.
Il Gallo Nero, Italian, M.
Imperial Inn, Chinese, I–M.
Irish Pub, American and Irish, I.
Jimmy's Milan, Italian, M.
Kelly's of Ludlow, Seafood, I–M.
Kyo Japanese Restaurant, Japanese, M.
La Camargue, French, M–E.
La Chaumiere, French, E.
L'Aigle D'or, International, E.
L'Americaine, French, E.
Latimer Deli and Restaurant, Etcetera, I.
Le Beau Lieu, French, E.
Le Bec-Fin, French, E.
Le Wine Bar, Continental, M.
Magnolia Cafe, American, M–E.
Magyar, Hungarian, M.
Mandana, American, M.
Marabella's, Italian, M.
Market Fair, Etcetera, I.
The Marketplace, American, I–M.
Mayflower Restaurant, Chinese, M.
Memphis, International, I.
More Than Just Ice Cream, Etcetera, I.
Morton's of Chicago–Philadelphia, American, M–E.
Natural Foods Eatery, Etcetera, I–M.
New London, American, M–E.
Nooner Lunch, Etcetera, I.
Nyala, African, I–M.
O'Dwyer's Dining Room and Pub, American, I.
Onassis, Greek, M.

Philadelphia Fish & Company, Seafood, I-M.
Pikkles Plus, Etcetera, I.
Portofino Restaurant, Italian, M.
Reading Terminal Market, Etcetera, I.
Restaurant School, International, I.
Rib-It, American, I-M.
Ristorante La Buca, Italian, M.
Saladalley, International, I.
Sansom Street Oyster House, Seafood, I-M.
Siam Cuisine, Thai,M.
Siam Lotus, Thai, M.
S.P.Q.R., Italian, M.
Szechuan Garden, Chinese, I-M.
Taylor's Country Store, Etcetera, I.
Thai Royal Barge, Thai, M.
The Three Threes, Continental, I-M.
Top of Center Square, Seafood, M-E.
20th Street Cafe, International, M.
Two Quails, American, M-E.
Warsaw Cafe, Eastern European, I-M.
Wok Chinese Seafood Restaurant, Chinese, I-M.

CENTER CITY— FAIRMOUNT PARK AREA

Adrian Cafe, International, I-M.
Fairmount Firehouse, American, M.
London, Continental, M.
Mirabelle, Continental, M-E.
Museum Restaurant, Brunches, I.
North Star Bar, American, I.
Rose Tattoo Cafe, International, I-M.
Tavern on Green, Brunches, I.

CENTER CITY—PARKWAY

Cafe Royal, French, E.

CHESTER COUNTY

Binni & Flynn's, American and Mexican, I.
Buoy 1, Seafood, I.
Chadds Ford Inn, Continental, M.
Chef Tell's, Continental, M-E.
The Columbia Hotel, American, M.

The Country House at Kimberton, American, M.
Coventry Forge Inn, French, M.
Dilworthtown Inn, Continental, M.
Duling-Kurtz House, Continental, M-E.
The Fox Barn, Cafeteria, I-M.
H. A. Winston, American, I-M.
The Inn at Historic Yellow Springs, French, M-E.
The Inn at St. Peters, Continental, M.
Kinterra, American, M-E.
La Cocotte, French,M.
Le Continental, Continental, M.
Marshallton Inn, Continental, M.
Mendenhall Inn, American, M.
The Mile Post Inn, Continental, M.
Orleans, American, M.
Steven Stars Inn, American, M-E.
Ship Inn, Brunches, I.
The Terrace, Continental, I-M.
Towne Hall, American, M.
Vicker's Tavern, French, E.
Warren Tavern, Continental, M.

CHESTNUT HILL

A Slice of Heaven, Etcetera, I-M.
Chautauqua, Continental, M.
Chiyo Japanese Restaurant, Japanese, M.
The Depot, American, M.
Flying Fish, Seafood, M.
The French Bakery and Cafe, Etcetera, I.
Roller's, International, M.
21 West, Continental, M.
Under the Blue Moon, International, I-M.
Valley Green Inn, American, M.

CITY AVENUE

Ristorante Alberto, Italian, M.
San Marco, Italian, M.
TGI Friday's, Brunches, I-M.

DELAWARE COUNTY

Clam Tavern, Seafood, I-M.
Crier in the Country, Continental, E.

The Greenhouse, Continental, M.
Hespe's, Continental, M.
La Fourchette, French, M.
L'Auberge, Continental, M-E.
Peking Restaurant, Chinese, I-M.
Towne House, Italian, M.

LANCASTER COUNTY

The Good 'n Plenty Restaurant,
Pennsylvania Dutch, I-M.
Groff's, Pennsylvania Dutch, M.
Jethro's, Continental, M.

MONTGOMERY COUNTY

Bala Rouge, American, M.
Casa Maria, Mexican, I.
Cutillo's, Brunches, I.
General Wayne Inn, American, M.
H.A. Winston, American, I-M.
Houlihan's Old Place, American,
I-M.
Hu-Nan, Chinese, M.
Hymie's, Etcetera, I.
Jefferson House, American, M.
La Coquille St. Jacques, French, E.
Lily Langtry's, Brunches, I.
Luchetta's Ristorante, Italian, M.
Mr. Ron's, American, I-M.
Mr. Ron's Louisiana Seafood
House, Seafood, M.
Morley's Pub and Saloon, American,
I.
Newport House, American, M.
The Old Guard House, Continental,
M.
Old Norrington Tavern, American,
I-M.
Over the Rainbow, Etcetera, M.
Quissett, Continental, I-M.
Sportster's, American, I-M.
Sunnybrook Farm, Brunches, I.
Tiffany Dining Saloon, American, M.
William Penn Inn, Continental, M.

NORTHEAST PHILADELPHIA

Country Club Diner, Etcetera, I-M.
Kawabata, Japanese, I-M.

94th Aero Squadron, Continental,
M-E.
The Original Blue Point Seafood
House, Seafood, I-M.
Ristorante DiLullo, Italian, M-E.

NORTHWEST PHILADELPHIA

Cou's Canal View Inn, International,
I-M.
Green's United States Hotel Bar
and Grill, American, M.
Jamey's, Continental, M.
Thomas', Italian, M.

OLD CITY AND SOCIETY HILL

Alfredo's, Italian, M.
Bookbinders Seafood House,
Seafood, M-E.
The Bourse, Etcetera, I.
Bridget Foy's, American, M.
Cafe de Costa, French, M.
Cantina del Dios, Mexican, I.
City Tavern, American, M.
Cobblestone II, Continental, M.
Dickens Inn, English, M.
DiNardo's, Seafood, I-M.
H. A. Winston, American, I-M.
Head House Inn, American, M.
H. T. McDoogal's, American, I-M.
J. B. Winberie, American, I.
Kanpai, Japanese, I.
Kawagiku Japanese Restaurant,
Japanese, M.
La Famiglia, Italian, M.
La Truffe, French, M-E.
Lautrec, French, M.
Le Champignon, French, M.
Los Amigos, Mexican, I.
Miss Headly's Wine Bar, Brunches,
I-M.
Moshulu, Seafood, M-E.
October, American, M.
Pizzaria Uno, Etcetera, I.
Raymond Haldeman Restaurant,
Continental, E.
Rib-It, American, I-M.
Sannas, International, M.
Si Ristorante, Italian, M.

Siva's, Indian, M.
Society Hill Hotel, American, I.
Waldo's, American, I–M.

QUEEN VILLAGE/ SOUTH STREET

Alouette, French, M.
Bangkok House, Thai, I.
Bridget Foy's, American, M.
Cafe Nola, American, M.
Catherine's Paris Bistro, French, M.
Copa Banana, Etcetera, I.
Downey's, Continental, M.
The Famous Delicatessen, Etcetera, I.
Giovanni's, Italian, I–M.
Hikaru, Japanese, M.
Judy's Cafe, International, I–M.
Knave of Hearts, International, M.
La Cucina, Italian, M.
La Grolla, Italian, M.
Le Bistro, Continental, M.
Lickety Split, Continental, I–M.
Luchetta's Ristorante, Italian, M.
Marrakesh, Moroccan, M.
Monte Carlo Living Room, Continental, E.
Montserrat, American, I.
Old Original Levis, Etcetera, I.
Pyrenees, Continental, M.
Reisha's, Seafood, I–M.
South Street Lobster House, Seafood, M.
South Street Souvlaki, Greek, I–M.

Spaghetti Factory, Italian, I.
Tang's, Chinese, I.
Ulana's, Continental, M.
Walt's King of Crabs, Seafood, I.

SOUTH PHILADELPHIA

Cent Anni, Italian, I–M.
Francesco's, Italian, M.
The Good, the Bad and the Ugly, Italian and Seafood, I–M.
Mama Yolanda's, Italian, M.
Marra's, Italian, I.
Melrose Diner, Etcetera, I.
Osteria Romana, Italian, M.
Palumbo's, Italian, M.
Pat's King of Steaks, Etcetera, I.
Ralph's, Italian, I.
Saigon, Vietnamese, I.
Saloon, Italian, M.
Snockey's, Seafood, I.
Strolli's Restaurant, Italian, I.
Torano's, Italian, M.
Triangle Tavern, Italian, I.
Vinh Hoa, Vietnamese, I.

UNIVERSITY CITY

Cavanaugh's, American, I–M.
Eden, Cafeteria, I.
Gold Standard, International, I–M.
La Terrasse, French, M.
Le Bus, Etcetera, I.
Sweet Basil, International, I.
The White Dog Cafe, American, M.

RESTAURANTS

American

Apropos, 211 S. Broad St.; 546-4424. M. Inspired by new wave cooking techniques of California, this bistro, bar, and cafe features mesquite-wood grilling and wood-oven baking for pizzas. European bakery produces Russian breads. Breakfast, Lunch and Dinner daily.

Arturo's, 1512 Walnut St.; 735-2590. M. Formerly Arthur's, this restaurant is a Philadelphia tradition. Mesquite-grilled meat, fish, poultry, and Italian specialties served. Lunch and Dinner Mon–Sat.

Bala Rouge, 222 Bala Ave., Bala Cynwyd; 667-5127. M. Louisiana fare with Cajun specialties in a Mardi Gras atmosphere. Dinner daily.

Black Bass Hotel, River Rd., Lumberville; 297-5770. M. Dine in this 18th-century inn overlooking the Delaware River, a setting that is enhanced by the beauty of the surrounding countryside. With a fireplace crackling in the background, choose from a wide range of superior dishes that include roast duck and breast of chicken. Dinner every day, 4:30–8 pm. Sunday brunch, 11am–3pm.

Bridget Foy's, 2nd and South Sts.; 922-1813. M. This popular East Philly Cafe now has hearty meals featuring pasta, seafood, burgers and salads. Casual dining in upholstered booths and a fireplace enhances the warm setting. Lunch and Dinner daily, Brunch Sun.

Cafe Nola, 328 South St.; 627-2590. M. Authentic Creole and Cajun cooking is created by knowing chefs in this turn-of-the-century saloon. Hot appetizers include oysters Rockefeller and from the raw bar the shrimp remoulade is a winner. Try the ever-popular jambalaya and Big Daddy's Fish Fry. Lunch in raw bar daily, Lunch Tue–Sat, Dinner daily, Brunch Sun.

Cavanaugh's (see NIGHTLIFE Cabarets, Dinner Theater and Supper Clubs.)

Cavanaugh's, 120 S. 23 St.; 561-4097. I–M. Steaks, chops, and seafood are served here, a former Irish taproom. Lunch and Dinner Mon–Sat.

City Tavern, 2nd and Walnut Sts.; 923-6059. M. This 18th-century tavern is a faithful recreation of the one on the same site that was a favorite of George Washington, Ben Franklin, Thomas Jefferson, and John Adams. Waitresses in colonial costumes serve up such traditional dishes as beef pie, roast duckling, fresh flounder in crust, and baked crab. The desserts feature excellent apple, cherry, and pecan pies. Lunch and Dinner daily.

The Columbia Hotel, 148 Bridge St., Phoenixville, 933-9973. M. Built in 1892, this authentic Victorian hotel presents excellent steaks and seafood and some of the best French fries in the East. There are four dining rooms, but eating in the dimly-lit, panelled barroom is the most fun. Excellent specials include prime rib on the weekend, New York strip steak on Tuesday night, and lobster tail on Wednesday night. Lunch and Dinner Mon–Sat, Sun 3:30–7:30 pm.

The Country House at Kimberton, Route 113 near Phoenixville; 933-8148. M. This 1796 inn offers excellent dining amid crackling fireplaces and a colonial setting accented by a host of antiques. The waterwheel mill house and the duck pond outside can be seen from the main dining room. The Kimberton crabmeat au gratin and original salmon Kimberton highlight a large, comprehensive menu, and the breads, cheesecake, and pies are made on the premises. Lunch and Dinner Tue–Sat, Sun 2–9 pm.

The Depot, 8515 Germantown Ave.; 247-6700. M. Even non-railroad buffs will be fascinated by the memorabilia at the depot—a 110-year-old caboose, a piece of metal from the railroad car that bore Abraham Lincoln to his funeral, and a model train that courses through the glass-enclosed bar. The cuisine is equally enjoyable; the meats, seafood, catch of the day, and the daily specials all are first rate. Dinner daily.

Fairmount Firehouse, 2130 Fairmount Ave.; 236-3440. M. This 1904 firehouse has been transformed into a striking restaurant. The dark wood walls are highlighted with attractive posters and paintings, along with a shiny brass pole to remind you of the days when it was an actual firehouse. A large racing shell and its oars hanging from the high ceilings remind one of Philadelphia's rowing heritage. The menu is as interesting as the restaurant and features traditional American dishes with a nouveau flair. Lunch Mon–Fri, Dinner Mon–Sat.

Flynn's Landing, 208 Race St.; 922-8046. I. This former blacksmith shop, with its wood-burning stove, hardwood floors, and brick walls, offers a rough-hewn atmosphere and American cuisine at attractive prices. Lunch Tue–Fri, Dinner Tue–Sat, Sunday Brunch noon–3 pm.

General Wayne Inn, 625 Montgomery Ave., Merion; 667-3330. M. This is a national historic restaurant that has been serving up hearty food since 1704. Turn back the clock and let the award-winning chef lavish you with one of his superior chicken, seafood, or veal dishes. The steaks, too, are outstanding. Lunch Tue–Sat, Dinner Tue–Sun, Brunch Sun.

Green's United States Hotel Bar and Grill, 4439 Main St., Manayunk; 483-9222. M. Owned by former Philadelphia mayor Bill Green, this restaurant features a raw bar, New York strip steak, blackened Louisiana redfish, etc. Lunch Mon–Sat, Dinner daily.

H. A. Winston & Co., seven locations, including Lancaster Ave., Paoli; 644-5120. I–M. This popular chain of restaurants is known for gourmet hamburgers with more than 20 different toppings. There are also fine quiches, omelettes, salads, and a wide variety of stuffed potato skins.

Head House Inn, 2nd and Pine Sts.; 925-6718. M. In an 18th-century setting of solid brass chandeliers, hurricane wall sconces, and wood beams, you'll enjoy fine smoked brook trout, tenderloin tips of beef bordelaise, and chicken cordon bleu. The chef's specialty is scallops of veal sauteed in white wine and topped with gruyere cheese. The Head House apple pie, made with Granny apples and sour cream, is a dessert favorite. Lunch and Dinner daily.

Houlihan's Old Place, 18th and Chancellor Sts.; 546-5940. Several locations. Also, King of Prussia Mall; 337-9522. I–M. These popular restaurant-bars offer American and international dishes in a relaxed atmosphere of greenery, antiques, art posters, and soft woods. Lunch and Dinner daily.

H. T. McDoogal's (see NIGHTLIFE Music for Listening and Dancing).

J. B. Winberie, 120 Locust St.; 923-6112, and 8229 Germantown Ave., Chestnut Hill; 247-6710. *I*. Warm, casual atmosphere and menu featuring steaks, seafood, pasta, salads, etc. Brunch Sun.

Jefferson House Restaurant, 2519 Dekalb Pike, Norristown; 275-3407. *M*. Country dining in this beautiful nine-room Georgian mansion is a delightful experience. The house is surrounded by ten acres that include a duck pond and a spring house, and the menu is highlighted by such specialties as rack of lamb Dijon, spaghetti Albania and shrimp scampi. Lunch Mon–Fri, Dinner Mon–Sat, Sun 1–8 pm.

Kinterra, 139 E. Lancaster Ave., Wayne; 687-5005. *M–E*. This charming restaurant, in the Wayne Hotel, serves popular nouvelle American cuisine at its best. Enjoy live jazz on Saturday evenings. Breakfast and Lunch Mon–Fri. Brunch Sat–Sun. Dinner daily.

Magnolia Cafe, 1602 Locust St.; 546-4180. *M–E*. Enjoy live jazz and Cajun/Creole specialties such as gumbo, crawfish etouffe, rabbit pasta, and New Orleans bread pudding. Saturday and Sunday brunch, too. Lunch and Dinner daily.

Mandana, 18 S. 20 St.; 569-4050. *M*. A Victorian townhouse with an intimate European atmosphere, serving regional American cuisines and international foods. Lunch Mon–Fri, Dinner Wed–Sat.

The Marketplace, 2400 Market St.; 569-4044. *I–M*. The building as a whole may only be opened to decorators and their clientele, but everyone is welcome to enjoy this fine American cuisine with a European flair. Among the specialties are chicken and artichoke hearts in lemon sauce over pasta, spinach and mushroom strudel, and a different souffle every day. Lunch only Mon–Fri.

Mendenhall Inn, Kennett Pike, Mendenhall; 388-1181. *M*. In the quiet rolling hills of Chester County is this lovely country inn, once an 18th-century barn and working mill. It now presents consistently outstanding food, including baked stuffed oysters, South African lobster tail, and calves liver saute. There's also a fine selection of imported and domestic wines. Lunch Tue–Sat, Dinner Tue–Sun, Sun 3–8 pm.

Montserrat (see NIGHTLIFE Bars).

Morley's Pub and Dining Saloon (see NIGHTLIFE Bars).

Morton's of Chicago—Philadelphia, One Logan Square; 557-0724. *M–E*. This classic steakhouse specializes in aged prime steaks, veal chops, and lobster. Relaxed, sophisticated atmosphere. Lunch Mon–Fri, Dinner Mon–Sat.

New London, 114 S. 12th St.; 922-5875. *M–E*. In the Victorian atmosphere of what once was a turn-of-the-century florist's shop, you can select from a menu of regional American dishes that include chicken Georgia, veal medallions, Mississippi mud pie, and "carpetbagger" steak. Lunch Mon–Fri, Dinner Mon–Sat.

Newport House, Bethlehem Pike at Dager Rd., Ambler; 542-7760. M. This restaurant is handsome with off-white walls, green wainscot, matted, softly-lit watercolors of old sailing vessels, and accented by the large brass chandeliers overhead. The menu offers basic, well-prepared food that includes robust soups, fine salads (especially the spinach), and hearty entrees highlighted by veal Newport and prime rib. Indulge in the homemade pumpkin pie or the chocolate chip cheesecake for dessert. Lunch and dinner Mon–Sat, Brunch Sun.

North Star Bar (see NIGHTLIFE Cabarets, Dinner Theater and Supper Clubs).

October, 26 S. Front St.; 925-4447. M. Fine regional American cooking is the rule in this relaxed setting of soft fall colors and fresh flowers. Among the wide variety of specialties are Philadelphia pepper pot and snapper soups, Maine baked mussels, Virginia pan-fried rabbit, Maryland veal, New Orleans jambalaya, and San Francisco cioppino. Lunch Mon–Fri, Dinner daily.

O'Dwyer's (see NIGHTLIFE Bars).

Old Norrington Tavern, Germantown Pike and Trooper Rd., Norristown; 539-5770. I–M. This former home of David and Benjamin Rittenhouse, which dates back to 1705 with the original brass and wood fully restored, offers everything from sandwiches and omelettes to full course dinners. In addition to the homemade breads and European coffees, there are also "stress hours" from 4–7 pm Tuesday through Saturday. Daily 11 am–1 am.

Orleans (see NIGHTLIFE).

Rib-It (see NIGHTLIFE Music for Listening and Dancing).

Seven Stars Inn, Ridge Rd. and Route 23, Phoenixville; 495-5205. M–E. Few who come to this 1736 inn for dinner leave without remnants of their meals to nibble on later. Portions are large and the food is simply too good to leave behind. Among the most popular selections are the surf and turf, lobster tail, and prime rib, and all are served with a choice of two of the seven fresh vegetable dishes. Dinner Tue–Sat.

Society Hill Hotel, 301 Chestnut St.; 925-1919. I. Inexpensive and creative dining and a cozy jazz piano bar. Lunch, Dinner, and late-night snacks daily.

Sportster's, Route 202 South at the Schuylkill Expressway, King of Prussia; 265-RIBS. I–M. Philadelphia, being the fanatical sports city that it is, took an instant liking to this place. Fans of all sports enjoy spicing the events on the seven-foot screens with barbecued babyback ribs, chicken, steaks, seafood, and the special of the day. The bar scene is a lively one, too. Breakfast, Lunch and Dinner daily.

Tiffany Dining Saloon, Route 202 north of Route 73, Center Square; 272-1888. M. In a plush Victorian decor accented with antiques, the "light meat" entrees are popular here. Included are breast of chicken, broiled scallops, flounder, and the day's fresh fish. You're welcome to create your own salad and grace it with the creamy oil and vinegar dressing. Dinner Mon–Sun, Brunch Sun.

Towne Hall, 15 S. High St., West Chester; 692-6200. M. Built as West Chester's town hall in 1912, this building once housed the offices of city government and police headquarters; in fact, what is now the kitchen used to be a block of jail cells. Both main dining rooms are decorated with Victorian antiques and softly-lit with 19th-century sconces and chandeliers. The Garden Room offers a more airy, casual atmosphere for lunch; try the crab cakes or London mixed grills. All the food, American with a touch of Italian, is superior here, especially the pheasant sauteed in brandy and fruit sauce and the veal piccante for dinner. Lunch Mon–Fri, Dinner Mon–Sat, Brunch Sun.

Two Quails, 1312 Spruce St.; 546-8777. M. In this contemporary spot with soft pastel colors and stenciling on the walls (it's the former site of Le Bec-Fin), you'll find a variety of excellent nouvelle American cuisine on three different menus. Among the more innovative dishes are buffalo with juniper berries and wild rice, breast of chicken in lemon marmalade sauce, and rib steak with wild mushrooms and bourbon sauce. Lunch Mon–Fri, Dinner Mon–Sat.

Valley Green Inn, Springfield Ave. and Wissahickon Creek, Chestnut Hill; 247-3450. M. You won't be able to resist the charm of this 18th-century inn located along the picturesque paths of Fairmount Park. Tempting hot dishes are especially satisfying on the dining porch in fair weather but they can also be enjoyed inside, where George Washington and Lafayette once dined on their way to Germantown. The inn does not serve liquor, so bring your own wine. Lunch and Dinner Mon–Fri, Brunch Sun.

Waldo's, 125 Sansom Walk; 627-4407. I–M. A casual, friendly place offering soups, salads, burgers, sandwiches, and pasta. Lunch and Dinner daily. Brunch Sun.

The White Dog Cafe, 3420 Sansome St.; 386-9224. M. New American cuisine in the heart of University City. Old favorites are combined with innovative dishes for an eclectic mix. Funky. Lunch daily. Brunch Sun.

Chinese

China Castle Restaurant, 939 Race St.; 925-7072. I. Authentic Cantonese Chinese cooking. Lunch and Dinner daily.

China Gate Restaurant, 153 N. 10th St.; 925-1906. *I.* Cantonese, Szechuan and Hunan cuisine with seafood, meat, and vegetarian specialties. Lunch and Dinner daily.

Chun Hing Restaurant, 1506 Spruce St.; 546-3888. *I.* Specializing in Szechuan cooking. Everything done to order. Lunch Mon–Fri, Dinner daily.

Ho Sai Gai I, 1000 Race St.; 922-5883, **Ho Sai Gai II,** 10th and Cherry Sts.; 925-8384. *I.* Also at 17th and Synder in South Philadelphia; 389-0300. These highly-acclaimed Chinatown restaurants rank among Philadelphia's finest. The decor in Ho Sai Gai II is more elaborate than that of its predecessor, but the food at both is consistently top-flight and a little more innovative than you'll find elsewhere in the area. You can choose from Szechuan, Mandarin, and Taiwanese soups and, from among the entrees, a spectacular dish called "Seven Stars Around the Moon" (lobster, tenderloin beef, chicken and roast pork sauteed in Chinese vegetables and surrounded by fried jumbo shrimp). A fine selection of vegetarian dishes, including superior stir-fries, are available too. Lunch and Dinner Mon–Sat.

Hu-Nan, 1721 Chestnut St.; 567-5757, 47 E. Lancaster Ave., Ardmore; 642-3050. *I–M.* These award-winning restaurants shun the stir-fry dishes for the more sophisticated and complex, and the results are the most stylish Chinese eateries in the Philadelphia area. Both specialize in the peppery cuisine of China's Hu-Nan region; the shrimp, with scallions and peppers in a sherry sauce, is like none other. Lunch, Mon–Fri, Dinner daily.

Imperial Inn, 142–146 N. 10th St.; 627-2299, 941 Race St.; 925-2485. *I–M.* Both offer a splendid selection of Szechuan, Mandarin, and Cantonese dishes, but if you can arrange for a party of at least 10, the fixed-price banquet is the way to go. Lunch and Dinner daily.

Mayflower Restaurant, 1010 Cherry St.; 923-4202. *M.* This restaurant serves Chinese cuisine such as deep-fried duck, Szechuan style, and seafood combinations in bird's nest. Lunch and Dinner daily.

Peking Restaurant, Granite Run Mall, Routes 1 and 352, Media; 566-4110. *I–M.* Unlike most shopping center Chinese restaurants, here you'll find dashes of haute cuisine with the more familiar Chinese-American favorites. Among the more creative specialties are shark's fin soup, beef sinews, and Peking duck. Lunch and Dinner daily.

Szechuan Garden, 1322 Walnut St.; 735-3334. *I–M.* One of the few Chinese restaurants located in Center City, Szechuan Garden caters to shoppers and business people with such spicy cuisine as Tung Ting shrimp, crabmeat with garlic sauce, and the tingly scallo beef. Lunch Mon–Sat, Dinner daily, Sun from 3 pm.

Tang's, 429 South St.; 928-0188. *I.* Owner Phillip Tang insists upon serving exclusively food traditional to China. In fact, all the food is served on painted china "from China," he says. With the entire menu based on all-natural Chinese ingredients, the shredded pork with Peking sauce is a favorite, along with the Thai chicken with broccoli. Tang's soups and vegetables are a delight, too. Dinner Mon–Fri.

Wok Chinese Seafood Restaurant, 1613 Walnut St.; 751-9990. I–M. Dishes from Szechuan, Mandarin, and Hunan cuisines represented. Lunch Mon–Sat, Dinner daily.

Continental

Arline, 1823 Sansom St.; 569-2754. M. Both intimate and casual continental dining are the stories in this elegant restaurant. Upstairs is a romantic Victorian dining room accented by pink and burgundy booths, while downstairs is a more clubby, casual atmosphere. The menu is select, innovative, and the chef is known for his specials. A pianist furnishes music Wednesday, Friday, and Saturday from 9 pm. Lunch and dinner Mon–Sat.

Blue Ram (see NIGHTLIFE Music for Listening and Dancing).

Bogart's, 17th and Walnut Sts.; 563-9444. M–E. In remembrance of the great actor, the Latham Hotel has a Casablanca atmosphere of ceiling fans, palms, and wicker. Many of the fine dishes are prepared at tableside. Breakfast and Lunch Mon–Sat, Dinner daily.

Carolina's, 261 S. 20th St.; 545-1000. M–E. This wildly popular restaurant appeals to the "Beautiful People" with eccentric but discriminating palates. Service is a bit shaky, and it's not a romantic or glamorous place, but the selection emphasizes Mexico, the Orient, and small-town USA. Reservations are a must. Lunch Mon–Sat, Dinner Mon–Sat, Brunch Sun.

Chadds Ford Inn, Routes 1 and 100, Chadds Ford; 388-7361. M. This historic inn has been satisfying customers since 1736, and the splendor of the surrounding countryside is now captured by the Wyeth paintings that adorn the walls. Among the more popular dishes are bay scallops in sherry sauce and heavy cream, veal Oscar, and roast duck a la Maison. Lunch Mon–Fri, Dinner Mon–Sat.

Chautauqua, 8229 Germantown Ave., Chestnut Hill; 242-9221. M. The basic decor and innovative dishes all contribute to the success this restaurant has enjoyed on the second floor of a renovated hotel. The oyster bar offers light snacks, primarily seafood, while the menu has interesting versions of pasta primavera, beef en brochette, and an intriguing selection of seafood, veal, and chicken dishes. Entertainment in the bar area on weekends. Lunch Mon–Fri, Dinner daily.

Chef Tell's, 115 Strafford Ave., Wayne; 964-1116. M–E. Fine continental and American cuisine created by Chef Tell Erhardt. Served in elegant surroundings on Philadelphia's Main Line. Lunch Mon–Fri, Dinner Mon–Sat.

Conti Cross Keys Inn, Routes 611 and 313, Doylestown; 348-3539. M. This is an 18th-century inn that once was known to patronize only those loyal to King George. Now all are welcome to enjoy the fine beef, lamb, and seafood dishes. Lunch Mon–Fri, Dinner Mon–Sat.

Crier in the Country, Route One, Glen Mills; 1-358-2411. E. Continental cuisine elegantly served in a restored Victorian mansion. Dinner daily.

The Cypress Restaurant, 301-305 S. 11th St.; 238-9967. M–E. Transcontinental cuisine in a subdued setting. Veal, lobster, prime rib. Dinner Tue–Sat.

Dilworthtown Inn, Route 202 at Brinton's Bridge Rd. and Old Wilmington Pike; 399-1390. M. Built in 1758 and now authentically restored, this inn presents fine continental and French cuisine that includes such dishes as crab imperial, filet mignon, and roast duckling. All are enhanced by an excellent wine list. Dinner daily.

Downey's, Front and South Sts.; 629-0526. M. An authentic Irish pub. You can get Irish stew, corned beef and cabbage, steaks, chops, and a complete continental menu. Lunch Mon–Fri, Dinner daily.

Duling-Kurtz House, 146 S. Whitford Rd., Exton; 544-1830. M–E. A quiet evening in the country can be spent in this charmingly renovated 19th-century mansion. Unusual continental and French dishes are served in eight intimate dining rooms, each with its own fireplace. Lunch and Dinner, Mon–Sat.

Ecco, 1700 Lombard St.; 735-8070. M–E. This tiny restaurant (it seats 30 in relative comfort) opened in 1986 and features flawlessly executed food—sometimes incredibly unusual, sometimes very successful. The menu changes seasonally, and the desserts are always a treat. Lunch Mon–Sat, Dinner Mon–Sat, Brunch Sun.

Friday, Saturday, Sunday, 261 S. 21st; 546-4232. M. Everything in this tiny rowhouse restaurant has been done with care and imagination. The decor is intimate yet casual, with the tapestry ceiling, mirrors, and reflected candlelight. The freshest ingredients are used in dishes you'll select from the blackboard menu. Breakfast and Lunch, Mon–Fri, Dinner Mon–Sat, Brunch Sun.

The Garden, 1617 Spruce St.; 546-4455. M. This townhouse restaurant, with a popular outdoor garden for summer dining, has forged a well-deserved reputation for great food. The interior dining rooms are decorated with charm and warmth, and the award-winning menu offers outstanding versions of steak tartare, veal medallion with ginger, roast duckling a l'orange, and breast of chicken with cepes. All are prepared with the utmost care. Lunch and Dinner Mon–Sat.

The Greenhouse, King of Prussia Rd. and Belrose Lane, Radnor; 687-2801. M. Part of this restaurant is actually a greenhouse, which underscores the bright, plant-filled atmosphere throughout. An excellent selection of wines applauds a menu of such delights as lobster and shrimp in fish stock and heavy cream, and rack of lamb glazed with coffee and sugar. Lunch Mon–Fri, Dinner daily, Brunch Sun.

Harry's Bar and Grill, 22 S. 18th St.; 561-5757. M. There's an upstairs dining room and another dining room downstairs, each with its own bar. Eighteenth century oil paintings of thoroughbred race horses and hunting scenes grace the walls, providing a clubby atmosphere for those dining on the fine pastas and aged beef. Lunch and Dinner Mon–Fri.

Hespe's, 115 Strafford Ave., Wayne; 688-9442. M. This lovely country mansion has served a Main Line clientele for more than 45 years. In five separate dining rooms with Victorian decor, you'll find owner and chef William Hespe serving excellent steak au poivre and broiled seafood. He is also known for his soups, especially the snapper. Lunch and Dinner Mon–Sat.

Horizon's (see NIGHTLIFE).

The Inn at St. Peters, off route 23, St. Peters Village; 469-9074. M. Nestled among the craft, fudge, and antique shops of St. Peters is this lovely restaurant, restored to its Victorian past. There are two dining rooms; one is glass-enclosed and overlooks the serenity of French Creek. Among the wide range of interesting dishes are the seafood bisque, chicken curry, and rainbow trout. Bed-and-breakfast accommodations also are available. Lunch Mon–Sat, Dinner Mon–Sun, Sun 1–7 pm.

Jamey's, 4417 Main St., Manayunk; 483-5354. M. An alternative to Center City fine dining. Upscale romantic restaurant serves seasonal specialties, many grilled over hardwood charcoal and mesquite. Lunch Mon–Fri, Dinner Mon–Sat.

Jenny's, Route 202 and Street Rd., Lahaska; 794-5605. M. Surrounded by the quaint shops of The Yard, this exquisite restaurant is resplendent in gray and burgundy hues. Three dining rooms serve carefully prepared dishes that include chicken and pasta primavera for lunch and chicken dijon and scallops tarragon for dinner. Lunch Mon–Sat, Dinner Tue–Sat, Brunch Sun.

Jethro's, First and Ruby Sts., Lancaster; 717-299-1700. M. The decor is very simple, plywood panelled walls and sparse furnishings, but you'll find some outstanding dishes arriving at tables graced with crisp linen and flowers. The hot and cold hors d'oeuvres are fresh and taste-filled, and the carefully prepared entrees include crabmeat in Mornay sauce and chicken stuffed with sausage and glazed with cider. Dinner Tue–Sun, Brunch Sun.

L'Auberge, Spread Eagle Village, Lancaster Ave., Strafford; 687-2840. M–E. This lovely restaurant has the ambiance of a French country inn with its blazing fireplace, shining copper pots hanging from the mantle, and fresh flowers on the tables. The cuisine is as delightful as the surroundings and includes innovative presentations of sweetbreads in Madeira sauce and chicken curry with peanuts, raisins, and coconut. Lunch and Dinner Tue–Sat.

Le Continental, Lancaster and Lakeside Aves., Berwyn; 647-2540. M. European elegance and grace is to be found in the decor here where the menu is highlighted by such dishes as steak Dianne, lamb en chemise, and filet of sole stuffed with spinach. Jazz is featured in the lounge on Wednesday and Friday nights. Dinner Tue–Sat, Brunch Sun.

Le Wine Bar (see NIGHTLIFE Cabarets, Dinner Theater and Supper Clubs).

Lickety Split, South St. at 4th; 922-1173. I–M. This was one of the first restaurants in the city to present nouvelle cuisine and it's still serving up an interesting array of soups, salads, and such entrees as stir-fried vegetables and broccoli topped with Alaskan king crab. The window comprising one complete wall offers a panorama of the neighborhood outside. Dinner daily.

London, 2301 Fairmount Ave.; 978-4545. M. Conveniently located across the street from the Art Museum, this cozy spot provides friendly service, sophisticated dishes, and, from Wednesday through Saturday nights, live entertainment. Lunch, Dinner and Late Snacks, Mon–Sat.

Marshallton Inn, Route 162, West Chester; 692-4367. M. You'll feel you are back in the 18th-century as you dine in this impeccably restored example of early Federal architecture. The excellent continental dishes are accompanied by a fine wine list, and an oyster bar adjacent to the restaurant serves light food from its own blackboard menu. Lunch Tue–Fri, Dinner Tue–Sat.

The Mile Post Inn, 644 Lancaster Ave., Strafford; 687-5640. M. In the tradition of the wayside inns that cropped up along this thoroughfare 200 years ago, The Mile Post offers fine food in a colonial atmosphere. It's particularly proud of its specialties, which include veal Marsala, rack of lamb, prime rib, and lobster. Lunch Mon–Sat, Dinner Sun–Sat. Sunday Brunch noon–3 pm.

Mirabelle, 1836 Callowhill St.; 557-9793. M–E. Sleek art-deco spot serving continental cuisine. Lunch Mon–Fri, Dinner Mon–Sat.

Monte Carlo Living Room, 2nd and South Sts.; 925-2220. E. This is easily one of the most exquisitely decorated restaurants in Philadelphia, with glass chandeliers and imported lace and crystal on the tables. An elegant club is upstairs. The menu features fisherman's baskets of lobster, salmon, and piettro, along with Dover sole in champagne sauce, veal, baby lamb chops, and steak. Dinner daily.

94th Aero Squadron, 2750 Red Lion Rd.; 671-9400. M. Many of you will find this restaurant a delightful place in which to dine, especially if you love aviation. The original headquarters for the 94th Aero Squadron features World War I memorabilia and offers a panoramic view of the Northeast Airport. While you dine on a fine selection of continental dishes, you'll also enjoy listening to the activity going on in the control tower. Lunch and Dinner Mon–Sat.

The Old Guard House, 953 Youngsford Rd., Gladwyne; 649-9708. M. Built in 1790 as a post office, this structure was later a hotel and a bar. Now a restaurant, the Old Guard House serves superior cuisine in a log-cabin setting of old cedar and oak. Among the specialties are calves liver with sage butter and bacon, medallions of veal in mushroom cream, and roasted farmhouse duckling with orange or pepper sauce. Lunch Mon–Fri, Dinner Mon–Sat.

Plumbsteadville Inn, Route 611 at Stump Rd., Plumbsteadville; 766-7500. M. The four dining rooms of this old inn are subtly decorated in a colonial motif, accented by a glowing fireplace and gleaming chandeliers. The continental and American cuisine is excellent, and the lounge presents entertainment nightly. Lunch and Dinner Tue–Sat, Brunch Sun.

Polo Bay Club (see NIGHTLIFE).

Pyrenees, 2nd and Bainbridge Sts.; 925-9117. M. Named after the mountains between Spain and France, this is a lovely, romantic restaurant that offers dishes traditional to both sides of the Pyrenees. Dinner Tue–Sat.

Quissett, Lancaster Ave., Haverford Square, Haverford; 896-0400. I–M. Nouveau continental cuisine is served in this unusual cafe. The decor is sparse, but the portions are anything but. A lot of care and imagination goes into everything on the blackboard menu which includes such delights as chicken saffron, seafood pasta, and pinbone sirloin steak. Afterwards, top off your meal with one of the scintillating desserts. Lunch Mon–Sat, Dinner daily.

Raymond Haldeman Restaurant, 110–112 S. Front St.; 925-9888. E. Spacious, elegant and comfortable European atmosphere featuring American, French, and Italian specialties from a Philadelphia restaurant legend. Lunch Mon–Fri, Dinner daily.

The Terrace, Route 1, Chadds Ford; 388-6741. I–M. This restaurant, built at a cost of $3 million, has been a welcome addition to the world-famous splendor of Longwood Gardens. A self-service cafe which resembles a country market, the Terrace serves hot and cold soups, salads, sandwiches, and a special of the day. The dining room offers a continental fare that includes a fine version of mushrooms stuffed with crabmeat and glazed with lobster sauce. Mon–Sat 11 am–5 pm, on days of special events 11 am–8 pm.

The Three Threes, 333 S. Smedley St.; 735-0667. I–M. Three generations and 50 years later, this family-owned restaurant is still serving up fine food at reasonable prices. Specialties include veal sauteed with mushrooms and sherry and roast duckling in orange sauce. Mon–Sat 11 am–10:30 pm.

21 West, 21 W. Highland Ave., Chestnut Hill; 242-8005. M. Tucked away in a tiny courtyard amid the quaint shops of Chestnut Hill. This restaurant has been popular for its fine continental food many years. Some of her best dishes are the veal chop Fontinea, roast leg of lamb, and chicken Eugene. Lunch offers an assortment of omelettes, crepes, sandwiches, and specials. Lunch and Dinner Mon–Sat.

Ulana's (see NIGHTLIFE Music for Listening and Dancing).

Upper Black Eddy Inn, River Rd. (Route 32), Upper Black Eddy; 982-5554. M. You'll find superior country dining in this 150-year-old inn that overlooks the Delaware River. The aroma of homemade breads enhances the cozy colonial atmosphere as you enjoy such favorites as sweetbreads in shallots and pork medallions with apple and port wine sauce. Lunch Wed–Sat, Dinner Wed–Sat, Brunch Sun.

The Walking Treaty Inn, River Road, Point Pleasant; 297-5354. M. This 18th-century inn offers charm and elegance, along with an interesting collection of continental dishes. They offer an excellent choice of wines and entertainment is available on Friday and Saturday evenings. Lunch Tue–Sun, Dinner Tue–Sat, Sun 5–9 pm.

Warren Tavern, Old Lancaster Ave., Malvern; 296-3637. M. Soft candlelight glows amid the crystal in this gracious inn that dates back to 1745. Dine on such favorites as veal Oscar Warren Tavern, rack of lamb, Caesar salad prepared for two, and a wide range of homemade pastries that include French chocolate ice cream with walnut crust. Dinner Mon–Sat, Brunch Sun noon–3 pm.

William Penn Inn, Route 202 and Sunnytown Pike, Gwynedd; 699-9272. M. In a colonial inn that dates back to 1714, the Mayfair dining room and the Seafood Tavern offer 35 different entrees and more than 150 wines. The portions are the he-man variety and include country-style roast rack of lamb, a mixed grill of lamb chop, filet mignon, pork cutlet and lobster tail, and other specialties. Lunch and Dinner Mon–Sat, Brunch Sun.

Eastern European

Annie's Place, 1206 Sansom St.; 592-6596. I. Homemade creations include blintzes, borscht, and stuffed cabbage. Traditional Philly fare offered too. Lunch Mon–Fri.

European Dairy Restaurant, 20th and Sansom Sts.; 568-1298. I. Homemade Eastern European Kosher dishes with an old country taste. Lunch and Dinner Mon–Fri.

Warsaw Cafe, 306 S. 16th St.; 546-0204. *I–M.* This friendly restaurant prepares superior versions of such hearty cuisine as borscht, German vegetable salad, beef stroganoff, sauerbraten, stuffed cabbage leaves, and Norwegian strudel (chicken, vegetables, almonds, raisins, and herbs in a light pastry crust). Lunch and Dinner Mon–Sat.

English

Dickens Inn, Head House Square, 2nd and Lombard Sts.; 928-9307. *M.* Dining in the historic 1788 Harper House is like dining in an old English pub. The cuisine is typically British, including Beef Wellington, rack of lamb, and of course, Yorkshire pudding. The outstanding desserts are fresh from the downstairs bakery. Lunch and Dinner daily, Tea Mon–Fri 3–5 pm.

French

Alouette, 334 Bainbridge St.; 629-1126. *M.* This charming restaurant presents nouvelle cuisine with Oriental touches. Specialties range from escargots wrapped in puffed pastry and glazed with egg yolk, to filet mignon spiced with peppercorn sauces. Dinner daily, Brunch Sun.

Cafe de Costa, New Market, Lower Courtyard, 2nd and Pine Sts.; 928-0844. *M.* Featuring "La Cuisine Provencale" from the south of France. Brick and stone Old World decor. Lunch and Dinner daily.

Cafe Royal, 18th St. and Benjamin Franklin Parkway; 963-2244. *E.* With its standard set by London's Cafe Royal since 1865, this new restaurant in the Palace Hotel has been a welcome addition to Philadelphia's discriminating dining scene. Superb haute cuisine is served with grace and style in an elegant setting designed by the noted Maria Bergsen. Chopin and Cole Porter music emanates from the grand piano. Lunch Mon–Fri, Dinner Mon–Sat.

Catherine's Paris Bistro, 782 S. Third St.; 592-6580. *M.* Authentic French menu featuring fish, meat, and game. Dinner Tue–Sat.

Chez Odette, South River Rd., New Hope; 862-2773. *M.* Built in 1794 and once a tavern for travelers on the Delaware Canal, Chez Odette offers superior French and continental dining in the serenity of a country-nautical atmosphere. Among the favorites are Chateaubriand, steak au poivre, and trout stuffed with escargots and langoustine. Lunch and Dinner Tue–Sat, Brunch Sun.

Coventry Forge Inn, Route 23, Coventryville; 469-6222. *M.* For more than a quarter century, this carefully maintained 18th-century inn has served basic French cuisine with an emphasis on freshness and simplicity. Dine on the enclosed porch in the summer or enjoy the cozy, romantic atmosphere the fireplaces lend the dining rooms in the winter. Hot cream watercress soup is a favorite, as well as the excellent rack of lamb. A fine selection of wines is available. The inn also offers colonial lodging in a quiet, rural setting. Lunch Tue–Fri, Dinner Tue–Sat.

Deja Vu, 1609 Pine St.; 546-1190. E. Owner Sal Montezinos is an individualist who has invested the same time and money on the interior of Deja Vu as he has on its menu. The result is that both are uniquely his own, from the luxurious Baroque atmosphere to the innovative touches he brings to traditional French dishes. His wine cellar, stocked with both rare and current vintages, is Philadelphia's oldest. Dinner Tue–Sat, Lunch Tue–Sat.

Deux Cheminees, 251 Camac St.; 985-0367. M–E. This 19th-century townhouse was the site of Philadelphia's first French restaurant, La Coin d'Or. Now beautifully restored, it presents fine classic French cuisine in a setting that suggests an invitation to the home of friends for dinner. Deux Cheminees has earned a four-star rating. Among the highlights are fresh bay scallops sauteed in an herbed butter sauce and the fresh catch of the day as prepared in the chef's own style. Dinner Tue–Sat, seatings at 5:30, 7, and 8 pm, Sun one seating from 5:30–7:30 pm.

Hotel du Village, North River Rd. and Phillips Mill Rd., New Hope; 862-5164. M. Here you'll find the delightful combination of traditional French cuisine served in an atmosphere of an old English manor house. The delicious dishes include lamb chops with green herbs, sole in curried butter, and filet with artichoke heart and choron sauces. Bring your own wine, as no alcoholic beverages are served. Dinner Mon, Wed–Sat, Sun from 3 pm.

The Inn at Historic Yellow Springs, Art School Rd., Chester Springs; 827-7477. M–E. This country inn was once a fashionable 18th-century resort. Much effort has been made to retain its historic appearance while creating intimate dining areas in an elegant, country atmosphere. An innovative selection of French gourmet dishes are served daily. Lunch and Dinner Tue–Sun.

The Inn at Oley, Friedensburg Rd., Oley; 987-3459. M. Many find this spot irresistible with its country French decor and traditional yet imaginative dishes that include steak au poivre, fresh trout poached in champagne, and baked red snapper in lobster sauce. Dinner Tue–Sat.

La Camargue, 1119 Walnut St.; 922-3148. M–E. Named by owner Marcel Brosette after the small province in the south of France where he once lived, this charming restaurant offers splendid dining in the coziness of a small country inn. Brosette worked under some excellent chefs in Europe (as well as under George Perrier at Le Bec-Fin) and presents formal dining in a friendly, relaxed atmosphere with classical guitar music in the background. Among his specialties are filet of sole dieppoise and rack of lamb. Lunch Mon–Fri, Dinner Mon–Sat.

La Chaumiere, 2040 Sansom St.; 567-8455. E. For more than 20 years chef-owner William Zimmerman has served excellent French cuisine in this intimate Gallic setting. His consistently fine food is highlighted by such dishes as coquille de bergerac duck l'orange, and crab marguerite. Dinner Tue–Sat. Prix fixe.

La Cocotte, 124 W. Gay St., West Chester; 436-6722. M. Located in a row house in this charming college community, La Cocotte is one of the better French restaurants in the Philadelphia area. All the classical French favorites are here, prepared with care and served in a friendly, relaxed atmosphere. Lunch Mon–Fri, Dinner Mon–Sat.

La Coquille St. Jacques, 314 Old York Rd., Jenkintown; 572-5411. E. Chef-owner Jacques Colmaire brings such magnificence to his classical French cuisine that some critics are convinced his classic dishes are the finest in the city. Given 24 hours notice, he will prepare any French dish you desire; but his menus, which are adjusted seasonally, are outstanding. The food is sumptuous, the atmosphere relaxed. Lunch Tue–Fri, Dinner Mon–Sat.

La Fourchette, 110 N. Wayne Ave., Wayne; 687-8333. M. This cozy, candlelit spot specializes in nouvelle cuisine and seafood, and is a favorite of the Main Line crowd. Lunch Mon–Fri, Dinner Mon–Sat.

L'Americaine, 135 S. 24th St.; 977-8917. E. A blend of French and regional dishes with awesome desserts. Art-deco atmosphere. Lunch Tue–Fri, Dinner Mon–Sat.

La Petite Auberge, Route 562 between Reading and Boyertown; 689-5510. M. Jean Maurice Juge's quaint little country restaurant is a minor challenge to find, and it is well worth the trip. All of his cuisine, from French classical to regional dishes to game, is prepared to perfection and served in delightfully warm and cozy surroundings. Don't overlook the puff pastries and daily specials. Lunch Mon–Fri, Dinner Mon–Sat.

La Terrasse, 3432 Sansom St.; 387-3778. M. Situated in three renovated 18th-century townhouses, La Terrasse features a terrace, glass-enclosed in the winter, open-aired in the summer, with brick floors and hanging plants everywhere. There is also a lively bar for a few pre-dinner cocktails before perusing a menu led by such favorites as roast duckling with orange Grand Marnier sauce and filet of west coast salmon grilled in beaujolais butter sauce. Dinner daily.

La Truffe, 10 S. Front St.; 925-5062. M–E. This restaurant, one of the city's first to offer strictly nouvelle cuisine, is delightful and romantic with gilt-framed mirrors, fresh flowers, and candlelight. Lunch Tue–Fri, Dinner Mon–Sat.

Lautrec, 408 S. 2nd St.; 923-6660. M. In an intimate, elegant setting accented by the art of Toulouse Lautrec, enjoy such fine French dishes as boneless breast of duck flambe, fresh bay scallops with madeira and cream, and heart of rack of baby lamb served with duxelles and spinach in puff pastry. A lighter fare and jazz music is available downstairs in the Borgia Cafe. (see NIGHTLIFE). Dinner Tue–Sat, Brunch Sun.

Le Beau Lieu, The Barclay Hotel, 18th St. and Rittenhouse Sq.; 545-0300. *E.* Luxury dining with French cuisine right in Philadelphia's classiest neighborhood. Breakfast, Lunch and Dinner Mon–Sat, Brunch and Dinner Sun.

Le Bec-Fin, 1523 Walnut St.; 567-1000. *E.* Twenty years ago, this restaurant was the first to introduce Philadelphians to superior French cuisine. Now it is one of Philadelphia's finest restaurants, having received a host of awards, and some national critics believe it is the best French restaurant in the East. What is incredible about Le Bec-Fin is that, under the endless quest for perfection by owner George Perrier, it somehow gets a little better every year. The Walnut Street location is also larger than the previous location on Spruce Street. Enhanced by its Louis XVI atmosphere, sophisticated, warm, intimate, the service is also as polished as the crystal. Lunch and Dinner Mon–Sat. Prix fixe.

Le Champignon, 122 Lombard St.; 925-1106. *M.* In this Gallic setting (the name is French for "mushroom"), you can choose between the elegance of a formal dining room or the homey atmosphere of the country room. The menu reflects the differences in both, offering classical French dishes and hearty cooking, as well as some splendid nouvelle cuisine. Lunch Mon–Fri, Dinner daily.

Sign of the Sorrel Horse, Old Bethlehem Rd., Quakertown; 536-4651. *M.* There are no distractions here, just superior French dishes prepared to meet the most discriminating taste. Located in the serene countryside of Quakertown, this restaurant presents an array of tantalizing dishes that include lobster in puff pastry, chicken stuffed with lemon and crushed walnuts, and daily specials. Dinner Mon–Sat, Brunch Sun.

Vicker's Tavern, Gordon Dr. and Welsh Pool Rd., Lionville; 363-7998. *E.* This is a 19th-century farmhouse where pottery was once manufactured. Now carefully restored, it houses five cozy dining rooms where owner-chef Arturo Burigutto presents creative French and continental cuisine that includes lobster tail in champagne sauce, quail with chestnut stuffing, and tournedos with artichokes and Bernaise sauce. Lunch Mon–Fri, Dinner Mon–Sat.

German

Hoffman House, 1214 Sansom St.; 925-2772. *M.* In the pleasantly haunting atmosphere of an old gasthaus with beer steins and dark woods, wainscoting and prints on the walls, you'll find gourmet German cuisine highlighted by steak tartare and superior fresh fish and wild game dishes. Lunch Tue–Fri, Dinner Tue–Sat.

Greek

South Street Souvlaki, 509 South St.; 925-3026. *I–M.* Once a takeout gyro and ice-cream stand, this restaurant now specializes in Greek and Middle Eastern dishes for takeout or eating on the premises. The menu changes frequently, but there's always moussaka and a wide range of Greek pastries, seafood, lamb, and chicken dishes. Monday night, you'll find Greek music, dancing, and fun. Lunch and Dinner daily.

Hungarian

Magyar, 2048 Sansom St.; 564-2492. *M.* If there were any other Hungarian restaurants in the Philadelphia area, Magyar would keep them on their toes. In a warm, charming atmosphere of linen, candles, and flowers, this tiny spot features Hungarian cuisine that soars well beyond goulash—lemon chicken in raisin sauce, noodles layered with ground sirloin, shard cheese and sour cream, and roast pork stuffed with sausage. Of course, the "guylash" is outstanding, too, as are the coarse breads and smooth, thick soups. Bring your own wine.

Indian

Siva's, 34 S. Front St.; 925-2700. *I–M.* This is one of the top restaurants in Philadelphia, offering truly unique dining pleasure. The kitchen is enclosed in glass and features a clay tandoor oven that produces everything from fantastic barbecued meats to tantalizing breads. The menu seems thick as an encyclopedia, but just let your waitress guide you; Siva's cuisine is prepared by the expert chef from Northern India and is first-rate. Lunch Tue–Fri, Dinner Tue–Sun.

International

The Abbott Cafe in the Abbott Building, 201 N. Broad St.; 977-9988. *I–M.* This new restaurant offers an innovative menu for the eighties. Light lunches offered, some Creole/Cajun dishes for dinner. Lunch and Dinner Mon–Fri.

Adrian Cafe, 747 N. 25th St.; 978-9190. You won't find any frills in this restaurant, but you will find great food. An interesting array of international dishes are listed on the blackboard and everything is cooked to perfection.

Astral Plane, 1706 Lombard St.; 546-6230. *M.* This restaurant occupies two converted townhouses where the decor is as intriguing as the food; the collection of antiques includes an old draped parachute suspended from the ceiling. The small menu features eclectic entrees and daily, in-season specials. Lunch Mon–Fri, Dinner daily, Brunch Sun.

The Commissary, 1710 Sansom St.; 569-2240. M. Owner Steve Poses offers a choice between two fine dining experiences in this bilevel restaurant. His small upstairs cafe, *USA Café,* features a different menu daily, but all the food—which always includes interesting stir-fries, pastas, seafood, and curried dishes—are accented by an exotic blend of ingredients. Downstairs is a bright, cheery cafeteria that offers the same menu and as fascinating a wine list as upstairs but also breakfasts of fresh fruits, omelettes, hot and cold cereals, and homemade pastries. Upstairs Lunch Mon–Fri, Dinner Mon–Sat. Downstairs, Breakfast, Lunch and Dinner daily.

The Fountain, One Logan Sq.; 963-1500. E. Elegance prevails in this restaurant in the Four Seasons Hotel, where pastel marble and gleaming brass are graced by windows with a magnificent view of Benjamin Franklin Parkway. Dishes from an international menu are carefully prepared and beautifully presented. Breakfast, Lunch, and Dinner daily. Brunch Sun.

Golden Pheasant, Route 32 and Erwinna, Bucks County; 294-9595. Romantic dining is available in this lovely 1857 country inn. International dishes are served in three dining rooms, including the Greenhouse, a glass-enclosed solarium.

Gold Standard, 3601 Locust Walk; 387-DINE. M. Two economics professors, Duane Ball and Roger Harman, enjoyed so much success with their original Gold Standard that they decided to expand their horizons with a larger restaurant; and this in the Christian Association Building is the admirable result. Restored red oak panelling is highlighted by leaded glass windows, a warm fireplace and friendly bar area, and an outdoor cafe. Downstairs you'll find a 200-seat cafeteria called the Silver Diner. The same menu is offered on both levels, and it includes a delightful collection of international dishes. Lunch and Dinner Mon–Sat.

The Hacienda, 36 W. Mechanic St., New Hope; 862-2079. M. The award-winning menu here offers consistently fine, hearty food that includes no-frills steak, prime rib, and chicken. Lunch features lighter dishes in wine sauces, creamed casseroles, cold platters, and salads. The four dining rooms are small and intimate, with the main room graced by mirrors and a warm fireplace. Lunch and Dinner Tue–Sun.

Judy's Cafe, 3rd and Bainbridge Sts.; 928-1968. I–M. This friendly neighborhood bistro attracts a regular clientele with hearty meals at prices that can't be beat. Among the most popular specialties are the sesame chicken and sauteed sweetbreads. Dinner daily.

Knave of Hearts, 230 South St.; 922-3956. M. For the romantically inclined, this is the perfect place to woo that special person. Soft candlelight flickers throughout, and there's a glass-enclosed garden in the back. It won't take long to discover that a lot of imagination has gone into the dishes on the small but varied menu. Lunch Sat–Sun, Dinner Mon–Sat.

L'Aigle d'Or, 1920 Chestnut St.; 567-0855. *E.* Amid the elegant surroundings, owner and chef Soren Arnoldi, a native of Denmark, prepares first class Danish, Australian, Hungarian, Japanese, and even African dishes, many of them at tableside. Examples of the variety from which you can choose are the Hungarian fresh lobster in creamy paprika sauce, Balkan sturgeon with eggs and mushrooms and baked in pastry, Grecian marinated lamb wrapped in strudel dough, and the African duck stuffed with forcemeat of pork and served in honied green peppercorn sauce. Lunch Mon–Fri, Dinner Mon–Sat.

Memphis, 2121 Arch St.; 569-1123. *I.* The downstairs restaurant serves lunch on Mon–Fri, dinner on Tues–Sat. Upstairs, a club features contemporary music, appealing to a 20- to 40-year-old crowd. Live jazz on Wednesday nights, too.

Mother's Restaurant, 4 N. Main St., New Hope; 862-9354. *I–M.* After you've wandered through the quaint shops on Main Street, you'll find the comfortable surroundings and friendly service of this restaurant most inviting. In addition to the contemporary indoor dining room, there's also a lovely outdoor garden where you can dine in the warm months. Among the favorites here are the German pancakes, the Vietnamese seafood basket, and the chutney chicken salad. Don't leave without some homemade goodies from the bakery and delicatessen. Lunch and Dinner daily.

Nyala Restaurant and Cafe, 123 S. 18th St.; 557-9401. *I–M.* Specializing in Ethiopian and African cuisines. Vegetable entrees, curries. Lunch and Dinner Mon–Sat.

The Restaurant School, 2129 Walnut St.; 561-3446. *I.* This charming Victorian restaurant offers the opportunity to watch future chefs displaying their culinary talents. The school has received considerable acclaim for its interesting assortment of dishes, many of which are prepared at tableside, and the menu is constantly changing. Prix fixe. Dinner Tue–Sat.

Roller's, 8705 Germantown Ave., Chestnut Hill; 242-1771. *I.* Perched on the top of Chestnut Hill is this small cafe, well known for its interesting dishes. The menu is forever changing, and if you're in a rush, takeouts are available at Roller's Market, right next door. Lunch Tue–Fri, Dinner Tue–Sat.

Rose Tattoo Cafe, 19th and Callowhill Sts.; 569-8939. *I–M.* Downstairs is a lively bistro. Upstairs, an intimate dining room features international and American dishes with an emphasis on seafood. Lunch Mon–Fri, Dinner Mon–Sat.

Saladalley, 1720 Sansom St.; 564-0767. Five locations. *I.* A sumptuous salad bar features an assortment of fresh greens and vegetables along with a selection of soups chosen from a collection of international recipes. Several dinner entrees are offered each evening and a special seafood salad bar is featured on the weekends. A selection of wines is also available. Lunch and Dinner daily.

Sannas, 239 Chestnut St.; 925-4240. M. Previously the site of a bank, this restaurant offers an eclectic gourmet menu in surroundings that are a delightful blend of the old and the new. The menu features a seafood soup that changes daily, appetizers such as shredded lobster wrapped in spring rolls, deep fried and served with a spicy Thai sauce, and entrees like fresh spinach pasta tossed with seafood or poultry and vegetables of the season. Lunch Mon–Fri, Dinner daily.

Sweet Basil, 4006 Chestnut St.; 387-2727. I. This restaurant has received a warm welcome in the University City area. The prices are reasonable and the variety of Asian and European cuisine is extensive. Even the salads are unique as they may include Brazilian shrimp, Thai beef, or Korean chicken. Among the more popular grilled entrees are Mongolian beef, Lebanese lamb, and tarragon chicken. Sweet Basil hasn't forgotten the red, white, and blue, however; its homemade apple pie is outstanding. Breakfast Mon–Fri, Lunch and Dinner daily.

20th Street Cafe, 261 S. 20th St.; 546-6867. M. The emphasis is on fine cooking rather than the decor, which is stark white. The menu is always changing, but it has included an award-winning boneless sliced duck breast and pasta primavera. The "Chili Elizabeth Taylor" is always available, and small wonder; it's an extremely popular hot and spicy dish topped with cornbread and served with black beans and vegetable chutney. Lunch and Dinner Mon–Sat, Brunch Sun.

Under the Blue Moon, 8042 Germantown Ave.; Chestnut Hill; 247-1100. I–M. As its name suggests, this restaurant offers a blue-moon motif highlighted by banners and linens, Mexican tile, and blond wood. The bar is open and airy, the waitresses attired in blue jeans, and the menu features hearty meals that are colorfully presented. Dinner Tue–Sat.

Irish

Downey's, 526 S. Front St.; 629-0526. M. This is an Irish spot so authentic that the downstairs bar, before it wound up here, was once part of a bank in Dublin. The hours are great (meaning late) and the food matches. In addition to a magnificent oyster bar which is laden with the freshest of seafood, you'll find a menu filled with such hearty delights as super sirloin steaks, green pasta with scallops in cream sauce, duckling with green peppercorn sauce, and of course, Irish stew. Lunch Mon–Sat, Dinner daily, Brunch Sun. Upstairs Dinner Fri–Sat, Late Supper until 2 am.

Irish Pub (see NIGHTLIFE Bars).

Italian

Alfredo The Original of Rome, The Bourse Building, 21 S. 5th St.; 627-4600. M. The fettucini is truly special here, courtesy of the former chef of the ocean liner *Michelangelo*. Excellent scampi and veal dishes are among the other favorites. Lunch and Dinner daily.

The Cafe Borelli, 117 S. 19th St.; 751-9494. M-E. Regional Italian dishes of pasta, veal, chicken and seafood. Lunch and Dinner Mon-Fri, Sat Dinner only.

Cent Anni, 770 S. 7th St.; 925-5558. I-M. In the old American-Neapolitan tradition, here you'll find red-checked tablecloths, a warm and cozy atmosphere, and a wide selection of seafood, pastas, and chicken dishes served in healthy portions. The prime sirloin can be exceptional. Dinner Mon-Sat.

Cou's Canal View Inn, 4348 Main St., Manayunk; 487-2330. I-M. Here's the place to feast on a seven-course dinner at a fixed price. Seafood specialties. And Main Street Manayunk is one of the fastest growing, and most fascinating, commercial districts in Philadelphia, a great place to walk off your dinner. Lunch Mon-Thu, Dinner daily.

Dante and Luigi's, 762 S. 10th St.; 922-9501. I-M. The room is simple, the food straightforward. Check out the calamari. Open daily.

DiLullo Centro, 1407 Locust St.; 546-2000. M-E. Northern Italian dishes prepared and served with flair in one of the prettiest new restaurants in the city. Across the street from the Academy of Music. Lunch Mon-Fri, Dinner daily.

Francesco's, 1430 S. Front St.; 398-0411. M. Authentic Italian cuisine including a variety of pasta and seafood. Lunch Tue-Fri, Dinner daily.

Frankie's Trattoria, 274 S. 20th St.; 546-3247. M. Northern Italian menu includes milk-fed veal, homemade pasta, and desserts. Lunch Mon-Fri, Dinner Mon-Sat.

Fratelli, 1701 Spruce St.; 546-0513. I-M. With its pink and green pastel decor, Fratelli's may not look like one of South Philadelphia's family-run restaurants, but it is. The homemade pastas are outstanding and complemented by delicate sauces and fresh vegetables. Among the most popular specialties are linguini primavera, fettucini Alfredo, and a half-dozen veal and chicken dishes as well. Don't overlook the Chocolate Decadence for dessert. Lunch Mon-Sat, Dinner daily.

Gaetano, 705 Walnut St.; 627-7575. E. This newer version lives up to the past glory of the old Ristorante Gaetano; in fact, some say it's the best Italian restaurant in the city. Everything served in this restored, handsomely-furnished townhouse, from the salads and pastas to the entrees and desserts, is outstanding. Of course, owners Inez and Gaetano Schinco are always around to make it so. All their five- and seven-course dinners are fixed price. Dinner Tue–Thu, seatings at 6 pm and at 8:30 pm, Fri–Sat, seatings at 6 pm and at 9:30 pm.

Giovanni's, 428 South St.; 592-1130. *I–M.* Giovanni's Italian restaurant is small and close. This adds to the charm of the place because you hear the oohs and aahs greeting the splendid dishes arriving at the adjoining tables. The menu is crammed with winners, including superior clams oreganata for appetizers. The entrees are paced by several outstanding veal dishes, especially the Rollentini. Giovanni's is uncompromising in its commitment to freshness. Dinner daily.

Il Gallo Nero, 254 S. 15th St.; 546-8065. *M.* Distinctly Northern Italian cuisine with a Florentine accent. Pheasant, wild hare, fresh white and black truffles in season. Lunch Mon–Fri, Dinner daily.

Jimmy's Milan, 39 S. 19th St.; 563-2499. *M.* For more than 30 years, this popular restaurant has specialized in basic Italian fare with the accent on quality. You can't go wrong here with the ziti, lasagna, manicotti, rigatoni, veal, bracciloa, chicken, and steaks. A specialty is the steak-and-a-half, which is broiled, or for an extra dollar, served with one of several toppings. Lunch Mon–Fri, Dinner Mon–Sat.

La Cucina, 121 South St.; 925-3042. *M.* An alleyway through a bricked courtyard leads to this restaurant that specializes in fine veal and seafood dishes, including a superior chippiano. Dinner Mon–Sun, Brunch Sun.

La Famiglia, 8 S. Front St.; 922-2803. *M.* Some say this is the city's finest authentic Italian restaurant. Mamma and Papa Sena fashion their dishes from personal recipes they gather each year in Italy. An exceptional Milanese appetizer combines mozzarella cheese and Italian ham, breaded in cornbread and eggs. The wine list is one of the most extensive in Philadelphia. Lunch Tue–Fri, Dinner Tue–Sun.

La Grolla, 782 S. 2nd St.; 627-7701. *M.* La Grolla translated into English means "cup of friendship," a traditional phrase from the Italian and French sides of the Northern Alps. In this quiet, elegant, formal dining room, the cuisines of both areas have been united with care and success. Lunch and Dinner daily, Brunch Sun.

Luchetta's Ristorante, 753 S. 2nd St.; 629-9518. Also, 3011 Jenkintown Ave., Glenside; 885-7992. *M.* These restaurants may be sparsely decorated, but there's nothing sparse about the seven-course, home-style Italian feasts they serve. Included are an assortment of appetizers, soup, flounder francese, grocci, and chicken franchese. All the portions are large and the obvious result of fresh ingredients. There is no liquor license here, so bring your own wine. Dinner Tue–Sun. Prix fixe.

Mama Yolanda's, 746 S. 8th St.; 592-0195. This charming Italian restaurant has become a popular spot, noted for its excellent veal, chicken, seafood, and pasta with homemade sauces. Dinner Tue–Thu, 5–11 pm; Fri–Sat, 5 pm–midnight; Sun, 3–10 pm.

Marabella's, 1420 Locust St.; 545-1845. M. A contemporary Italian restaurant in the theater district, featuring innovative cuisine in an upbeat setting. Pasta is handmade daily. Desserts are sinful. Lunch and Dinner daily.

Marra's, 1734 Passyunk Ave.; 463-9249. I. As Philadelphia's oldest Italian restaurant, this family-owned dining spot has years of experience in preparing homemade pasta, veal, chicken, and seafood dishes. The hot brick oven also produces a delectable thin-crust pizza that proves to be an ideal companion to a selection from the extensive list of imported beers and wines. Lunch and Dinner Tue–Thu, 11 am–11:30 pm, Tue–Sun, 11 am–1 am, Fri, Sun 1–11 pm.

Osteria Romana, 935 Ellsworth St.; 271-9191. M. As perhaps Philadelphia's most authentic Roman restaurant, Osteria Romana features angel hair pasta with caviar, mussels with brandy, and veal saporita. Leg of lamb Osteria Romana is a recommended special. To dine here is like sitting in the dining room of an Italian home. Dinner Tue–Sun.

Palumbo's (see NIGHTLIFE Cabarets, Dinner Theater, and Supper Clubs).

Piccolo Mondo, 21 S. 4th St. in the Bourse Building; 627-4600. M. Nothing flamboyant about this place, just good Italian cuisine at affordable prices. Lunch and Dinner daily.

Portofino Restaurant, 1227 Walnut St.; 923-8208. M. Central and Northern Italian cuisine served here, with daily specials. Lunch Mon–Fri, Dinner Mon–Sat.

Ralph's, 760 S. 9th St.; 627-6011. I. Dining at this family-operated restaurant has been a Philadelphia tradition for years. All the Italian dishes, especially the veal, linguini, and chicken varieties are exceptional, especially when accompanied by the homemade pastas. And it must be said—the mussels are a must. Lunch and Dinner daily.

Ristorante Alberto, City and Haverford Aves.; 896-0275. M. This Italian spot has been a hit ever since its doors opened. The stylish Main Line crowd loves the quality and ample portions on a menu featuring canneloni, linguini, veal, and seafood dishes. Dinner daily.

Ristorante DiLullo, 7955 Oxford Ave., Fox Chase; 725-6000. M–E. There is much to look forward to at this world-class Italian restaurant—the mirrored, airy atmosphere, the small chic bar, and Northern Italian dishes prepared and served to perfection. You'll even be able to watch the pasta creations being made in the open air kitchen. Entree favorites include the veal dishes, lamb parmigiana, and steaks broiled the Florentine way. Dinner daily.

Ristorante La Buca, 711 Locust St.; 928-0566. M. This cozy restaurant features regional Italian cuisine and Old World service in a softly-lit dining room with brick and stucco walls. The catch of the day will be brought to your table before it is prepared. Lunch Mon–Fri, Dinner Mon–Sat.

Saloon, 750 S. 7th St.; 627-1811. M. This is a most attractive restaurant, with its carved-wood molding and panelling, antiques, stained glass, and white-tiled floors. The whole-wheat pasta with crabmeat is a rare treat and the fettucini Alfredo certainly is a credit to its name. However, the Saloon's reputation has been forged by its treatment of steaks, sirloins, and filet mignon. Lunch Mon–Fri, Dinner Mon–Sat.

San Marco, 27 City Ave., Bala Cynwyd; 664-7844. M. The accent is on Northern Italian dishes in an atmosphere of a converted mansion. Some of the fine pastas include penne arrabiata (spicy hot), cannelloni, and cappelletti. The chicken Florentine is a winner and the veal, fish, and beef specialties are highly recommended. Music from the piano bar. Lunch Mon–Fri, Dinner Mon–Sat.

Si Ristorante, 212 Walnut St.; 238-1528. M. This new restaurant, ideally located across from the Ritz 5 movie theater, serves a Northern Italian cuisine featuring pasta, meat, and seafood. Lunch and Dinner daily; late snacks, too.

Spaghetti Factory, 530 South St.; 627-5595. I. Pasta, anyway you like it, in a festive atmosphere. Lunch and Dinner daily.

S.P.Q.R., 2029 Walnut St.; 496-0177. M. To answer your first question, the name comes from the call letters of the Latin phrase that means, "The Senate and the people of Rome." Owner-chef Vincent di Donato spends most of his time in the kitchen working with fresh, quality ingredients. You can't miss with anything on the menu—lamb, rib chops, pasta, veal, chicken, and seafood—but the mussels are outstanding. Lunch Mon–Fri, Dinner Mon–Sat.

Strolli Restaurant, 1528 Dickinson St.; 336-3390. I. This family-operated restaurant has been delighting patrons with homemade Italian foods for years. Don't expect fancy decor, only fine cooking with the freshest ingredients. Included on the menu are veal piccante, chicken cacciatore, grocchi, and a variety of pastas. Lunch and Dinner Mon–Sat.

Thomas', 4201 Main St., Manayunk; 483-9075. M. A Northern Italian menu and a 100-year-old bar. Lunch daily, Dinner Mon–Sat.

Torano's, 11th and Christian Sts.; 925-2282. M. In the atmosphere of an Italian villa, you'll enjoy large portions of excellent lasagna, baked rigatoni, veal parmigiana, and chicken cacciatore. The lobster dishes are outstanding; the salads superior. The Empire Room upstairs has entertainment once a month, accompanied by a special menu. Lunch and Dinner Mon–Sat.

Towne House, 117 S. South Ave., Media; 566-6141. M. Families have been known to fill up Babe D'Igazio's ten dining rooms for his homemade pasta, large salads, and Italian and seafood specialties. He also offers prime rib of beef and a 2½-pound Porterhouse steak, both of which rank among the largest in town. Lunch daily, Dinner Mon–Sat.

Triangle Tavern, 10th and Reed Sts.; 467-8683. *I.* This neighborhood restaurant and bar is the epitome of South Philadelphia Italian food, fun, and festivity. It specializes in pasta, pizza, mussels, and antipasta salads. Local bands, musicians, and singers Friday and Saturday nights. Dinner Mon–Sat.

Japanese

Chiyo Japanese Restaurant, 8136 Germantown Ave., Chestnut Hill; 247-8188. M. Traditional Japanese favorites. Special treats are Japanese salad and green tea ice cream. Bring your own wine. Dinner daily.

Chocho Japanese Restaurant, 1824 Ludlow St.; 567-9679. *I.* A small, unassuming restaurant featuring an extensive menu. Open daily.

Hikaru, 607 S. 2nd St.; 627-7110. M. Take your shoes off in the tatami room and enjoy sushi or sukiyaki. Lunch Mon–Fri, Dinner daily.

Kanpai, at Head House Sq.; 925-1532. *I–M.* Overlooking the New Market shopping complex, this restaurant offers Japanese Teppanyaki cooking in which everyone generates an appetite while watching steak, seafood, chicken, and vegetables sizzle to perfection at tableside. There's also a sushi bar and an intimate cocktail lounge. Lunch, Tue–Fri, Dinner daily, Sun from 3 pm.

Kawabata, 2455 Grant Ave.; 969-8225. *I–M.* Kimono-clad waitresses serve from an authentic Japanese menu. The sushi bar features more than 20 varieties of fresh fish. Lunch Mon–Fri, Dinner Mon–Sun.

Kawagiku Japanese Restaurant, 110 Chestnut St. at Front St.; 928-9564. M. Elegant yet homey, Kawagiku is perfect for enjoying the light cuisine of Japan. Scallop kushi and salmon batayaki are impressive. All-vegetable sushi is very popular. Lunch Mon–Fri, Dinner Mon–Sat.

Kyo Japanese Restaurant, 228 S. Broad St.; 545-7144. M. Gourmet selections of fresh sushi and sashimi, teriyaki and tempura dishes. Lunch Mon–Sat, Dinner daily.

Mexican

Binni & Flynn's (see NIGHTLIFE Bars).

Casa Maria, 145 W. DeKalb Pike, King of Prussia; 337-2303. *I.* This beautifully decorated restaurant glows with bright pinatas and flowers, and it's all warmed by the Mexican music and friendly service. Try Maria's special, if you're undecided, but don't pass up at least one of the frozen margaritas. Lunch Mon–Thu, Dinner Mon–Sun, Fri–Sun from 3 pm.

Cantina del Dios, 225 Church St.; 625-8686. *I.* Beneath an old sugar refinery is this charming restaurant, the name of which means "eating place of the gods." Decked out with brightly colored Mexican ornaments, if offers a wide variety of fine Mexican food that includes stuffed tortillas and beef and eggplant casseroles. Lunch Mon–Sat, Dinner daily, Brunch Sun.

El Sombrero, 1046 Bustleton Pike, Feasterville; 357-3337. *I.* This no-frills, family-run restaurant serves truly authentic Mexican dishes. But expect to wait, for each is cooked to order with the finest of ingredients, and the ultimate takes a little time. Along with the traditional guacamole, nachos, and burritos, try the fish house soup or the pierna al horno (roast pork in a succulent gravy). Bring your own beer or wine. Lunch Mon–Fri. Dinner daily.

Los Amigos, 50 S. 2nd St.; 922-7061. *I.* This cantina serves traditional Mexican dishes along with margaritas that are reputed to be the best in the city. The six-page menu features a combination of platters, special entrees, appetizers, and a wide selection of Mexican beers. Lunch Mon–Fri, Dinner daily.

Moroccan

Marrakesh, 517 S. Leithgow; 925-5929. *M.* Dining in Marrakesh is truly a unique experience; you sit close to the floor on pillowed benches and are served on revolving brass circles. Eating Moroccan style means using the fingers of your right hand; your hands will be cleansed with warm water poured from a brass kettle. A typical dinner starts with a nibbling of three vegetables, three salads, some breads, and bastilla, a pastry filled with eggs and poultry. Then comes lemon chicken, skewered lamb, and couscous tinged with the flavor of zucchini, turnips, and a nice hot sauce. Dinner daily.

Pennsylvania Dutch

Good 'n Plenty Restaurant, East Brook Rd., Route 896, Smoketown; 717-394-7111. *I–M.* In this old farmhouse, sect ladies whip up family-style Pennsylvania Dutch meals of pork, chicken, and beef with sauerkraut and rich egg noodles. Breakfast, Lunch, and Dinner until 8 pm Mon–Sat.

Groff Farm, RD 3, Mount Joy; 717-653-2048. *M.* This working farm was once the home of Betty and Abe Groff. Now it is one of the best places to eat in Lancaster County. In the Early American farmhouse that has been converted into a series of small dining rooms, you'll enjoy robust, family-style meals that include country ham, Chicken Stoltzfus (chicken with tiny bits of pastry in thick gravy), and prime rib. Seconds are encouraged, and after the bean soup embellished with chunks of ham, the fresh, steamed vegetables, homemade breads and butter, and whatever you choose for your main course, you'll depart filled to the brim. Lunch Tue–Fri, Dinner Tue–Sat.

Moslem Springs Inn, Routes 222 and 662 between Reading and Allentown; 944-8213. M. Built more than 130 years ago as a place for food, drink, and lodging for travelers headed to and from Philadelphia, this inn has retained an atmosphere of an era gone by. The dining rooms are graced with flickering fireplaces; you'll love the tasty meats from the smokehouse in the back, the fresh vegetables, homemade breads, and dark butter. Lunch and Dinner Mon–Sat.

Russian

Borscht and Tears, 202 S. Quince St.; 923-1853. M. Just a few steps from the Forrest Theater, this restaurant offers robust a la Russe dining in neat, comfortable surroundings. For appetizers, the herring in pink beet sour cream, the buckwheat blini, and the salmon caviar are highly recommended. For main dishes, the Chicken Kiev is superior, as are the veal with mushrooms, nuts and buckwheat, the medallions of lamb in juniper sauce, the duck with apple bread stuffing, and stroganoff on homemade noodles. Dinner Mon–Sat.

Seafood

Bookbinder's Seafood House, 215 S. 15th St.; 545-1137. M–E. The fourth generation of Bookbinders, Sam and Richard, continue to operate the family business that long ago became an institution in Philadelphia. In an atmosphere of oak panelling, nautical chandeliers, and captain's tables, the menu boasts live Maine lobsters up to 3½ pounds in size, super fresh oysters, clams and jumbo shrimp, and a variety of fresh fish dishes. The mussels in red sauce are truly special. Also, don't hesitate to order from Booky's selection of prime meats; they are first-rate. Lunch and Dinner daily.

Buoy 1, Route 30 at 401, Frazer; 644-0549. I. This no-frills place may be the best catch for the price in the Philadelphia area. You'll use paper plates and plastic utensils, but this only helps keep the price of excellent seafood in line. Specialties include shellfish and fresh fish, and the daily chowders are robust and flavorful. Sandwiches are excellent and the entire menu is available for takeout. Bring your own beer and wine. Daily 9 am–11 pm.

Clam Tavern I, 339 E. Broadway Ave., Clifton Heights; 623-9537. Also 615 MacDade Blvd., Collindale; 532-1938. I–M. This tavern's highlights include the broiled lobster tails, steamed shrimp and clams, and fried fish. The volume here enables them to produce quality food at very appealing prices. Dinner Mon–Sun.

DiNardo's, 312 Race St.; 925-5115. I–M. The menu includes most of the usual seafood favorites, but practically everyone comes to roll up their sleeves and dig into the metal trays brimming with steamed Louisiana crabs. You can thank the DiNardo family for the super seasoning and sauces. Lunch Mon–Sat, Dinner daily.

The Dockside Fish Company, 815 Locust St.; 925-6175. M. Fresh fish hot from the grill is the specialty in this friendly neighborhood restaurant. Enjoy your meal with a lovely view of the outside through the glass wall of the beige and lavender dining room. Lunch and Dinner daily.

The Fish Market, 124 S. 18th St.; 567-3559. M. With its butcher block, blond wood, and touch of neon and Scandinavia, this became the city's first gourmet seafood restaurant in 1975. Still attached to the little retail fish market that provided its name, the restaurant has since been greatly expanded to accommodate its devotees. The menu is chic and seasonal. For dessert try the apple pie; it might be the best apple pie in town. Lunch Mon–Fri, Dinner daily.

Flying Fish, 8142 Germantown Ave., Chestnut Hill; 247-0707. M. This is a casual but elegant restaurant featuring seafood and luscious desserts. Lunch Mon–Sat, Dinner daily.

Kelly's on Ludlow Street, 1620 Ludlow St.; 567-4333. I–M. Kelly's is so fanatical about quality that a new menu, based on the freshest seafood and fish available each morning, is printed every day. Their meats, too, are outstanding. Visit the "standup" oyster and clam bar. Kelly's has been doing things this way since 1901. Lunch Mon–Fri, Dinner Mon–Sat.

Moshulu, Chestnut St. and Delaware Ave.; 925-3237. M–E. More than $2 million was spent to transform this ship, the largest steel sailing vessel afloat 75 years ago, into a restaurant. Now moored at Penn's Landing, it offers the standard fare of seafood and beef in a unique Victorian setting on the Delaware River. Lunch Mon–Sat, Dinner daily.

Mr. Ron's Louisiana Seafood House, Route 73 and Penllyn Pike, Blue Bell; 542-9090. M. The decor is early New Orleans and the menu features more than 80 items from Cajun country. There is an excellent seafood bar, where the Mardi Gras sampler includes raw oysters and clams, shrimp, and crabmeat. The bouillabaisse leads a parade of hearty portions. Lunch and Dinner daily, Late Snacks Fri–Sat.

Old Original Bookbinder's, 125 Walnut St.; 925-7027. M–E. Dining here has been a Philadelphia tradition since it was opened in 1865. All done up in mahogany, antiques, and tables laden with superior seafood, this is where the locally-important and out-of-town famous go to dine (and be seen). Seven rooms, each different, seat a total of 1000 customers. Start with the peerless snapper soup, then move on to a menu that includes live Maine lobster, crabmeat, oysters, shrimp, and clams. The sole, scrod, swordfish, and bluefish are tops, broiled to perfection. Lunch and Dinner daily, Sun 1–10 pm except July and August 3–10 pm.

The Original Blue Point Seafood House, corner of Bridge and Harbison; 289-3344. I–M. At a new location, this restaurant is still keeping customers happy with a large selection of seafood dishes. Specialties include platters of hard shelled crabs and shrimp, lobster, and steamed mussels, clams, and oysters. Take out service is available. Open daily Mon–Sun.

Philadelphia Fish & Company, 207 Chestnut St.; 625-8605. I–M. This restaurant specializes in mesquite grilling, and the desert hardwood that burns so hot brings out the best of flavors in the seafood and chicken served here. Order from the blackboard and then watch your meal being grilled in the kitchen through the large picture window. Lunch Mon–Fri, Dinner daily.

Reisha's, 646 South St.; 592-8899. I–M. Relax in a casual setting with buckets of steamed garlic crabs, or try lobster burgers. Cajun cheesecake for dessert is a must. Lunch and Dinner Tue–Sun.

Sansom Street Oyster House, 1516 Sansom St.; 567-7683. I–M. The emphasis is strictly on the seafood here, not the decor. The floors are bare and the walls are "decorated" by a collection of oyster plates, some of them antique. All the clams and oysters are shucked on the premises and can be bought individually. In addition to the raw delights of the oyster bar, succulent clam and oyster stews, broiled and fried fish, and shellfish platters are available. Lunch and Dinner Mon–Sat.

Snockey's Oyster House, 1020 S. 2nd St.; 339-9578. I–M. In this family-owned restaurant, Mrs. Snockey has been preparing the specialty of the day, oyster stew soup, for more than 70 years. Other seafood favorites are made with lobster, shrimp, clams, and mussels. Lunch Mon–Sat, Dinner daily.

South Street Lobster House, 431 South St.; 238-1830. M. Pasta, veal, poultry, and steaks in addition to fresh seafood. European rustic decor. Open daily.

Top of Centre Square, First Pennsylvania Bank Tower, 15th and Market Sts.; 563-9494. Here, 41 stories above Philadelphia, you can enjoy a spectacular view of Center City while dining on a menu of fine seafood and other dishes.

Walt's King of Crabs, 804-06 S. 2nd St.; 339-9124. I. This is a truly low overhead spot, a fact that is reflected in the winning prices on huge platters of high quality seafood. Walt's features hard-shell crabs all year round and the special is a pair of jumbo shrimp stuffed with crab meat. Friendly folks abound, with pitchers of ice cold beer, wine, and mixed drinks available at the two bars. Lunch and Dinner daily.

Thai

Bangkok House, 117 South St.; 925-0655. I. This house is white and spartan, but then it's in the business of fine Thai food, not interior decorating. The "satay," a marinated meat kabob, is the appetizer to start with; then move on to a menu of sweet, sour, and hot delights. The number of asterisks beside each dish indicates just how hot each will be. Dinner daily.

Siam Cuisine, 925 Arch St.; 922-7135. M. Surrounded by an elegant atmosphere, this restaurant offers a unique blend of dishes from Thailand. Some of their specialties include fried fish cakes and Thai beef salad, along with an assortment of exotic desserts. Lunch Tue–Sun, Dinner Mon–Sat.

Siam Lotus, 931 Spring Garden St.; 235-6887. M. Unusual Thai dishes. Beautifully served in "late art-deco" atmosphere. Located in a changing area of Philadelphia. Lunch Mon–Fri, Dinner Tue–Sun.

Thai Royal Barge, 23rd and Sansom Sts.; 567-2542. M. Classic and authentic Thai food. The degree of spiciness is suited to your palate. Dinner daily.

Vietnamese

Saigon Restaurant, 935 Washington Ave.; 925-9656. I. Le Hop and his wife operate this restaurant beneath their rowhouse home, preparing excellent meals with fresh ingredients and vegetables from the nearby Italian Market. Their curry dishes, a Vietnamese beef soup called "pho," and their spring rolls are out of this world. Lunch and Dinner Mon–Sat.

Vinh Hoa, 746 Christian St.; 925-0307, 8919 Ridge Ave.; 482-3760. I. Although there are 24 Vietnamese dishes from which to choose, carefully prepared fish specialties are the highlights at both locations. Everything—including Korean, Chinese, and Japanese cuisine—is cooked to order, and the "happy pancakes" alone are worth a visit. Lunch and Dinner daily.

ETCETERA

A Slice of Heaven, 8225 Germantown Ave., Chestnut Hill; 248-3888. I. Sinful desserts, elegant afternoon teas, Sunday brunch and now, dinner. Closed Tuesdays.

The Bourse, Independence Mall, between 4th and 5th Sts.; 625-0300. I. The third level of this historic merchant's exchange building has 14 fast-food eateries that feature international as well as local specialties. Choose from Philadelphia's own cheese steaks, sandwiches from Bain's, soups, salads, and more. There's a wine bar on Saturday. Desserts? Try the unforgettable cheesecake from Katz's, as well as the homemade pastries and ice cream. It's all to be enjoyed from the tables of the open-air, third-floor balcony. Mon–Sat 10 am–6 pm, Sun noon–6 pm.

Copa Banana, 4th and South Sts.; 923-6180, and **Copa Too,** 263 S. 15th St.; 735-0848. *I.* These two Center City cantinas serve great burgers and Tex-Mex food, fiery Spanish fries, and fresh margaritas. Lunch and Dinner Mon–Sat.

Corned Beef Academy, 121 S. 16th St.; 665-0460, 18th St. and JFK Blvd.; 568-9696, 4th and Market Sts.; 922-2111. *I.* This trio of spots is among the busiest in town at lunchtime. The reason is that they offer hearty salads, fantastic sandwiches, and some of the best French fries to be found anywhere. Breakfast Mon–Fri, Lunch Mon–Sat.

Country Club Restaurant, 1717 Cottman Ave., Northeast Philadelphia; 722-0500. *I.* A landmark diner with famous baked goods, at least five varieties of chicken daily, brisket, blintzes, matzoh ball soup, etc. Open 24 hours.

Diner on the Square, 19th and Spruce Sts.; 735-5787. *I.* Friendly neighborhood diner with reasonable prices. Breakfast served all day. Open daily.

The Famous Delicatessen, 700 S. 4th St.; 922-3274. *I.* This Philadelphia institution for more than 70 years is still "famous" for its blintzes, corned beef, and chopped herring sandwiches, as well as for its kniches and kugels. The chocolate chip cookies are a must. Daily 7 am–6 pm.

The French Bakery and Cafe, 8624 Germantown Ave. (rear), Chestnut Hill; 247-5959. *I.* Continental breakfast and light lunches featuring croissant sandwiches, quiches, and soups. A neighborhood hangout. Open daily.

Hymie's, 342 Montgomery Ave., Merion; 664-3544. *I.* For 30 years this award-winning deli has been serving a loyal following with generous portions of homemade cabbage and matzo ball soup, blueberry, cheese, and cherry blintzes, and lox and bagels. The roast turkey and chicken are specialties, too. Daily 7 am–11 pm, Fri–Sat until 1 am.

Latimer Deli and Restaurant, 255 S. 15th St.; 545-9244. *I.* All entrees are homemade, including turkey, brisket, roast beef, whitefish salad, quiche, kugel, etc. Daily dinner specials. Lunch and Dinner daily.

Le Bus, 3402 Sansom St.; 387-3800. *I.* Located in University City, this restaurant has the best muffins and cornbread in town. Also, soups, salads, and pasta dishes. Light breakfast, lunch, and dinner daily.

Market Fair, The Gallery at Market East, 9th and Market Sts.; 925-7162. *I.* Here you'll find 25 local and international fast food eateries on the lower level of the magnificent indoor mall. They serve everything from Chinese and Mexican foods to clams and pizza. Mon–Sat 10 am–8 pm, Sun noon–5 pm.

Melrose Diner, 1501 Snyder Ave.; 467-6644. *I.* Started in 1932, this 24-hour Philadelphia institution is now serving good, old-fashioned American food to an average of 3000 people per day! All the fresh ingredients for the dishes on the standardized menu are weighed to the fraction; as a result, there's consistent excellence from week to week with such winners as the bean and vegetable soup, lamb stew, roast chicken, crab cutlets, and ever-popular apple pie. The Melrose Diner may be strictly "diner" in decor, but with the exception of Christmas Eve and Christmas Day, it's always open with wholesome, hearty food. 24 hours.

More Than Just Ice Cream, 1141 Pine St.; 574-0586. *I.* This place caters to the entire family with much more than just ice cream. Using the freshest ingredients, Kay, the owner, whips up quiches and chili daily, and, for dessert, has apple cobbler, apple pie, and pumpkin pie that is out of this world. Hot loaves of honey bread also are on sale. Daily from 7:30 am.

Natural Foods Eatery, 1345 Locust St.; 546-1350. *I.* This expanded eatery on the second floor features gourmet health foods and a view of the Academy of Music and the Hershey Hotel. Lunch and Dinner Mon–Sat.

Nooner Lunch, 115 S. 10th St.; 351-9191. *I.* Up-to-date diner specializes in country American home cooking. Fabulous breakfasts. Breakfast and Lunch Mon–Fri.

Old Original Levis, 507 S. 6th St.; 627-2354. *I.* For 85 years this spot has been grilling the same (and best) beef hot dogs in town. The neon hot dog sign outside is proof you've arrived. The fishcakes are legendary too, as is the "champ" cherry soda from the oldest operating soda fountain in the nation. Not much has changed at Levis in the last 90 years except a little redecorating here and there, and, considering the cost of everything today, a very modest increase in prices. Daily in the winter 10 am–7 pm, other seasons 10 am–11 pm.

Over the Rainbow, 856 Montgomery Ave., Narberth; 664-8589. *M.* Imaginative healthy cuisine offers Pritikin and vegetarian specialties. Lunch and Dinner Tue–Sat.

Pat's King of Steaks, 1237 E. Passyunk Ave.; 339-9872. *I.* This is another Philadelphia institution where, 24 hours a day, people from all walks of life line up for the thinly-sliced beef on fresh rolls, doused with hot melted cheese. "Philadelphia cheese steaks" originated with Pat's, and you can get them "wid" or wid'out" onions. How good are they? Well, rumor has it that Sinatra sent his chauffeur up from Atlantic City to pick up a limousine full. 24 hours. Closed Christmas Day and New Year's Day.

Pikkles Plus, 113 S. 16th St.; 561-0990. *I.* Fresh cooked turkey every day and all fresh deli selection. Center City lunch crowd. Breakfast and Lunch Mon–Sat.

Pizzeria Uno, 509 S. 2nd St.; 592-0400. *I.* This is a fun, bustling spot with a saloon decor where you'll find no less than ten varieties of deep dish pizza along with an interesting selection of sandwiches, salads, soups, and drinks. Sun–Thu 11 am–1 am, Fri–Sat until 2 am.

Reading Terminal Market, 12th and Filbert Sts.; 922-2317. *I.* Built in 1893, this bustling marketplace, now on the National Register of Historic Places, has more than 700 shopping stalls, with 20 of them comprising a veritable smorgasbord of over-the-counter delights. Clearly, the challenge here is choosing from local specialties, country cooking, or an international array that includes French, Italian, Mexican, Middle Eastern, Indian, and Asian dishes. The Terminal's recent facelift also provided a beer garden, where there is always a piano playing on weekdays. Mon–Sat 8 am–6 pm.

Taylor's Country Store, 609 Sansom St.; 563-7627. *I.* The posters, antiques, and tropical plants make this three-tiered restaurant a most delightful place in which to dine. Among the award-winning sandwiches are the white turkey, smoked Gruyere, and chopped liver with sweet onions and chopped mustard. The homemade chili and soups are thick and filled with flavor, and, for dessert, you can't miss with the cheese, chocolate, or carrot cake. Everything on the menu is available for takeout or delivery. Mon–Sat 10 am–3pm.

CAFETERIAS

Chameleon, 1519 Walnut St.; 636-4434. *I.* Lively gourmet foods in a bright cafeteria. Take out, too. Lunch Mon–Fri, Dinner Mon–Sat, Brunch Sat.

The Commissary (see DINING, International).

Eden, 1527 Chestnut St.; 972-0400, in International House, 3701 Chestnut St.; 387-2471. *I.* This pair of gourmet cafeterias offers an interesting assortment of dishes that include a different stir-fry every day, fish, chicken, and quiches. You'll also find homemade desserts, with takeout and delivery of all items. Mon–Fri 7:30 am–9 pm, Sat 11 am–9 pm.

The Fox Barn, Great Valley Corporate Center, Route 29, Malvern; 648-0680. *I.* In this old barn overlooking the corporate center, you'll find a rustic cafeteria with lots of exposed wood and brass. Lunch includes a Wellington dish that changes daily, and dinner offers a choice between dining cafeteria-style or sitting down with a menu that has everything from steamed mussels to pasta primavera and roast duck. The bar has become a great spot for drinks afternoon and night. Breakfast and Lunch Mon–Fri, Dinner Mon–Sat.

The Gold Standard (see DINING, International).

The Terrace (see DINING, Continental).

BRUNCHES

Sunday brunch can be enjoyed in many restaurants and interesting locations throughout the Philadelphia area. Some are to be found amid the scenic beauty of rolling hills, old barns, creeks and streams; others are conveniently located near historic sights, museums, and seasonal activities. Some may have a harpist or a jazz quartet playing in the background, while others are loads of fun for the whole family.

With variety as our criterion, we have selected a number of restaurants for Sunday brunch in and around Philadelphia, and have included some that do not appear in our regular dining section. You may wish to call in advance for any changes in times and format. Also, remember that in Pennsylvania, alcoholic beverages cannot be served until 1 pm. on Sunday.

Black Bass Hotel, River Rd., Lumberville; 297-5770. M. The champagne brunch is a lovely experience in this historic inn on the Delaware River. 1–3 pm.

Houlihan's Old Place, 18th and Chancellor Sts.; 546-5940, King of Prussia Mall; 337-9522. I–M. A six-item brunch menu is offered and for an extra dollar you have access to an Emporium table laden with salads, bagels, and muffins. After 1 pm there's bottomless champagne for 99¢. From 11 am–3 pm, Sunday only.

La Terrasse, 3432 Sansom St.; 387-3778. M. One of the city's first restaurants to offer Sunday brunch, La Terrasse features quiches, omelettes, fettuccine, crepes, and salads among other delicious items. 11:30 am–2:30 pm. Classical music is presented on the grand piano.

Le Beau Lieu, Rittenhouse Sq.; 545-0300. M. This beautiful restaurant in the Barclay Hotel offers an elegant buffet that changes weekly. Dine to the music of a harp duet. Reservations required. From 11 am–12:30 pm on Sunday.

Le Bistro, 757 S. Front St.; 389-3855. I. Sunday brunch in Rick's Cabaret theater offers six entrees, including egg dishes, chicken, pasta, seafood, and champagne. Chocolate mousse is a favored dessert.

Lily Langtry's, Route 363, King of Prussia; 337-LILY. I. This Las Vegas dinner theater features an all-you-can-eat buffet with egg dishes, bacon and link sausages, Swedish meatballs, chicken, homemade baked goods, pancakes, hash browns, and a large assortment of salads. A harpist plays. 9:30 am–2 pm.

Miss Headly's Wine Bar, upstairs, 56 S. 2nd St.; 922-0763. M. In a draped interior of colorful Pakistani gypsy wedding tents, brunch features eggs benedict, omelettes, homemade breads, curry dishes, and cheese boards. Tarot card readings are also available. Located upstairs in the Khyber Pass pub. Noon–3 pm.

The Oyster Bar, 1300 West Strasburg Rd.; West Chester; 692-5702. *I.* The blackboard menu features simple, quality preparations of shrimp, fish of the day, homemade pasta, quiche, and French toast. 11 am–2 pm.

Ship Inn, Lancaster Ave. at Ship Rd., Exton; 363-7200. *I.* In this turn-of-the-century tavern enjoy a variety of homemade breads, egg and chicken dishes, and sumptuous desserts. 10 am–2 pm.

Society Hill Hotel, 3rd and Chestnut Sts.; 925-1919. *I.* In Philadelphia's first bed-and-breakfast hotel you can partake of a fixed price menu that includes eggs benedict, egg dishes, Belgian waffles, and homemade breads along with a Bloody Mary or Mimosa. 11:15 am–2:15 pm.

Sunnybrook Farm, East High St., Pottstown; 326-6400. *I.* Sunday buffet is a festive occasion in this 20-acre countryside setting. The huge, high-quality servings include eggs scrambled on an open grill, spare ribs, salads, and a lavish selection of desserts. The giant theater organ adds to the congenial atmosphere, 9:30 am–2 pm.

Tavern on Green, 21st and Green Sts.; 235-6767. *I.* This cheery, plant-filled restaurant offers a dozen entrees that include crabmeat benedict, Mexican ranch-style eggs, crepe du jour, deep fried brie, and eggs. Super fresh salads and excellent desserts will accent your visit. 11:30 am–3 pm.

TGI Friday's, 4000 City Ave.; 878-7070. *I M.* The Sunday menu here is highlighted by Belgian waffles, quiches, puffed pancakes, croissants, and eggs benedict. Special price on champagne. From 10:30 am.

PERFORMING ARTS

With its world-famous orchestra and ballet, its opera company, the Curtis Institute, and such landmarks as the Academy of Music and the Forrest, Shubert, and Walnut theaters, Philadelphia's roots in the performing arts are well-established. Philadelphia's music is a great tradition. So is its dance. With theater soaring on the wings of such groups as the Philadelphia Drama Guild, the People's Light Theater, and the Philadelphia Festival for New Plays, the city's entire performing arts scene has come alive with innovation, diversity, and creativity. The reaction has been extraordinary; audiences are rising with unbridled applause, media critics can't say enough good things about what they're seeing and, perhaps most revealing of all, a great number of Philadelphia's finest talents in music, dance, and theater are staying home to perform.

PERFORMING ARTS BY AREA

BUCKS COUNTY

Bucks County Playhouse, Theater

CENTER CITY

Academy Boys Choir, Vocal
Academy of Music, Music
All-Star Forum, Music
American Music Theater Festival, Summer Concerts
Ann Vachon/Dance Conduit, Dance
The Avante Theater Company, Theater
AVA Opera Theater, Opera
Collegiate and Archdiocesan Choirs, Vocal
Concerto Soloists of Philadelphia, Music
The Curtis Institute of Music Recitals, Music
1807 and Friends, Music

Forrest Theater, Theater
Jazz Dance Center, Dance
Mendelssohn Club of Philadelphia, Vocal
Mozart on The Square, Music
Music from Marlboro, Music
Neighborhood Concerts, Summer Concerts
Opera Company of Philadelphia, Opera
Opera Ebony, Opera
Orchestra Society of Philadelphia, Music
Pennsylvania Ballet, Dance
Pennsylvania Opera Theater, Opera
Philadelphia Baroque Orchestra, Music
Philadelphia Boys Choir and Chorale, Vocal
Philadelphia Civic Ballet, Dance
Philadelphia Classical Guitar Society, Music

Philadelphia College of Performing
Arts, Music
Philadelphia Company, Theater
Philadelphia Dance Company,
Dance
Philadelphia Festival Chorus, Vocal
Philadelphia Oratorio Choir, Vocal
Philadelphia Orchestra, Music
Philadelphia Singers, Vocal
Phillyfest, Summer Concerts
Philly Pops, Music
Plays & Players, Theater
Savoy Company, Opera
Seminole Dance Coalition, Dance
Serenata, Music
Shubert Theater, Theater
Singing City, Vocal
Theater Center Philadelphia,
Theater
Voloshky Ukrainian Dance
Ensemble, Dance
Walnut Street Theatre, Theater
Wanamaker Organ Concerts, Music
Wilma Theatre, Theater
Youth Orchestra of Greater
Philadelphia, Music
Zero Moving Dance Company,
Dance

CENTER CITY–
FAIRMOUNT PARK AREA

Laurel Hill Candlelight Concerts,
Summer Concerts
Mann Music Center, Summer
Concerts
Robin Hood Dell East, Summer
Concerts

CHESTER COUNTY

The People's Light and Theatre
Company, Theater
Valley Forge Music Fair, Theater
Yellow Springs Institute for
Contemporary Studies, Theater

CHINATOWN

Trocadero Theater, Theater

DELAWARE COUNTY

Hedgerow Theater, Theater
Tower Theater, Music
Villanova Theater, Theater

MONTGOMERY COUNTY

Cheltenham Playhouse, Theater
Keswick Theater of Performing
Arts, Theater
Philadelphia Folk Festival, Summer
Concerts

NORTHEAST

The Settlement Music School, Music

NORTH PHILADELPHIA

New Freedom Theater, Theater
Temple University Theater, Theater

NORTHWEST

The Afro American Dance
Ensemble, Dance
Basically Bach Festival, Music
Germantown Theater, Theater
LaSalle College and Music Theater,
Theater
Philomel, Music
Serenata, Music
The Settlement Music School, Music
Summer Opera Festival, Summer
Concerts

OLD CITY SOCIETY HILL

Group Motion Multi Media Dance
Theater, Dance
Painted Bride Art Center, Theater
Penn's Landing Summer Music
Festival, Summer Concerts
Pennsylvania Pro Musica, Vocal
Philomel, Music
Port of History Museum, Theater
Society Hill Playhouse, Theater

QUEEN VILLAGE–
SOUTH STREET

Delaware Valley Opera Company,
Opera

South Street Dance Company,
Dance

SOUTH PHILADELPHIA

Mummers String Bands, Summer
Concerts
The Settlement Music School, Music

UNIVERSITY CITY

Annenberg Center, Theater
Collegium Musicum, Music

Gallery Concerts, Music
Mandell Theater, Theater
Philadelphia Drama Guild, Theater
Philadelphia Festival for New
Plays, Theater
Philadelphia Folksong Society,
Vocal
Relache, Music
University Museum Concerts, Music
University Museum Summer Series,
Summer Concerts

DANCE

The Afro American Dance Ensemble, 2544 Germantown Ave.;
225-7565. Founded in 1968 by Arthur Hall, the ensemble traces black dance
from its African origins to contemporary expression in American jazz. When
they're not on tour, this group can be enjoyed at the Ile Ife Center and various other locations in Philadelphia.

Ann Vachon/Dance Conduit, 1518 Broad St.; 564-6810. This young
company was named "Conduit" by Ms. Vachon because she wanted to con-
vey to the group her own learning experiences under renowned choreographers Doris Humphrey and Jose Limon. The result is an energetic ensemble
with a fresh and varied repertory of original music and choreography. Performs in concerts, lecture-demonstrations, master classes and workshops
throughout the Philadelphia area.

Group Motion Multi Media Dance Theater, 623 S. Leithgow St.;
928-1495. Formed in West Berlin in 1962, this group came to the United
States six years later after performing and touring in Germany. Now performing extensively in colleges and theaters on the East Coast, its emphasis
is on dance accented by live and taped electronic instrumental music, films,
slides, video tapes, and lighting. Studio performances throughout the year
with weekly workshops open to the public.

Jazz Dance Center, 2030 Sansom St.; 569-2033. Founded in 1981, the
Center introduced Philadelphia to a new form of jazz dance with choreog-
rapher Shimon Braun's series of "WAVES" shows. In Braun's words, "It's like
an album (of music), only translated into dance." Performances at the Schu-
bert, Walnut, and Annenberg theaters, as well as at fashion shows and promotional events throughout the city.

Pennsylvania Ballet, 2333 Fairmount Ave.; 978-1400. For over 20 years,
this nationally-acclaimed company has been performing both classical and
contemporary ballet. The Academy of Music, where the ballet last performed in the early 70s, became its permanent home starting with the

1984–85 season. Four subscription series are offered, and the company performs an annual holiday production of "The Nutcracker." Also offered are performance series for young people, lecture-demonstrations, master classes, and educational programs for schools, colleges, and community groups.

Philadelphia Civic Ballet Company, 1615 Sansom St.; 546-4405. Founded in 1955, this is the oldest continuing dance organization in the Philadelphia area. In addition to its performances at the Academy of Music and local theaters, the company is also at home performing in schools, streets, parks, colleges, historical sites, hotels, and department stores. A dance school, which was started in 1949, remains a part of the company.

Philadelphia Dance Company, 9 N. Preston St.; 387-8200. Founded in 1970 and known more informally as "Philadanco," this company specializes in classical ballet and modern dance forms. Maintains a year-round schedule of 75 to 100 performances in Philadelphia and on tour.

Seminole Dance Coalition, 45 E. Church Lane; 848-5726. A group of five choreographers that presents modern dance performances throughout the Philadelphia area. Seminole Works, a division of the coalition, is directed by John Gamble and has developed a highly energetic and athletic style based on traditional dance forms, gymnastics, martial arts, and contact improvisation.

South Street Dance Company, 700 Sansom St.; 483-8482. This modern dance theater's repertoire includes group and solo works. Directed by Ellen Foreman, the company performs in theaters, colleges, elementary and secondary schools, street festivals, and churches throughout Philadelphia, the East, and the Midwest. Also offered throughout the year are lectures, lecture-demonstrations, and workshops for adults and children.

Voloshky Ukrainian Dance Ensemble, 700 Cedar Rd.; 769-8159. Founded in 1972, this group continues to develop a style that is clearly native to Ukrainian folk dancing in character, yet with a style that is classical enough to be appreciated by audiences everywhere. Performs at colleges, universities, and various ethnic festivals and community affairs throughout Pennsylvania.

Zero Moving Dance Company, 151 W. Harvey St.; 843-9974. Founded in 1972, Zero Moving has become one of the most innovative and creative modern dance companies in the world—performing to critical acclaim throughout the East and Europe. The company's popularity is rooted in its exciting integration of dance, theater, and the visual arts.

MUSIC

Academy of Music, Broad and Locust Sts.; 893-1935. As the oldest auditorium in the United States still in use in its original form and for its original purpose, the Academy is the official home of the Philadelphia Orchestra (although a new home for the orchestra will soon be built after an exhaustive search for an architect). Its magnificent interior of crimson, cream, and gold, as well as its matchless acoustics, have been the setting for the world's finest concerts, recitals, opera, and ballet. Among the legends that have performed at the Academy, often with the Philadelphia Orchestra, are Paderewski, Caruso, Mahler, Rachmaninoff, Horowitz, Rubinstein, and Cliburn. The Academy is also home for the Philly Pops, the Opera Company of Philadelphia, and the All-Star Forum series. Named a National Historic Landmark in 1963, it has also been the site of speeches by numerous Presidents and such orators as Susan B. Anthony and Mark Twain. Available for tours (see SIGHTS).

All-Star Forum, 1530 Locust St.; 735-7506. As the city's foremost presenter of the performing arts at the Academy of Music, the Forum has brought renowned American and international orchestras, ballet companies, artists, ensembles, theatrical attractions, and, of course, the Philly Pops, to Philadelphia for more than 50 years.

Basically Bach Festival of Philadelphia, 8419 Germantown Ave.; 247-4020. Started in 1976 by music director Michael Korn as a local celebration of beautiful music, this has evolved into a major festival that has attracted capacity audiences and critical acclaim. Up to six concerts a year are performed by international artists specializing in solo, ensemble, and orchestral presentations of Johann Sebastian Bach's music. Performances are held at Chestnut Hill churches, colleges, and art galleries.

Collegium Musicum, University of Pennsylvania; 898-6244. Director Mary Anne Ballard has presented concerts of the Medieval and Renaissance periods for more than ten years. The ensemble consists of vocalists and musicians performing songs and playing instruments that entertained the nobility and the peasants during the Middle Ages and the Renaissance. Concert series are held at the University Museum and there is an annual festival in the spring.

Concerto Soloists of Philadelphia, 2136 Locust St.; 735-0202. Modeled after the orchestras of Bach and Mozart, this renowned chamber orchestra specializes in a wide range of baroque and classical music. Under the direction of Marc Mostovoy, who founded the soloists in 1964, it performs 15 concerts yearly at the Academy of Music and the Holy Trinity Church on Rittenhouse Square, as well as on national and international tours.

The Curtis Institute of Music Recitals, 1726 Locust St.; 893-5260. Founded in 1924, this highly respected music school is one of the superior training grounds for the musical elite. Free concerts, as well as 60 to 70 free recitals by the Institute's faculty and students, are performed each year, including opera and chamber music. Pre-recorded concerts on Tuesday nights on WFLN-FM.

1807 & Friends, 1807 Sansom St.; 636-9605. Deriving its name from the Center City residence where professional musicians have gathered for more than 40 years to perform chamber music, this ensemble includes members of every major Philadelphia performing group, such as the Philadelphia Orchestra, Philadelphia Opera Company, and Concerto Soloists.

Gallery Concerts, 518 Annenberg Center, University of Pennsylvania; 898-6244. Donations requested. A series of five gallery concerts are presented once per month from January through May in conjunction with Collegium Musicum.

Mozart on The Square, Rittenhouse Square; check newspapers. This free annual festival in May consists of 22 events in and around The Square and celebrates the music of Mozart and his contemporaries. Also lectures and a film series.

Music from Marlboro, 135 S. 18th St.; 569-4690. Since 1965, the Marlboro Music Festival has brought the finest of chamber music to Philadelphia from Marlboro, Vermont. Ten concerts from November to May at the Port of History Museum.

Orchestra Society of Philadelphia, 32nd and Chestnut St.; 895-2453. Founded in 1964, this group of professional musicians is the resident orchestra of Drexel University. Three free annual concerts are held in the Main Hall or in Mandell Theater on campus.

Philadelphia Baroque Orchestra, 420 W. Mermaid Lane; 248-2028. This new group has been applauded for its 17th- and 18th-century works as performed on period instruments.

Philadelphia Classical Guitar Society, 110 S. 20th St.; 567-2972. The Society has provided the finest in guitar concerts and workshops for Philadelphia since 1968. Ten concerts during the season.

Philadelphia College of Performing Arts Concerts, 250 S. Broad St.; 875-2200. Founded in 1870, the college has built an outstanding reputation for training performing artists. Free annual concerts in chorus, jazz, dance, opera, and orchestral music are held in the fall and spring at the Shubert Theater.

Philadelphia Orchestra, 1420 Locust St.; 893-1900. From its first concert on November 16, 1900, the Philadelphia Orchestra has been heralded as one of the finest orchestras to be found anywhere. Over the years more than a few experts have called it "the greatest orchestra in the world." It was the first American symphony orchestra to make a recording (1917) and now boasts 500 long-playing albums to its credit. It was also the first orchestra to be featured in films (1937) and on television (1948). Fourteen years ago it became the first orchestra to perform in the People's Republic of China. Under the direction of Riccardo Muti, who succeeded the legendary Eugene Ormandy, the Orchestra performs at the Academy of Music from September through May. A series of free concerts are held at the Fredric R. Mann Music Center in Fairmount Park in June and July. Thirty concerts are offered in its subscription series.

Philly Pops, 1530 Locust St.; 735-7506. This orchestra combines symphonic and popular music with outstanding guests provided by the All-Star Forum. Performances are at the Academy of Music, and directed by Peter Nero.

Philomel, 216 Dupont St.; 482-8575. The oldest group of its kind in Philadelphia, six to twelve musicians perform a series of concerts in area churches, colleges, and art centers, using all original or reproduction Baroque period instruments.

Relache, 308 Wharton St.; 387-4115. This Philadelphia-based ensemble has received considerable recognition for its contemporary music. It is currently in residence at Drexel University's Mandell Theater.

Serenata, 8871 Norwood Ave.; 247-4323. This group of 11 professional musicians has received high marks for their presentations of baroque music on original instruments. The players are joined by Julianne Baird, a soprano who specializes in baroque vocal practice. A series of concerts are held in churches throughout the Philadelphia area.

The Settlement Music School, 416 Queens St.; 336-0400. Founded in 1908, this school provides a solid education in music, theater, and dance. Its 3000 students and faculty members give free recitals throughout the year at its main location in South Philadelphia and at branches in Germantown and the northeast. An organization within the school, "Friends of Settlement School," offers a subscription series to the public at various locations throughout the city. At the end of the year, an annual concert is given at the main location to highlight the school year.

Tower Theater, 69th and Ludlow Sts.; Upper Darby; 352-0313. This theater features Electric Factory concerts in jazz, folk, and rock. Don't forget that the Factory also brings such concerts to the Spectrum, John F. Kennedy Stadium, the Mann Music Center, and the Academy of Music.

University Museum Concerts, University of Pennsylvania, 33rd and Spruce Sts.; 898-4015. Directed by Philadelphia Orchestra member Donald Montanaro and other artists, the Museum String Orchestra offers a series of free concerts four times per year at the Harrison Auditorium on the Penn campus. Also featured are various dance and musical programs.

Wanamaker Organ Concerts, 13th and Market Sts.; 422-2000. These free half-hour concerts are presented every shopping day on the largest organ in the world, which overlooks the Grand Court of John Wanamaker's department store. Concerts at 10 am, 12 noon and 5:30 pm, except Wednesday, when the 5:30 pm concert is held at 8 pm.

Youth Orchestra of Greater Philadelphia, 1421 Arch St.; 241-1200. This 100-piece orchestra is comprised of youths between the ages of 14 and 21. Conducted by Philadelphia Orchestra member Joseph Primavera, it gives five performances between December and May, plus an annual festival concert at the Academy of Music.

Opera

AVA Opera Theater, 1920 Spruce St.; 735-1685. In operation for over 50 years, this opera school and presenting company offers numerous recitals and master classes throughout the season. The recitals and first three operas are presented in the AVA's Helen Corning Warden Theater at the above address. Other performances are staged at The Walnut Street Theatre.

Delaware Valley Opera Company, Henry Ave. and Hermit Lane; 339-8132. Performing throughout the year, this company presents concerts, one-act operas, recitals by various members, and full-scale operas with orchestra. Performances at the opera company's outdoor theater and the Paul D. Osimo Theater near Hermitage Mansion in Roxborough. Feel free to bring lawn chairs and blankets (see Summer Concerts).

Opera Company of Philadelphia, Suite 700, 1500 Walnut St.; 732-5811. International stars present grand opera in five to six productions from October through April at the Academy of Music. Telecast annually on PBS.

Opera Ebony, 151 W. Susquehanna Ave.; 879-9029. Founded as a hopeful adjunct to the 1976 Bicentennial, this opera company has remained a solid addition to Philadelphia's music life, performing at the Academy of Music, colleges, and churches. Providing a forum for black singers, conductors, and directors, it has taken on the stature of an artistic institution with performances by Pavarotti, Jessye Norman, and Mirella Freni.

The Pennsylvania Opera Theater, 1345 Chestnut St.; 972-0904. Founded in 1975 to bring the Philadelphia area opera in English, this theater, informally known as "T-Pot," features spectacular singing and acting, exciting sets, and glorious costumes. It also has a community outreach program with special performances for children.

The Savoy Company, Broad and Chestnut Sts.; 735-7161. Founded in 1901, this is the second oldest Gilbert and Sullivan company in the world. At the Academy of Music in May, and at Longwood Gardens in June.

Summer Concerts

American Music Theater Festival, 1617 J.F. Kennedy Blvd.; 988-9050. The June and July festival offers an intensive three-week program of music, theater and opera. It also features minority art work, showcase productions, a musical for children, cabaret performances, and public debates with prominent artists. Performances are held at Port of History museum, The Walnut Street Theater, and Trocadero Theatre.

Laurel Hill Candlelight Concerts, Laurel Hill Mansion, Fairmount Park; 925-8197. Five to six concerts are presented by the Women of Greater Philadelphia from early June to the first week of August. They feature chamber music in the candlelit music room of the 18th-century Laurel Hill Mansion for audiences of 100 people or less. Piano accompaniment on an 1808 broadwood grand. Reception and refreshments follow each concert.

Mann Music Center, 52nd St. and Parkside Ave.; 567-0707. This pastoral setting is the site of 18 concerts by the Philadelphia Orchestra in June and July and by other top entertainment in August. Although there is free seating for 15,000 on the grassy slopes and bleachers, tickets are required. These may be obtained by clipping coupons appearing in *The Philadelphia Inquirer* and *Daily News* six weeks prior to each concert and mailing them with a self-addressed stamped envelope to the city's Department of Recreation, P.O. Box 1000, Philadelphia, 19105. Two tickets will be sent to you by return mail. Bring a blanket and picnic on the grass. Box suppers and refreshments are available at intermission. The August portion of the program is devoted to pop concerts, ballet, theater, and opera.

Mellon Jazz Festival, Mann Music Center, Academy of Music, and other locations. For seven days in June the festival offers top-notch groups playing big-band swing, small-group hard rock, and electric jazz fusion. Among the artists who have performed in this festival are Sonny Rollins, McCoy Tyner, Archie Shepp, and Miles Davis.

Mummers String Bands, Mummers Museum, 2nd St. and Washington Ave.; 336-3050. From May 17 through September 27, weather permitting, the Mummers play and strut for free in all their glory every Tuesday night at 8 pm in the Museum's parking facilities. Please bring your own chairs.

Neighborhood Concerts, Department of Recreation; 686-0156. These free concerts are sponsored by the Philadelphia Department of Recreation in July and August throughout the city's neighborhoods. Bring blankets and snacks to the Monday night entertainment on Rittenhouse Square and the Art Museum on Thursday, Friday, and Saturday nights. The fare includes folk, jazz, quartets, and dance groups.

Penn's Landing Summer Festival, Delaware Ave. and Spruce Sts.; 923-8181. From May to October there are free dockside concerts on Friday nights, and folk dancing, parties, and dancing other nights. Various festivals are held throughout the summer and include a wealth of ethnic foods, exhibits, music, and dancing. Join in the festival atmosphere and enjoy performances by the American Wind Symphony, Opera Ebony, and other groups.

Robin Hood Dell   *City of Philadelphia*

Philadelphia Folk Festival, 7113 Emlen St.; 247-1300. For three days and nights in late August, this festival offers international folk music performers and groups in concerts and workshops. There is also camping out, folk dancing, and special programs for children held at Suburban Poole Farm, Schwenksville.

Phillyfest, John F. Kennedy Plaza, JFK Blvd. and 15th St.; 686-3657. Free performances of folk music, jazz, string quartets, and dance groups are offered throughout the summer. Check newspapers for further information.

Robin Hood Dell East, East Fairmount Park; 567-0707. In July and August the Dell features top stars in music and dance in a series of low-cost concerts.

Summer Opera Festival, Hermitage Mansion, Roxborough; 339-8132. Bring a blanket or a lawn chair and enjoy these operas. Held by the Delaware Valley Opera Company on three Saturday nights in late July and August, they are staged at the outdoor Paul D. Osimo Theater on acreage surrounding the Hermitage in Fairmount Park.

University Museum Summer Series, University of Pennsylvania; 898-3024. Ethnic groups from throughout the world perform music and dance in the mosaic garden on the campus at 33rd and Spruce Streets, Wednesdays in July and August at 5:45 pm. Bring blankets and food for picnicking. Free iced tea and lemonade are served afterwards.

Vocal

Academy Boys Choir, 250 S. Broad St.; 875-2200. Sixty of the finest young voices, ages eight to fifteen, in the Philadelphia area perform at the Shubert Theater with the Philadelphia Orchestra, as well as at concerts throughout the area. The group, which is affiliated with the Philadelphia College of Performing Arts and is directed by Daniel Ford, also performs abroad in semi-annual tours which have taken it to England, Europe, Scandinavia, and the Caribbean.

Collegiate and Archdiocesan Choirs, 222 N. 17th St.; 587-3696. These choirs perform independently and together in concerts and special liturgies at the Cathedral-Basilica and elsewhere in the Philadelphia area.

Mendelssohn Club of Philadelphia, 260 S. Broad St.; 735-9922. Founded in 1874 by William W. Gilchrist, this nationally-recognized choral ensemble produces a series of subscription concerts each year, equally divided between large concerts and Mendelssohn Singers performances. Directed by Tamara Brooks, it has performed with the Philadelphia Orchestra and has at least one major concert every year at the Academy of Music. Its concert at the Cathedral of St. Peter and St. Paul is an annual sellout.

Pennsylvania Pro Musica, 1700 Sansom St.; 222-4517. Founded in 1968, this is the oldest professional soloist, choral, and orchestral performing organization in Pennsylvania. It performs six to eight concerts per year at Old Christ Church, featuring music of the Medieval, Renaissance, and Baroque eras. It also offers lectures, panel discussions, and concert previews.

The Philadelphia Boys Choir and Chorale, 311 S. Juniper St.; 222-3500. A select group of 75 boy and 35 adult male singers, this group has received national and international recognition for its White House appearances, performances with Luciano Pavarotti and the Philadelphia Orchestra, and a Bob Hope television special from Peking, China. Directed by Robert G. Hamilton, the choir performs music primarily by American composers, as well as classical, spiritual, and folk music. It has travelled 700,000 miles to every major continent in the world, performing in 13 languages for royalty, heads of state, and millions of people.

Philadelphia Festival Chorus, 1433 Spruce St.; 985-0202. This ensemble of 100 professional-level singers has performed with the Philadelphia Orchestra, the Pittsburgh Symphony, the Philly Pops, the Pennsylvania Ballet, and the Pennsylvania Opera Theater, as well as in solo concerts. Its performances are held in Philadelphia area concert halls, churches, museums, sports arenas, retirement homes, and hospitals. The chorus also tours Europe on occasion.

Philadelphia Folksong Society, 7113 Emlen St.; 247-1300. The Society presents monthly formal concerts, followed by informal gatherings of performers and members of the audience at International House. Other annual events include the Philadelphia Folk Festival in August, The Blue Grass and Old Time Festival in March, and the Spring Thing in May.

Philadelphia Oratorio Choir, First Baptist Church, 17th and Sansom Sts.; 563-0397. An all-professional choir of 36 to 40 members, this group performs during the winter at the First Baptist Church. Directed by Earl Ness, it has a number of outstanding concerts, among them "Amahl and the Night Visitors" at Christmastime.

The Philadelphia Singers, 1830 Spruce St.; 732-3370. This ensemble of 30 professional singers, directed by Michael Korn, and founded in 1972, performs more than 200 works from every part of the choral repertoire. The singers have established a tradition of performing special programs in unusual locations, such as the "Music from San Marco" program in Great Stair Hall of the Philadelphia Museum of Art, and Handel's "Samson" in Temple Shalom. Its Christmas performances of Handel's "Messiah" in local churches have become a local institution.

Singing City, 2031 Chestnut St.; 561-3930. As Philadelphia's world-famous community choir, this 125-voice group combines a tradition of musical excellence with human service by singing at hospitals, senior citizens' centers, and often on city streets. It continues to draw critical acclaim with its performances at the Academy of Music and with the Philadelphia Orchestra.

THEATER

Annenberg Center, University of Pennsylvania, 3680 Walnut St.; 898-6791. This four-theater performing arts center is one of the most exciting in Philadelphia, offering a wide variety of entertainment. From October to April, the Center and its primary tenant, the Philadelphia Drama Guild, each sponsors a series of plays selected from Broadway and from America's leading theater companies. Classicals, musicals, and premieres are held in the Zellerbach Theater and the Annenberg School; national artists and local groups present dance, music, and plays in the Studio Center and the Harold Prince Theater, which is also the home of the Festival for New Plays. The Center offers three productions of children's plays from late December through late March.

The Avante Theatre Company, 106 West Logan St.; 844-4040. Founded in 1973, this company performs at the Academy of Music's Cabaret Theater.

Bucks County Playhouse   *Bucks County Tourist Commission*

Its objectives are to provide opportunities for black performers, to bring socially relevant theatre to black audiences, to provide the black experience for white audiences, and to provide opportunities for black playwrights.

Bucks County Playhouse, Main St., New Hope; 862-2041. Located in a former grist mill built in 1790, this is the official State Playhouse of Pennsylvania. It has featured such stars as Helen Hayes, Walter Matthau, and George C. Scott performing in plays by Noel Coward, Tennessee Williams, and George Bernard Shaw. It now looks much as it did when it was first converted into a playhouse in 1939.

Cheltenham Playhouse, Cheltenham Art Center, 439 Ashbourne Rd., Cheltenham; 379-4027. This charming community theater founded in the 1930s seats 150 people and presents semi-professional actors and actresses with professional goals. The plays dare to be different and include Agatha Christie's mysteries and a series of children's productions at Christmas and Easter.

Forrest Theater, 1114 Walnut St.; 923-1515. Named after the legendary actor Edwin Forrest (1806-1872), the Forrest presents four to five Broadway productions each year. Originally opened as a movie house, it now seats 1440 and in recent years has featured top stars in such smash hits as "Annie," "The Elephant Man," and "42nd Street."

Germantown Theatre, 4821 Germantown Ave.; 849-0460. One of the oldest regional theaters in the country (formed in 1933), the guild has produced over 200 plays, including classics and contemporary works. Despite a busy schedule of national tours, it's still headquartered in the 150-seat "Little Theater," a converted 18th-century carriage house. Large productions are performed at the John B. Kelly School Theater, but most local performances are conducted in schools, libraries, community theaters, day camps, and hospitals.

Hedgerow Theatre, Rose Valley Rd., Moylan; 565-4211. Formed in the 1920s, this 134-seat theater has a resident company of professionals from across the country. A wide variety of performances unfold in the playhouse which was originally built as a grist mill in 1840 and later used as a bobbin mill.

Keswick Theater of Performing Arts, 291 Keswick Ave., Glenside; 572-7650. The Keswick, designed by Horace Drumbauer (designer of the Art Museum), used to be a vaudeville stop for Fanny Brice, the Marx Brothers, and Stepin Fetchit. Now it's a performing arts center with 50 performances annually, including plays, dance concerts, and variety shows.

LaSalle College and Music Theater, 146 W. Laurel St.; 951-1410. Founded in 1962, this is the nation's only college-sponsored professional theater that operates in the summer months. It thrives on youthful exuberance, colorful sets and costumes, and highly professional choreography rather than on "name" performers. In September and May, the Masque Theater of LaSalle offers a fall and spring production and holds student drama workshops during the winter.

Mandell Theater, Drexel University, 32nd and Chestnut Sts.; 895-ARTS. Since the early 1970s, this theater has offered a number of presentations in the performing arts. Its main stage also has three major productions annually by students and faculty. Professional dance companies also use the theater for major productions.

New Freedom Theatre, 1346 N. Broad St.; 765-2793. Founded in 1966, the New Freedom continues to provide performing arts training and/or employment for gifted inner-city residents. Under the direction of John E. Allen, Jr., it has received critical acclaim for its energy and creativity, and was cited by the John F. Kennedy Center for the Performing Arts as one of the nation's best black theaters. Located in the old mansion of the 19th-century stage actor Edwin Forrest, the theater continues to perform at area colleges, schools, libraries, churches, hospitals, and prisons.

Painted Bride Art Center, 230 Vine St.; 925-9914. The center features professional and experimental performances in music, dance, theater, and poetry, as well as a regular series of jazz, chamber, and folk music. There are also appearances by Philadelphia-area and nationally-recognized artists, as well as exhibits of unusual art in all forms of media.

The People's Light and Theatre Company, 39 Conestoga Rd., Malvern; 647-1900. One of the most attractive regional theaters in the country, People's Light offers main stage subscription series and an annual New Play Festival. It also operates a four-part Outreach program, taking live professional productions to non-traditional audiences.

The Philadelphia Company, The Bourse Building; 592-8333. This professional theater company is Philadelphia's only resident theater directed toward producing contemporary American plays. Its performances are held at the historic Plays & Players Theater at 17th and Delancey Streets. The theater school, which is housed in the Walnut Street Theatre, operates year-round and provides extensive training in theater arts for both professionals and theater enthusiasts.

Philadelphia Drama Guild, 112 S. 16th St.; 563-7530. Founded in 1956 as an amateur group, the guild evolved into a professional company 15 years later. It presents new works of living American playwrights in the Philadelphia area, offering five productions between October and May.

Philadelphia Festival for New Plays, 3900 Chestnut St.; 222-5000. Only seven years old, this theater has already been termed a rousing success by critics who see it growing in scope and importance. Its presentations are staged at the Annenberg Center's Harold Prince Theater.

Plays & Players, 1714 Delancey St.; 735-0630. This club, founded in 1911, presents at least four main attractions a year, along with a Children's Theater and Children's Theater Workshop Series. The theater hall, purchased in 1922, is listed in the National Register as an historical monument.

Port of History Museum Theater, Delaware Ave. and Walnut St.; 925-3804. This theater is consistently rented to such performing organizations as the Curtis Institute, the Philadelphia Boys Choir and Chorale, and Music from Marlboro. Check newspapers for information.

Shubert Theater, 250 S. Broad St.; 732-5446. The Shubert belongs to the Philadelphia College of Performing Arts, one of only a handful of fully-accredited private music colleges in the nation. It presents pre-Broadway musicals, dramas, and touring companies, and draws upon the student body for a wide range of concerts, musical events, dance, and theater.

Society Hill Playhouse, 507 8th St.; 923-0210. Having celebrated its 25th anniversary, this is Philadelphia's original professional off-Broadway theater. The playhouse is devoted to contemporary American and European works. It has presented 175 area premieres and developed and encouraged many performers, technicians, and playwrights while maintaining an on-going community services program.

Temple University Theater, 13th and Norris Sts.; 787-8414 and 787-1122. This is one of only 11 collegiate companies in the United States with a membership in the League of Professional Theater Training Programs. All of Temple's shows are produced, directed, and performed by students and faculty. Two major productions are held each year in the Thomlinson Theater on the main campus, with others staged at the Stage Three Theater and the Uptown Randall Lab Theater. A popular children's series unfolds annually at the Stage Three.

Theater Center Philadelphia, 622 S. 4th St.; 925-2682. Founded in 1976, the Theater Center's main purpose is to develop and present new plays and to encourage the artistic growth of writers, directors, actors, composers, and designers. Audiences are drawn into the creative process through discussions after the performances. Its main stage season highlights original plays from the workshops.

Valley Forge Music Fair, Route 202, Devon; 644-5000. This theater-in-the-round is known for presenting the finest shows in musical comedy, variety, rock, road shows, and international productions. Name any star and he or she has most likely performed at the Music Fair. It also hosts a series of special theater presentations for children in the summer.

Villanova Theatre, Ithan and Lancaster Ave., Villanova University; 645-4760. A year-round program of productions are staged in the Vasey Theatre on the Villanova campus. Five contemporary and European classics are presented during the school year, three semi-professional productions in the summer.

The Walnut Street Theater, 825 Walnut St.; 574-3550. Since 1809 this playhouse has been the oldest theater in continuous use in the English-speaking world and has premiered countless plays that went on to Broadway and worldwide acclaim. Formerly a presenting theater, it is now a major regional theater company producing significant works in drama, music, and dance.

The Wilma Theatre, 2030 Sansom St.; 963-0345. Founded in 1973 this theater entered its first professional season in 1982. A variety of productions include drama, original works, multimedia productions, and visiting shows.

Yellow Springs Institute for Contemporary Studies and the Arts, Art School Rd., Chester Springs; 827-9111. Set in a renovated 18th-century stone barn amid 15 acres of pasture and trees, this institute, whose avant-garde performance spaces are among the finest in the area, combines performing arts by professional artists with conferences, seminars, and Arts Laboratory residences.

NIGHTLIFE

With the revitalization of Center City and its hundreds of new restaurants, nightlife in Philadelphia has taken off. In a city where the question used to be "Should we go out?" the question has now become "Which place tonight?" From lavish nightclubs to intimate piano bars, from Irish pubs to throbbing jazz spots, from comedy houses and cabarets to Las Vegas revues, Philadelphia's night spots are alive with unprecedented energy, quality, and yes, sheer fun.

For the young—or the young-at-heart—or the curious, Philadelphia's South Street can be considered a nightlife entity in itself. Not only is it home to dozens of restaurants, bars, and comedy clubs, but it is the place to stroll, to gawk at some of the more bizarre Philadelphians and to shop in some oddball boutiques that stay open until the wee hours.

NIGHTLIFE BY AREA

BUCKS COUNTY

Blue Ram, Music for Listening and Dancing
Paso Doble Ballroom, Music for Listening and Dancing

CENTER CITY

All That Jazz, Cabarets, Dinner Theaters, and Supper Clubs
Bacchanal, Bars
The Barclay, Bars
Cabaret at Equus, Cabarets, Dinner Theaters, and Supper Clubs
Comedy Factory Outlet, Comedy
Delancey Street, Music for Listening and Dancing
Digby's Saloon Restaurant, Bars
Doc Watson's Pub, Bars
Frank Clements, Bars
Houlihan's Old Place, Bars

The Irish Pub, Bars
Jewels, Cabarets, Dinner Theaters, and Supper Clubs
The Kennel Club, Music for Listening and Dancing
Maxwell's, Bars
Not Quite Cricket, Bars
O'Dwyer's, Bars
The Piano Bar, Bars
The Piano Bar at The Commissary, Bars
Polo Bay Club, Music for Listening and Dancing
Rib-It, Music for Listening and Dancing
Roxy Screening Room I & II, Film
Second Story Club, Music for Listening and Dancing
16th Street Bar & Grill, Bars
Social Club, Music for Listening and Dancing
Temple Cinematheque, Film

The Troc, Music for Listening and Dancing
Up the Square, Bars

CENTER CITY–FAIRMOUNT PARK AREA

Kopia Dinner Theater, Cabarets, Dinner Theaters, and Supper Clubs
North Star Bar, Cabarets, Dinner Theaters, and Supper Clubs
Philadelphia Museum of Art, Film

CENTER CITY–PARKWAY

Academy of Natural Sciences, Film
Free Library of Philadelphia, Film
Mace's Crossing, Bars

CHESTER COUNTY

Binni & Flynn's, Bars
Cabaret, Music for Listening and Dancing
Devon Ballroom, Music for Listening and Dancing
Orleans, Music for Listening and Dancing
The Stone Barn Dinner Theater, Cabarets, Dinner Theaters, and Supper Clubs

CITY AVENUE

Carney's, Music for Listening and Dancing
City Line Dinner Theater, Cabarets, Dinner Theaters, and Supper Clubs
Quincy's, Music for Listening and Dancing
Pierre's, Bars
TGI Friday's, Bars

DELAWARE COUNTY

Alpine Inn, Music for Listening and Dancing
Brandywine Club, Music for Listening and Dancing
Huntingdon Valley Dinner Theater, Cabarets, Dinner Theaters, and Supper Clubs

Pulsations, Music for Listening and Dancing

MONTGOMERY COUNTY

Ambler Cabaret, Music for Listening and Dancing
Bennigan's, Bars
Eon's, Music for Listening and Dancing
Lily Langtry's, Cabarets, Dinner Theaters, and Supper Clubs
McSorley's Pub, Bars
Morley's Pub and Dining Saloon, Bars
Popcorn's, Music for Listening and Dancing
Scintillations, Music for Listening and Dancing
Sunnybrook Ballroom, Music for Listening and Dancing

NORTHEAST PHILADELPHIA

Kristopher's, Music for Listening and Dancing

NORTHWEST PHILADELPHIA

The Blushing Zebra, Music for Listening and Dancing
Campbell's Place, Bars
McNally's Tavern, Bars

OLD CITY–SOCIETY HILL

Borgia Cafe, Cabarets, Dinner Theaters, and Supper Clubs
Cafe Sassafras, Bars
Comedy Works, Comedy
Dickens' Inn Tavern, Bars
Khyber Pass, Music for Listening and Dancing
The Middle East, Music for Listening and Dancing
Monte Carlo Living Room, Music for Listening and Dancing
President's Room, Bars
P.T.'s, Music for Listening and Dancing
Revival, Music for Listening and Dancing
Ritz 5, Film

Riverfront Dinner Theater,Cabarets, Dinner Theaters, and Supper Clubs
Society Hill Hotel, Bars

QUEEN VILLAGE AND SOUTH STREET

Downey's, Bars
Going Bananas, Comedy
J.C. Dobbs, Music for Listening and Dancing
Montserrat, Bars
23 East Cabaret, Music for Listening and Dancing
Ulana's, Music for Listening and Dancing

SOUTH PHILADELPHIA

Cahoots, Music for Listening and Dancing
Palumbo's, Cabarets, Dinner Theaters, and Supper Clubs

UNIVERSITY CITY

Cavanaugh's, Cabarets, Dinner Theaters, and Supper Clubs
Chestnut Cabaret, Music for Listening and Dancing
Exploratory Cinema, Film
Neighborhood Film Project, Film
University Museum, Film

Bars

Bacchanal, 1320 South St.; 545-6983. This art bar is home to poetry readings, live performances, music, multi-media shows, and an art gallery.

The Barclay, 18th St. on Rittenhouse Square; 545-0300. Just off the lobby of the hotel is this sophisticated little place that's accented by the high ceiling, period chairs, deep sofas, and music from a 1935 Steinway grand piano. The atmosphere is subdued, classy, elegant.

Bennigan's, 160 N. Gulph Rd., King of Prussia; 337-0633. Six locations. These friendly spots offer a happy hour, from 5–7 pm.

Binni & Flynn's, Gateway Shopping Center, Wayne; 293-0880. Three locations. Southwest cantina bars and restaurants where you can enjoy nachos, burritos, enchiladas and tacos. Guitar music is featured nightly.

Cafe Sassafras, 48 S. 2nd St.; 925-2317. Enjoy a typical French bistro where Philadelphians gather around an original bar that's more than 100 years old. The menu is highlighted by gourmet hamburgers, spinach salads, and onion soup.

Campbell's Place, 8337 Germantown Ave.; 242-2066. The upstairs cozy bar ranks among Philadelphia's best with soups, sandwiches, and homemade desserts. Come well-dressed.

Copa Banana, 4th and South Sts.; 923-6180. A fun spot, as the name suggests, with an island theme; three bars, two downstairs, one up, and a fine selection of Mexican food.

Dickens' Inn Tavern, 41 S. 2nd St.; 928-9307. This authentic Old English pub (separate from the well-known restaurant) offers a wide selection of imported beers and ales. Menu features Shepherd's Pie, beefeater sandwiches, and fish and chips served in English newspapers. Folk music and bag pipes on occasion. Dart board, of course.

Digby's Saloon Restaurant, 11 S. 21st St.; 561-3542. The young professional set likes this place with its mahogany bar and moderately priced dining room menu.

Doc Watson's Pub, 216 S. 11th St.; 922-3427. This rustic, woodsy saloon has three floors with a bar on each level and offers 32 domestic and imported beers. Guitar music and games can be enjoyed on the second floor nightly. Their complete menu features daily and weekly specials.

Downey's, Front and South Sts.; 629-0525. This is a very popular place for the after work crowd. You will often see some of Philly's star athletes here, too. Downstairs is a rustic bar (it used to be a Dublin bank) with walls covered with newspaper pages of historic significance. Upstairs, in the lovely brass and mahogany dining room, piano and guitar music can be heard nightly, and a strolling string ensemble can be enjoyed on Saturday nights and at Sunday brunch. See DINING.

Frank Clements, 224 S. 15th St.; 985-9600. Here's an interesting little saloon where Center City businessmen provide their own entertainment.

Houlihan's Old Place, 18th and Chancellor; 546-5940. Three locations. Surrounded by antiques, posters, greenery, and lots of art, one can indulge in one of the best happy hours at all locations. The lounges are always bustling with fun and socializing. The menu features everything from finger foods to full-course meals.

The Irish Pub, 2007 Walnut St.; 568-5603. St. Patrick's Day is always celebrated in this pub. Stained glass, posters, and maps of Ireland enhance the walls. The menu features corned beef and cabbage, Irish stew, and pork chops, along with imported beers.

Mace's Crossing, 1714 Cherry St.; 854-9592. At this popular little spot on the Parkway, the after-work crowd likes to unwind. While the sun is setting, enjoy a drink on the small outdoor patio.

Maxwell's, 17th and Locust Sts.; 545-4655. This restaurant and bar in the Warwick Hotel serves up omelettes and fresh salads, but is known for eggs benedict.

McNally's Tavern, 8634 Germantown Ave.; 247-9736. Since 1921, this has been a casual, friendly spot known for its scrumptious sandwiches. Outside, look for the green door. Inside, ask for the "Schmitter." Foreign and domestic beers on tap.

McSorley's Pub, 2330 Haverford Rd., Ardmore; 642-1370. Imported Irish beers and whiskies. Irish bands sing folk songs and ballads Friday and Saturday nights. Contemporary music other nights. Casual.

Montserrat, 623 South St.; 627-4224. This attractive, woodsy bar and restaurant is known for the large selection of food at reasonable prices. New outdoor cafe. Happy hour 4–7 pm Monday through Friday.

Morley's Pub & Dining Saloon, 36 E. Main St., Norristown; 279-5498. Situated directly across the street from the Montgomery County Courthouse, this fun spot has lots of Irish folk music. It's also known for its exciting eclectic menu. Lawyers from across the street love it for lunch.

Not Quite Cricket, 17th and Walnut Sts.; 563-7474. This very small, cozy lounge is in the Latham Hotel. Contemporary and jazz tunes can be heard at the piano bar.

O'Dwyer's, 30 S. 17th St.; 563-7995. O'Dwyer's is an old-fashioned Irish saloon and restaurant. You'll hear ragtime ringing from the upright piano.

The Piano Bar at The Commissary, 1710 Sansom St.; 569-2240. This spot adjoining The Commissary restaurant graces the singles crowd with good drinks, sandwiches, and desserts. Live entertainment Thursday through Saturday.

Pierre's, Adam's Mark Hotel, City Line Ave. at Monument Rd.; 581-5000. This elegant and comfortable lounge features piano or combo music Monday through Friday nights.

President's Room, 125 Walnut St.; 925-7027. The bar, from Old Original Bookbinder's, is one of the finest in Philadelphia. Enjoy the healthy drinks while you scan the antiques.

16th Street Bar & Grill, 264 S. 16th St.; 735-3316. This small, sophisticated bar attracts the Center City professionals with its light menus, chili, hamburgers, salads, and pasta dishes. A large selection of imported wines and beers.

Society Hill Hotel, 3rd and Chestnut Sts.; 925-1919. The first bed-and-breakfast hotel in Philadelphia features a modern, good-looking bar. There's lots of carved wood, stained glass, and flowers, with large windows overlooking Independence Park. Popular drinks are made with freshly-squeezed citrus juices. Piano music Tuesday through Saturday night and also during Sunday brunch.

TGI Friday's, 4000 City Line Ave.; 878-7070. Friday's is pleasantly cluttered with woodsy atmosphere, stained-glass, tile ceiling, catering to the after-work crowd. Happy hour 4:30–6:30 pm. Brunch Sunday.

Up the Square, 1907 Sansom St.; 567-2259. This small, friendly bar with casual Western decor has excellent hamburgers.

Cabarets, Dinner Theaters, & Supper Clubs

All That Jazz, 119 S. 18th St.; 568-5247. Located over Le Wine Bar, this is a cozy spot that seats fewer than 50 people. Jazz Wednesday through Saturday. Twenty-five wines available by the glass. The interesting menu offers continental cuisine.

Borgia Cafe, 408 S. 2nd St.; 574-0414. Situated beneath the lower level of Lautrec, this nice bar and restaurant has jazz six nights a week. An eclectic menu offers escargot, shrimp scampi, homemade pizza, and soups. Everything is moderately priced.

Cabaret at Equus, 254 S. 12th St.; 545-8088. This small, intimate spot seats 100 and is one of the finest cabarets in Philadelphia. There's also a cocktail lounge and a newly-renovated restaurant downstairs.

Cavanaugh's Jameson Room, 3132 Market St.; 386-4889. This cabaret features guitar and piano bar entertainment along with excellent steaks and seafood. The Friday night smorgasbord is a winner for seafood lovers, in particular, but also includes spareribs, salads, soups, and vegetables.

City Line Dinner Theater, 4200 City Line Ave.; 879-4000. With some 700 seats, this is one of the larger dinner theaters in the Philadelphia area, and has featured such hits as "Grease," "On Golden Pond," and "Barnum." The full-course luncheons and dinners are served buffet-style.

Huntingdon Valley Dinner Theater, 2633 Philmont Ave.; 947-6000. This theater is very popular for its lavish productions of Broadway musicals, performed on a stage with a turntable that makes scene changes possible within seconds. A sumptuous smorgasbord precedes the show and features more than 100 delicious items on the dessert tray alone.

Jewel's, 679 N. Broad St.; 236-1396. Specializes in jazz—some say it's the best in town—with everything starting at 9 pm and running until 2 am. Thursday is jam session night, and special guests appear in the Topaz Room and the lounge on Friday and Saturday nights.

Kopia Dinner Theater, 4942 Parkside Ave.; 877-4426. This is a unique dinner theater that produces standards and original works of both drama and comedy. It seats 275. A buffet and bar precedes each performance and changes with each new show.

Lily Langtry's, 363 King of Prussia Ave., King of Prussia; 337-5459. Located in the Sheraton Valley Forge, Lily's presents a highly-energetic Las Vegas revue and variety show. There are lavish production numbers and much changing of costumes in a Victorian atmosphere of handpainted skylights, glittering chandeliers, and balconies. Dinner is served before the show, but reservations are required and may not be cancelled within 48 hours of the date reserved.

North Star Bar, 27th and Poplar Sts.; 235-7827. Recently redecorated, this cabaret has comedians, poets, and lots of fun. Tuesday and Thursday nights feature music downstairs, which now includes a patio area. This spot is also known for its chili served in bread bowls.

Palumbo's, 824 Catharine St.; 627-7272. This is a nightclub and a Philly tradition where many of the town's famous entertainers (Joey Bishop, Frankie Avalon, David Brenner) got their start. Bobby Rydell still shows up frequently. Known for its excellent Italian dishes. A la carte menu in the Nostalgia Room.

Riverfront Dinner Theater, Delaware River at Poplar St.; 925-7000. Seats up to 400 and features luncheon and dinner buffet-style before its Broadway theater productions.

Stone Barn Dinner Theater, two miles west of Unionville off Route 842; 347-2414. Surrounded by a picturesque setting in the fox-hunting area of Chester county, this lovely dinner theater presents Broadway musicals and comedy. Their buffet dinner includes an assortment of meats and vegetables, a salad bar, and delicious desserts.

Comedy

Comedy Factory Outlet, 31 Bank St.; 386-6911. Comedians from all over the country make stops here. Local talent, too. Two shows Friday and Saturday at 8:30 and 11 pm. Two hours before Friday's show, there's a package dinner at Winners, the restaurant below, and reservations are required (922-2727). The show and dinner are included in one price. Thursday night is audition night, so if you think you're funny, why not see if others do, too.

Comedy Works, 126 Chestnut St.; 922-5997. Located on the third floor of the Middle East Restaurant, this 250-seat spot has shows Wednesday through Saturday nights. Wednesday is amateur night, Thursday is "Best of Philly" night, and Saturday night brings more laughs with special guest appearances.

Going Bananas, 2nd and South Sts.; 925-3470. A small club that seats 140, this spot features top comics from the Big Apple Friday and Saturday nights.

Music For Listening and Dancing

Alpine Inn, Baltimore Pike, Springfield; 544-1230. The dance floor here is flanked by two stages, and there are two bands every night except Tuesday and Thursday. There's also a large restaurant with one of the biggest salad bars anywhere.

Ambler Cabaret, 43 E. Butler Pike, Ambler; 646-8117. A recent addition to the nightclub scene, this spot is very popular. Tuesday is comedy night, featuring talent from both coasts. Live music is featured Thursday, Friday, and Saturday nights.

Blue Ram, Route 532, Washington's Crossing; 493-1262. You'll hear some of the best jazz around here. The continental dining is highlighted by a menu that changes every two weeks. Veal dishes are a specialty.

The Blushing Zebra, 7167-69 Germantown Ave., Mt. Airy; 242-2221. This new neighborhood club attracts folk singers, storytellers, and other unconventional acts.

Brandywine Club, Route 1 and Route 202, Chadds Ford; 459-4400. A large spot featuring the Brandywine Room and Club. The Room has a full dinner menu nightly, but you must be a member. The Club seats 1500 for top stars, including 400 at "ringside."

Cabaret, 15 N. Walnut St., West Chester; 436-9569. This is one of the nicest nightclubs in the area. Small and cozy, its three seating levels make excellent use of the available space. Very friendly, with live music Wednesday through Saturday nights.

Cahoots, 10th St. and Packer Ave.; 755-9500. In the Philadelphia Airport Hilton, this is a popular spot for fans after events at Veterans Stadium and the Spectrum.

Carney's, 4190 City Line Ave.; 473-0300. This singles spot features live bands, a friendly bar, and a dining room where you can get a filet for one of the lowest prices in town. Drinks are reasonably priced, too.

Chestnut Cabaret, 30th and Chestnut Sts.; 382-1201. The lines outside can be long because this is the hottest spot in the University City area. Large stage, dance floor, and rock music in a subdued atmosphere of brick walls, hanging plants, and candlelit tables. It's also got afterhours permission (drinks can be served 'til 3 am). No sneakers or T-shirts.

Delancey Street, 1500 Market St.; 988-9334. Replete with an absolutely stunning mahogany and brass bar, it has live entertainment Wednesday through Friday nights. Happy hour 5–7 pm.

The Devon Ballroom, 28 Lehigh Ave., Devon; 964-1610. A full-time dancing school, this place opens its doors to the public every Friday night. Those who come waltz to Springsteen and rumba to the Beatles. It's really an interesting spot where you'll find students from other dance schools dancing, practicing, and getting to know each other.

Eons, Route 29, Graterford; 489-3000. It's outerspace dancing here with the myriad of overhead and multitubular lights. There's also a dazzling laser light show. A disc jockey plays current hits Friday and Saturday nights. Wednesday night is Ladies' Night.

J. C. Dobbs, 304 South St.; 925-4053. Hires performers that don't charge much, meaning that you'll have fun with beginners, newcomers to Philadelphia, or local groups putting together an act. Many who patronize this spot are fellow musicians and their friends.

The Kennel Club, 1215 Walnut St.; 592-7650. This video dance bar blasts new music by a DJ and attracts a blend of the Center City chic-arty-punk crowd.

Khyber Pass, 56 S. 2nd St.; 627-6482. Also, 18th and Callowhill Sts.; 567-8533. Both are British pub-style eating and drinking spots with entertainment nightly. Entertainment features blues, jazz, reggae, rock, bluegrass, and new wave. You've got a choice of more than 100 kinds of beers and imported wines. The 2nd Street location is located below Miss Headly's Wine Bar and features a candlelit restaurant with a continental menu.

Kristopher's, Cottman and Bustleton Aves.; 332-8900. Offers live entertainment geared for the 30s set, a big dance floor, and a menu of fine continental dishes at reasonable prices. (The $6.95 early bird special includes an entree that changes daily, a side order of spaghetti or one vegetable, soup, salad, and coffee or tea.)

The Middle East, 126 Chestnut St.; 922-1003. A Philadelphia tradition that starts with a Middle East dish then continues with music and the best in belly dancing.

Monte Carlo Living Room, 2nd and South Sts.; 925-2220. Situated above what may be the most handsomely appointed restaurant in town, this private club is one of the city's most exclusive night spots, and one of its most expensive. If you're not a member, there's an entrance fee for the chance to dance on imported Italian marble and stroll on carpets that seem like velvet. There's also a balcony, smoked mirrors, glass ceilings, and comfortable sofas.

Orleans, 1676 Lancaster Ave., Paoli; 296-8787. This large restaurant-nightclub has a 300-seat cabaret downstairs and a piano bar upstairs. You'll find gracious dining in "The Greenhouse" restaurant, where the creole dishes are all winners.

Paso Doble Ballroom, 4501 Falls Rd., Levittown; 547-2311. Those who want to show off their dancing talents will love this large ballroom and its live band music. For those who may require a few tips, dance lessons are available.

Polo Bay Club, 17th and Locust Sts.; 546-8800. A very chic club in the Warwick Hotel. Backgammon tables, dancing. Happy hour 5–6:30 pm with hot and cold hors d'oeuvres. Sunday brunch.

Popcorn's, 160 N. Gulph Rd., King of Prussia; 265-7226. Weekday happy hours from 5–7 pm. Smart decor of brass, wood, mirrors, and Tivoli lights. Buffet of hors d'oeuvres.

PT's, 6 S. Front St.; 922-5676. In the heart of Old City, this is a nice spot to mingle at the long bar, play backgammon, and dance. Thursday night features live big-band music; Friday and Saturday night, the sound system takes over.

Pulsations, Route 1, Glen Mills; 459-4140. This $6 million nightclub attracts large crowds Wednesday through Sunday nights for dancing with a live DJ and a 25,000-watt sound system. Each night is highlighted soon after midnight when a huge spaceship, scanning the dance floor with hundreds of lights, begins its descent from the ceiling. When it "lands," Pulsar, the dancing robot, emerges. This has to be seen to be believed.

Quincy's, City Ave. and Monument Rd.; 581-5000. Within weeks after the Adams Mark Hotel opened, this became the hottest singles spot in town. It's got an authentic Victorian flavor, but the dance music is very up-to-date. A DJ plays Top 40 tunes, followed by a live band doing the same from 8:30 pm–1:30 am. Happy hour Monday through Friday, 4–8:30 pm with hot and cold hors d'oeuvres. Jackets please.

Revival, 22 S. 3rd St.; 627-4825. This private dance club features new wave music, both live and recorded. Open Wednesday through Sunday from 9 pm to 3:30 am.

Rib-It, 1709 Walnut St.; 568-1555, and 52 S. 2nd St.; 923-5511. Jazz and contemporary music every night except Sunday at these popular spots. Known for their baby-back ribs, Irish rice pudding (for mature adults), and a new drink at owner Paul Rimmeir's whim. His latest—the Choo-Choo Train. ("It takes you where you want to go," he says.)

Scintillations, Sheraton Valley Forge Hotel, Route 363, King of Prussia; 337-2000. This dazzling nightclub with its special lights, sound system, and sunken dance floor features dancing from Monday through Saturday nights.

Second Story Club, 1127 Walnut St.; 925-1127. This singles spot is popular for dancing and mingling. For a minimal charge, you can also become a member.

Social Club, 2009 Sansom St.; 564-2277. Located above the Academy of Social Dance, this place features disco, Latin, slow dance, and waltzing to the sound system. A must are its Saturday night theme parties and dance contests. From 2 to 6 pm Saturday is the "tea dance," with free lessons included in your admission.

Sunnybrook Ballroom, Route 422, Pottstown; 326-6400. Tommy Dorsey, Guy Lombardo, and Art Mooney are just some of the big names who have performed in this legendary ballroom. It stages a big band night about once a month and always sells out, with everybody dancing 'til 1 am. The food is splendid, too.

The Troc, 10th and Arch Sts.; 592-8762. First opened in 1870 as the Arch Street Opera Theater, this building eventually became a home for vaudeville and burlesque. Now beautifully restored to its original grandeur, it is listed on the National Register of Historic Places. Occasionally, it is rented out to local groups for performances.

23 East Cabaret, 23 E. Lancaster Ave., Ardmore; 896-6420. This is the Main Line's most popular nightclub, bright and airy with white walls, a long bar, and stage. Features quality bands with original music.

Ulana's, 205 Bainbridge; 922-4152. Ulana's is a unique multistory Queen Village bar, restaurant, and club. Continental cuisine in the dim and cozy restaurant downstairs, and after dinner, go upstairs for the dancing.

Film

Following a nationwide trend, there is a growing interest in films in exciting Philadelphia. The following list offers the best schedules for repertory cinema, foreign film, and classics.

Neighborhood Film Project, International House, 3701 Chestnut St.; 387-5125, ext. 222. A showcase of works produced by independent film makers along with a series of foreign films. Shown September through April, Wednesday through Sunday evenings. Guest speakers often appear with their movies and occasionally a workshop is staged with the film program.

Ritz 5, 214 Walnut St.; 925-7900. This theater presents quality first-run foreign films. Classy clientele, extremely comfortable seats.

Roxy Screening Rooms I & II, 2021-23 Sansom St.; 561-0115. Recently expanded, now has two screening rooms of 132 seats each. Roxy I shows limited runs of obscure films and revivals. The II features more commercial movies.

Temple Cinematheque, 1619 Walnut St.; 787-1529. These two screening rooms located in the old KYW studio present classical movies along with some foreign films. At least five different films are screened every week. A film society membership is available, too.

Special films and series are presented at the following centers:

Academy of Natural Sciences, 19th St. and the Parkway; 229-1000. Throughout the year the Academy's 425-seat auditorium presents motion pictures and animated cartoons relating to animals, the history of dinosaurs, and nature. Free with admission. Check newspapers for times and schedules.

Exploratory Cinema, 3620 Walnut St.; 898-6701. Experimental and noncommercial movies are shown in the auditorium of the Annenberg School.

Free Library of Philadelphia, Central Library on Logan Square and at branches; 686-5322. A series of free films is shown on an irregular basis at

2 pm Sunday in the Montgomery Auditorium except during summer. Topics vary and include everything from MGM musicals to aviation, foreign movies, and travel. Regional libraries also present a free film series. Check newspapers for times and schedules.

Philadelphia Museum of Art, Van Pelt Auditorium, 26th St. and the Parkway; 763-8100. Special movies are shown in conjunction with the current exhibitions. Children's films are shown occasionally on Sundays.

University Museum, 33rd and Spruce Sts.; 898-4025. October through March, the museum features a series of films for children every Saturday morning. Sunday features adult archaeology and anthropology movies.

SIGHTS

As the birthplace of the American democratic process, Philadelphia is without question one of the most historic cities of the United States, a city flourishing with names like Washington, Jefferson, and Franklin as if these men were old and trusted friends, which in fact they once were. From stately Independence Mall to historic Germantown, from battle-scarred Old Fort Mifflin to the haunting Brandywine Valley and the rolling meadows of Valley Forge, Philadelphia with its surrounding counties is *the* place where the United States began, and an omnipresent reminder of when, why, and how.

While many visitors come in search of the nation's roots—in the historic buildings, churches, mansions, homes, and museums (there are more than 90 museums in Philadelphia alone)—they invariably discover much, much more than was originally expected. Among these new discoveries are the parks and arboretums, the wildlife refuges and bird sanctuaries, colonial plantations and homesteads, excellent zoos and amusement parks, even a 19th-century iron-making community meticulously restored.

One of Philadelphia's strongest attributes is its wealth of sights, many of which are free or available at a very nominal fee. Below we have listed as many historic, interesting, intriguing, and varied sights as space permits. In addition to these, you will find even more in our walking tours, Metro and Main Line/Brandywine Valley driving tours, and one-day excursions. Since there may be slight changes in the individual schedules or hours, we recommend that you call in advance of your visit.

SIGHTS BY AREA

BERKS COUNTY
Daniel Boone Homestead
Hopewell Village

BUCKS COUNTY
Andalusia

CENTER CITY
Academy of Music
Afro-American Historical and
   Cultural Museum

American-Swedish Historical
   Museum
The Atheneum of Philadelphia
Atwater Kent Museum
The Balch Institute for Ethnic
   Studies
Chinese Cultural and Community
   Center
Edgar Allen Poe House
Historical Society of Pennsylvania

Library Company of Philadelphia
Museum of American Jewish
  History
Mutter Museum
The National Shrine of St. John
  Neumann
Rosenbach Museum and Library
Shoe Museum
Wanamaker Museum
War Library Museum
Wistar Museum

CENTER CITY
AND THE PARKWAY

Academy of Natural Sciences
Franklin Institute Science Museum
  and Fels Planetarium
Free Library of Philadelphia
Please Touch Museum

CHESTER COUNTY

Chester County Historical Society
Historic Yellow Springs
Swiss Pines

DELAWARE COUNTY

Brinton 1704 House
Caleb Pusey House
Colonial Pennsylvania Plantation
Franklin Mint Museum
John Chad House
Newlin Grist Mill
Thomas Massey House
Tinicum National Environmental
  Center
Tyler Arboretum

LANCASTER COUNTY

Hershey Park

MONTGOMERY COUNTY

Clifton House
Elmwood Park Zoo

Graeme Park
Highlands Historical Society
Hope Lodge
Mill Grove
Morgan Log House
Peter Wentz Farmstead

NORTH PHILADELPHIA

Wagner Free Institute of Science

NORTHEAST PHILADELPHIA

Pennyback Environmental Center
Ryerss Museum and Library

NORTHWEST PHILADELPHIA

Historic Germantown
Morris Arboretum
Schuylkill Valley Nature Center

OLD CITY-SOCIETY HILL

Historic St. George's Methodist
  Church
Mikveh Israel Synagogue
Mother Bethel A.M.E. Church
Old First Reformed Church
Old Pine Presbyterian Church
Pennsylvania Hospital
St. Joseph's Church
Welcome Park

QUEEN VILLAGE

Gloria Dei Church

SOUTH PHILADELPHIA

Mario Lanza Institute and Museum
Mummers Museum
Old Fort Mifflin

SOUTHWEST PHILADELPHIA

Bartram's Gardens

UNIVERSITY CITY

University Museum

Academy of Music, Broad and Locust Sts.; 893-1930. CH. The official home of the Philadelphia Orchestra since 1900, the "Grand Old Lady of Locust Street" celebrated its 125th anniversary on January 23, 1982. Since most of the $250,000 that was raised to build the Academy was used in the magnificent crimson, gold, and cream interior, the exterior was left "plain like a market house" so that a marble front might one day be added. It never was, however, because through the decades the mellowed brick brownstone and cast-iron exterior became most representative of historical Philadelphia. The Academy, which was completely renovated in the early 1970s, is a Registered National Historic Landmark (see PERFORMING ARTS).

Academy of Natural Sciences, 19th St. and Benjamin Franklin Parkway; 299-1000. CH. Founded in 1812, this is the oldest natural history museum in the country. It exhibits animals in their natural habitat. The bird, fish, and plant collections are among the most comprehensive in the world and include bird specimens that were used as models by Audubon. Plant specimens were gathered by Lewis and Clark during their exploration of the West. Thomas Jefferson's own fossil collection even found a home here. Visitors are always fascinated by the exhibit of the 65-million-year old dinosaur. The Academy also features Outside-Inn, a nature museum designed especially for children. Those ages 12 and under can try to lift a meteorite, find dinosaur footprints in a slab of pre-historic rock, and crawl through a fossil cave. The Academy's division of education also presents a daily live animal "Eco-Show."

Afro-American Historical and Cultural Museum, 7th and Arch Sts.; 574-0380. CH. This is the world's most comprehensive museum of the Afro-American past, tracing the roots of black history, art, and culture from Africa to the United States. Five galleries are filled with maps, masks, hairstyles, model slave ships, art, and sculpture; the Fine Arts gallery features a wealth of graphics, oils, and watercolors. Tue–Sat 10 am–5 pm, Sun 12–6 pm.

American Swedish Historical Museum, 1900 Pattison Ave.; 389-1776. CH (*children under 12 NCH when accompanied by an adult*). Mod- eled after a 17th-century Swedish manor house, the museum is located on land that was settled by the Swedes prior to Penn's arrival in 1682. It has 14 galleries of materials depicting 300 years of Swedish contributions to American life that include early glass, textiles, paintings, drawings, and etchings. Many of the rooms are accented by the finest in 20th-century Swedish architecture. Library, gift shop. Tue–Fri 10 am–4 pm, Sat noon–4 pm.

Andalusia, north of Philadelphia, on the Delaware River, Andalusia; 848-1777. CH. This was the first mature Greek Revival mansion in America, and is one of the best known country estates from Philadelphia's Federal period. Built in 1795, it was later occupied by Nicholas Biddle, director of the Second Bank of the United States. Members of the Biddle family still live here. Hours by appointment.

The Atheneum of Philadelphia, 219 S.6th St.; 925-2688. *NCH.* Named for the classical Greek goddess of wisdom, The Atheneum was founded in 1814 by members of The American Philosophical Society and is housed in a National Historic Landmark building that was called "the handsomest edifice in the city" when it opened in the mid-19th century. As the first major structure in America to be built in the Italianate Revival style, it was authentically restored to its former grandeur in 1975. It maintains an independent research library specializing in 19th-century social and cultural history. Guided tours Mon–Fri 10:30 am and 2 pm.

Atwater Kent Museum, 15 S. 7th St.; MU6-3630. *NCH.* This handsome marble building is Philadelphia's own history museum, depicting everyday life in the city through its 300 years of existence. Displays include antique working clocks, hammers and saws, political posters, sunbonnets, train tickets, toys, guns, swords, ship models, even cigar store Indians. Tue–Sun 9:30 am–5 pm.

The Balch Institute for Ethnic Studies, 18 S. 7th St.; 925-8090. *NCH.* Founded in 1971, this museum and library explores the history of immigration and the melding of more than 100 ethnic cultures in the United States. Documents, clothes, household goods, and other artifacts reveal what immigrants brought and how and where they lived after arriving. You can sit on a genuine Ellis Island bench while learning about the millions of immigrants who sat on them before you. Museum Mon–Sat 10 am–4 pm, Library Mon–Sat 9 am–5 pm.

Bartram's Garden, 54th St. and Lindbergh Blvd.; 729-5281. *NCH (guided tours, CH).* Started in 1728 by John Bartram, a Quaker, this is the oldest botanical garden in the nation. Encouraged to pursue his botanical interests by Benjamin Franklin and James Logan, Bartram later traveled extensively, returning with seeds and roots that he planted in his garden, observed, propogated, and shipped abroad. In 1765 King George III appointed him a Royal Botanist. Bartram's former home is also on the 27-acre property, which is ideal for picnicking; afternoon teas or box lunches can be arranged in advance. April–October Tue–Sun 10 am–4 pm; November–March by appointment only.

Betsy Ross House, 239 Arch St.; 627-5343. *NCH.* This two-story Colonial home is where Betsy Ross lived and where she is credited with sewing the nation's first flag. Daily 9 am–5 pm.

The Brinton 1704 House, Oakland Rd., south of Dilworthtown; 692-4800. *CH.* In the rolling hills of the Brandywine Valley, this is one of the most authentic restorations in the state. It was built in 1704 by William Brinton, based on his memories of medieval English architecture. Inventories taken at his death in 1751 provided his descendants with the authentic basis upon which this restored house is furnished.

Betsy Ross House   City of Philadelphia

The Caleb Pusey House, 15 Race St., Upland; 874-0900. CH. This is the last remaining house in Pennsylvania William Penn is known to have visited. His good friend, Caleb Pusey, was Pennsylvania's first historian, and also managed the Chester Mills, a saw and grist mill set up by Penn and his partners. Pusey built this house in 1683. It is now completely restored. On the 12 acres there is also a 1790 log house, an 1849 schoolhouse museum, a gift shop, and picnic tables. May–September Sat–Sun 1–4:30 pm, other days by appointment.

Chester County Historical Society, 225 N. High St., West Chester; 692-4800. CH. This museum and library has an extensive collection of more than 50,000 examples of furniture, textiles, metals, and ceramics reflecting history of the area. Extensive printed materials, manuscripts, and genealogical data ideal for family research are also available. Tue, Thur, Fri, 10 am–4 pm, Wed 1–8 pm. Museum only Sat 10 am–4 pm. Groups by appointment.

Chinese Cultural and Community Center, 125 N. 10th St.; 923-6767. CH. This Mandarin palace-style building is the perfect spot to begin a tour of Chinatown. It features Chinese art, musical instruments, exhibits, tours of the center and of Chinatown itself, banquets, a tea house, movies, and special cultural events throughout the year. Mon–Fri 9 am–4:30 pm, tea house Mon–Fri 11 am–2 pm.

Clifton House, 473 Bethlehem Pike, Fort Washington; 646-6065. NCH. Located in the heart of the Whitemarsh encampment area, this house stands on the site of the original Sandy Run Inn, where the cold, hungry men of Washington's army once stayed in the tavern's common room. The tavern burned down in 1802, was rebuilt, burned down again in 1852, was rebuilt again and named Clifton House for the steep cliff that was in back of it at the time. Its museum is one of the finest small museums and historical libraries in Pennsylvania. It was on the 3 nearby hills that the Continental Army watched over British-occupied Philadelphia from November 2 to December 11, 1777, prior to its march to Valley Forge. Museum first and third Sunday of the month 2–4 pm, Library Wed 2–4 pm and 7–9 pm.

The Colonial Pennsylvania Plantation, in Ridley Creek State Park on Route 3, 3 miles west of its intersection with Route 252 in Newtown Square; 566-1725. CH. Watch an 18th-century farmer, his wife, and their helpers go about daily chores on this "Living History Farm," where the original acres date back to a patent by William Penn's commissioners. The farmhouse, springhouse, store, barns, even the horses, cattle, sheep, and pigs, are much the same as they were in the 1770s. April–November Sat–Sun 10 am–4 pm. Group tours Tue–Fri by reservation.

Daniel Boone Homestead, Route 82, just north of Route 422, Birdsboro; 582-4900. NCH. Though he's most identified with the settling of the West, Daniel Boone, son of Quaker parents, was born in a log house here in

November 1734. At the time, this area of Berks County was on the fringes of the wilderness, and it was here that Boone learned to hunt, trap, and shoot. Sometime in the 18th century, the log house was replaced by the two-story stone structure which has been carefully restored to its original flavor. Daily 8:30 am–5 pm, Sun 1–5 pm. During non-Daylight Saving Time, daily 9 am–4 pm, Sun 1–4:30 pm.

Edgar Allen Poe House, 532 N. 7th St.; 597-8780. *NCH.* The famed poet and writer enjoyed his most productive and contented years in Philadelphia, where he lived from 1838 to 1844. It was here that he resided in 1843 with his wife Virginia, and her mother, Mrs. Clemm, writing "The Black Cat," "The Tell Tale Heart" and "The Gold Bug." It was in Philadelphia that Poe achieved his greatest success as an editor and critic. Of Poe's several homes in Philadelphia, this is the only one that survives, and Congress has selected the site as the nation's memorial to him. Daily 9 am–5 pm, except Christmas Day and New Year's Day.

Elmwood Park Zoo, Harding Blvd., Norristown; 272-8089. *NCH (donations accepted).* If you've been touring the sites and battlefields of Valley Forge, this will provide an ideal break for the children. It's clean and friendly, with paths leading past cages housing all kinds of favorite animals, including monkeys and lions. There's a reptile house, an aviary, and a petting zoo. A special feature is "Zoo America," an exhibit of animals indigenous to this country (prairie dogs, Chincoteague ponies, deer, elk, and eagles). Tue–Sun 10 am–4:30 pm.

The Franklin Institute Science Museum and Fels Planetarium, 20th St. and Benjamin Franklin Parkway; 448-1200. *CH.* Founded in 1824 and named for Benjamin Franklin, the Institute and the Planetarium attract more than 600,000 visitors a year. You can walk through a human heart or play the world's largest pinball machine, and the Institute has pioneered the use of computer exhibitions. This is the nation's first push-button museum of science and technology and from the beginning included a 350-ton Baldwin locomotive. Under the dome of Fels Planetarium, one is introduced to the mysteries and wonders of the universe, and in particular the sun, moon, and stars. Multimedia shows are presented daily, and several public shows are given each year. It also is the site of the Benjamin Franklin Memorial, dedicated in 1938, and, in 1972, designated by Congress as the official national memorial to Franklin. Mon–Sat 10 am–5 pm, Sun noon–5 pm.

The Franklin Mint Museum, Route 1, Franklin Center; 459-6168. *NCH.* This is the world's largest private mint, producing limited edition coins, medals, and objects in honor of world figures and events. The museum features a remarkable range of art in precious metals, bronze, pewter, crystal, and porcelain, as well as books, recordings, graphics, jewelry, and furniture. The highlight is watching the mint's manufacturing process in various mediums and chances are you'll be able to watch a craftsman making a Franklin Mint

Benjamin Franklin Memorial,   City of Philadelphia
Franklin Institute of Science

collectible on the spot. The omnipresent film describes the art of minting from start to finish. Tue–Sat 9:30 am–4:30 pm, Sun 1–4:30 pm.

Free Library of Philadelphia, Logan Square; 686-1776. *NCH.* Designed by Julian Abele, this is a replica of the Ministry of Marine on the Place de la Concorde in Paris. More than 2 million books are housed here and in its 48 neighborhood branches. Among its treasures are the world's largest collection of automated history, the world's largest collection of orchestral scores, and Philadelphia's largest collection of children's books. Its rare-book department features, among a myriad of stunning collections, original manuscripts and first editions of works by Charles Dickens and Edgar Allen Poe. The exhibits in the main lobby change regularly.

Graeme Park, ½ mile west of Route 611 on County Line Rd., Horsham; 343-0965. *CH.* William Keith erected the buildings on this lovely rural setting in 1721–22, not so much for a residence as for a place to manufacture alcohol (he called it "Fountain Low"). Eventually he fell into conflict with the Penn family, which had appointed him Provincial Governor. After they removed him from office in 1726, Keith lived here briefly before returning to England. Dr. Thomas Graeme, a respected Philadelphia physician, bought the property as a country estate and entertained a great deal. His daughter Elizabeth, however, emerged as a tragic and controversial figure; according to legend, her ghost still walks the estate at night. Wed–Sat 9 am–5 pm, Sun noon–5 pm.

Hershey Park, Exit 20 on the Pennsylvania Turnpike, then follow the signs; 717-534-3900. CH. This is the centerpiece of the town which rose around Milton Snavely Hershey's chocolate factory. Started by Hershey shortly after the turn of the century as an amusement park for his employees, it now includes 76 acres, virtually in the center of town, with 7 theme areas, 36 rides, and 5 entertainment centers. Its roller coasters are among the scariest in the nation. The 10-acre ZooAmerica features 200 North American animals, birds and reptiles, and the Aqua Theater has performances by dolphins and sea lions. Adjacent to the park is Hershey's Chocolate World, where a tour highlights the history and manufacture of Hershey's chocolate, and the Hershey Museum, which features exhibits and artifacts from early Americana and serves as a tribute to the man who started it all. Open from mid-May to mid-September; call for specific times.

Highlands Historical Society, 7001 Sheaff Lane, Fort Washington; 641-2687. NCH. Built by Anthony Morris in 1796 as a "country house for entertaining," the Highlands were visited often by Morris' friends, among them Presidents Madison, Monroe, and Jefferson. Morris is credited with introducing Madison to the widowed Dolly Todd. The handsome Georgian house and the beautiful gardens surrounding it have since been faithfully restored. Office open Tue–Thu 10 am–1 pm. By appointment only.

Historical Society of Pennsylvania, 1300 Locust St.; 732-6200. CH. There is a veritable gold mine of Pennsylvania history here, including the most comprehensive research anywhere in the state, its largest collection of genealogical works, portraits and scenes of the colonial period by great artists, and the largest and most important historical manuscript collection in private hands in the United States. The manuscript collection includes the voluminous archives of the Penn family, maps, prints, and drawings of the Pennsylvania scene. There is also fine Philadelphia silver and furniture, and many other fascinating items once the property of the Penn, Franklin, Washington, and Jefferson families. Tue–Fri 9 am–5 pm, Mon 1–9 pm.

Historic Yellow Springs, off Route 113, east of its intersection with Route 401, Chester Springs; 827-7414. NCH (*donations accepted*). Started in 1722 as a popular colonial spa with lodging at the inn and baths in the iron, sulphur, and magnesium mineral springs, Yellow Springs and the inn ultimately became the only Revolutionary War hospital commissioned by the Continental Congress. It later became a spa once more, then an orphanage, then the summer campus of the Pennsylvania Academy of Fine Arts and a motion picture studio until 1974. The entire village is on the National Register of Historic Places and features an elegant restaurant. The inn was remade into a hotel. Mon–Fri 9 am–4 pm.

Hope Lodge, 553 Bethlehem Pike, Whitemarsh; 646-1595. *CH.* This beautiful home in the finest Georgian tradition was built in 1750. It was occupied by Samuel Morris, a successful grist mill operator who died here in 1770 and was in the middle of various military operations during the Revolutionary War. It is named for the Hope banking family, which purchased the home in 1784. Wed–Fri 9 am–5 pm, Sun noon–5 pm.

Hopewell Village, Route 345, 6 miles south of Birdsboro; 582-8773. *NCH.* As a magnificent restoration of this ironmaking community between 1820 and 1840, Hopewell Village brings back the time when it was famed for its stoves, pig iron, domestic and farm implements, and the cannon, shot, and shell it made for the Continental Army during the Revolutionary War. Mark Bird, who built Hopewell in 1771, was an ardent patriot who served as a colonel in the militia. Among the restored structures are the ironmaster's house, charcoal house, village barn, tenant houses, blacksmith shop, the church, and furnace. Of special interest from late June to Labor Day is the "Living History" program, in which employees in period costumes demonstrate the manufacturing, cooking, and domestic skills once used in this National Historic Site. Daily 9 am–5 pm.

John Chad House, Route 100 just north of Route 1, Chadds Ford; 388-1132. *CH.* Built in 1726, this charming stone building was the home of ferryman/farmer/tavern keeper John Chad, after whom Chadds Ford was named. It has since been restored, and aromatic baked goods emerge from the beehive oven every Sunday. June-August noon–5 pm. Tours year round; call for an appointment.

Library Company of Philadelphia, 1314 Locust St.; 546-3181. *NCH.* Benjamin Franklin founded this library in 1732, when its first books were brought from England. It is now the oldest circulating library in the nation, contains 300,000 books, and is highlighted by such historical minutiae as the metal box in which members placed requests for books to be imported, Thomas Jefferson's personal copy of his first published book, and Lewis and Clark's guidebook for their expedition in 1804.

Mario Lanza Institute and Museum, 1919 Wolf St.; 468-3623. *NCH.* The museum is a tribute to the great tenor who was born and raised in South Philadelphia. A large bust of the singer made by one of his fans in Hungary is on display, as are numerous photographs, gold records, personal items from his wallet, and newspaper and magazine articles recounting his thrilling yet tragic story. Recordings of Lanza's greatest hits provide background music. The museum is sponsored by the Mario Lanza Institute which provides outstanding young talents with scholarships to the Settlement Music School where Lanza received his early musical education. Mon–Sat 10 am–5 pm.

Mikveh Israel Cemetery, Spruce St. between 8th and 9th; 922-5446. *NCH.* Through the gates, you get an excellent view of the cemetery that was

Hopewell Village

founded in 1738 by Nathan Levy on ground he acquired from William Penn. Among those buried here are Levy, whose ship brought the Liberty Bell to Philadelphia, and Haym Salomon, one of the major financiers of the Revolutionary War. For special arrangements, call in advance.

Mill Grove: The Authentic Audubon Home and Wildlife Sanctuary, Audubon Rd. West of Route 363, Audubon; 666-5593. NCH. This beautiful 130-acre estate, whose mansion (circa 1762) is the only true Audubon home still standing in America, was owned for 17 years by John James Audubon's father, a French sea captain. In 1804 the father brought his son here to supervise the estate, and it was while he roamed the wooded hills along the Perkiomen Creek and the Schuylkill River that the young Audubon gained his first impressions of American birds and wildlife. The estate is now a wildlife sanctuary with miles of trails, feeding stations, nesting boxes, and trees and shrubs attractive to birds. The mansion serves as a museum with all the major works of the world-famous naturalist, artist, and author on display. Tue–Sat 10 am–4 pm, Sun 1–4 pm.

Morgan Log House, Weikel Rd., one block west of Route 363, Towamencin Township; 368-2480. CH. Built in 1695 by Daniel Boone's maternal grandparents, Edward and Elizabeth Morgan, the log house has been completely resorted and is furnished with antiques from the Philadelphia Museum of Art, the Dietrich Foundation, and the Finklestein Collection. After standing virtually unnoticed for almost 300 years, it is now on the National Register of Historic Places. Tours daily by appointment, Sat–Sun 1–5 pm.

Morris Arboretum, 101 Hillcrest Ave.; 247-5777. CH. The Morris Arboretum brought to Philadelphia an institution modeled after the great British botanic gardens—the Royal Botanic Gardens of Edinburgh and Kew, and of Cambridge and Oxford Universities. Administered to by the University of Pennsylvania, this 175-acre estate is alive with 3500 varieties of exotic and native shrubs and trees. It is particularly noted for its conifers, hollies, and azaleas, while winter accents the many evergreens and the tropical Fern House. Daily 10 am–5 pm, Thu 10 am–8 pm.

Mummers Museum, Two St. at Washington Ave.; 336-3050. CH. Designed as a permanent display of Philadelphia Mummery, its history, and traditions, this museum is filled with memorabilia representing the pageantry of the famed New Year's Day parade up Broad Street. The parade's roots date back to pre-colonial times, and it is all evident here. Tue–Sat 9:30 am–5 pm, Sun noon–5 pm.

Museum of American Jewish History, 55 N. 5th St.; 923-3811. CH. This is the only museum in the United States that is devoted exclusively to the role of Jewish people in the growth and achievements of America. A permanent exhibit is "The American Jewish Experience: From 1654 to the Present," with a smaller gallery featuring changing exhibits. Mon–Thu 10 am–5 pm, Fri–Sun 10 am–4 pm.

Mutter Museum, 19 S. 22nd St.; 561-6059, ext. 41. *NCH (donations accepted).* Named for Dr. Thomas Dent Mutter, who gave his unique collection of specimens and models to the College of Physicians of Philadelphia in 1858, the museum contains a host of skeletons, surgical instruments, and medical lore that includes a 7th-century B.C. prescription tablet from Assyria. Gracing the walls are artwork and sculpture busts by Thomas Eakins, Charles Wilson Peale, Thomas Sully, and William Rush. Tue–Fri 10 am–4 pm.

The National Shrine of St. John Neumann, St. Peter the Apostle Church, 5th St. and Girard Ave.; 627-2386. *NCH.* Saint John Neumann was the first American to be canonized by the Roman Catholic Church, the father of parochial education in America, and a former bishop in Philadelphia. This is his final resting place; his body lies in a glass casket. Tue–Fri 10 am–4 pm, Sat 10 am–5 pm, Sun 1–5 pm.

The Newlin Grist Mill, S. Cheney Rd. off Baltimore Pike, 7 miles west of Media; 459-2359. *CH.* This lovely property, which has grown to 140 acres from the original 3½, contains the mill, the stone house, log cabin, blacksmith shop, and picnic tables in the woods for a pleasant day in the country. The millrace is stocked with rainbow and brown trout, and fishing can be enjoyed for a fee, without a license. Three miles of paths wind past a giant ash tree and an oak which doubtless looked down upon the Lenni Lenape Indians long before Penn arrived. The mill was built in 1704 by Nathaniel Newlin, a Quaker who emigrated from Ireland in 1683. He built the house in 1739. Daily 8 am–dusk. For reservations to the picnic grove, call in advance.

Old Fort Mifflin, Fort Mifflin Rd. near Philadelphia International Airport; 365-5194. *CH (children under 12, 25¢, adults 50¢).* It was in 1772 that the British began to build this fort, but it was the Continental Army that completed it in 1776 under the direction of Benjamin Franklin. The British then won back the fort in fierce fighting, during which more than 250 patriot soldiers were killed. Twenty years after the war Fort Mifflin was rebuilt. During the Civil War, the fort served as a prison for military deserters. Now a National Historic Landmark, the fort is operated by the Atwater Kent Museum and contains such vivid reminders of the Revolution as cannons, officers' and soldiers' quarters, and their arsenal. Outside is one of the oldest houses in Philadelphia, built by a Swedish settler in the 1660s. After being scarred by cannon fire during the attack on the fort during the Revolution, it was dubbed the "Cannonball Farmhouse." Sat 12–5 pm, Sun 12–4 pm, weekdays by reservation only.

Pennsylvania Hospital, 8th and Spruce Sts.; 829-3000. *NCH.* This is the nation's oldest hospital, founded in 1751 by Benjamin Franklin and Dr. Thomas Bond. The Great Court features a gallery of portraits of the hospital's most famous men as well as colonial medical instruments and a library of rare books. There's also America's first surgical amphitheater, built in 1804 and last used in 1868. The History of Nursing Museum contains a wealth of materials tracing the development of the nursing profession. Mon–Fri 9 am– 5 pm, by reservation only.

Pennypack Environmental Center, Verree Rd. near Bloomfield Ave.; 671-0440. NCH. The center offers 150 acres of hiking trails, with maps for self-guided nature walks. It is also a bird sanctuary and wildlife preserve, with one section of the preserve devoted to exhibits of turtles, reptiles, and fish. Daily 9 am–5:30 pm.

Peter Wentz Farmhouse, Schultz Rd. off Route 73, Worcester; 584-5104. NCH (*donations accepted*). This restored colonial farmhouse was used by George Washington before and after the Battle of Germantown and is one of the top 10 tourist attractions in Pennsylvania. According to calculations of the commissioners and historical board of Montgomery County, the structure is *exactly* as it was in 1777—from the bright mortar between the stones of the main house to the crisp contrast between its black and white shutters. The farm includes typical 18th-century crops, a reception center with hostesses in authentic costumes, the barn that was built in 1744, 14 years before the main house, and an orchard of apples, peaches, and pears. Tue–Sat 10 am–4 pm, Sun 1–4 pm.

Please Touch Museum, 210 N. 21st St.; 963-0666. CH. This museum is designed specifically for children 7 years and younger. It is also ideal for handicapped children 12 and under. Here the arts, sciences, technology, natural sciences, and cultural subjects are offered with the accent on sound, watching and petting small animals, crawling and climbing, and acting out fantasies in masks, costumes, and uniforms, as well as with puppets. Tue–Sat 10 am–4:30 pm, Sun 12:30–4:30 pm.

Queen Village, south of Head House Sq. in Society Hill. This neighborhood is Philadelphia's oldest, originally settled in the early 1600s by the Swedes but quickly taken over by the English who made it their own. Now a neighborhood of many old homes that have been faithfully restored, Queen Village is also the site of Gloria Dei, or Old Swede's Church, at Swanson and Christian Streets. Opened in 1700, it is the oldest church in Philadelphia.

Rosenbach Museum and Library, 2010 Delancey St.; 732-1600. NCH. This museum has earned world-wide recognition for its priceless books and manuscripts, which include the *Bay Psalm Book*, the first Bible printed in the Western Hemisphere, James Joyce's manuscript of *Ulysses*, and the manuscript of Chaucer's *Canterbury Tales*. It also has the only known first copy of Benjamin Franklin's *Poor Richard's Almanac* and a letter sent to Stalin by Franklin Roosevelt and Winston Churchill. Also included are superior collections of silver, furniture, porcelain, and works of art, all initiated by the brothers Rosenbach, Philip, and Dr. A.S.W. Tue–Sun 11 am–4 pm.

Ryerss Estate, Cottman and Central Aves.; 745-3061. NCH. The estate offers a jewel of a museum and library with a tower that has a stunning view of the Philadelphia skyline. The hilltop mansion was built in 1859 as the country home of Joseph Waln Ryerss, a wealthy Philadelphia merchant. In 1978 it was restored by architects specializing in the Victorian period, and it stands as a tribute to their expertise today. Museum Sun 1–4 pm, Library Fri–Sun 10 am–5 pm. Tours of the entire estate by appointment.

Schuylkill Valley Nature Center, 8480 Hagy's Mill Rd., Upper Roxborough; 482-7300. CH. Just as Philadelphia is blessed with the largest urban park in the country, Fairmount Park, it also has the largest urban outdoor education center of any city—the Schuylkill Valley Nature Center. Only 5 miles from Center City are 360 acres of fields, thickets, ponds, streams, and woodlands, with 6 miles of winding trails. On clear days enjoy a spectacular view of Center City from the Upper Fields trail. Indoor facilities include a 5000-volume library, the Discovery Museum, a teaching resource center, an auditorium, and a book store. Mon–Sat 9 am–5 pm, Sun 1–5 pm.

Shoe Museum, Pennsylvania College of Podiatric Medicine, 8th and Race Sts.; 629-0300. NCH. Children as well as adults will be amused with the college's display of more than 500 foot coverings dating from early Egyptian times to the present. Included are the skates Bernie Parent wore when the Flyers won their first Stanley Cup, and the shoes Joe Frazier wore when he defeated Muhammed Ali. By appointment only.

Swiss Pines Park, Charlestown Rd. near Phoenixville; 933-6916. NCH. Known as the "little Longwood," this magnificent spot of quiet beauty is most worthy of the nickname. Covering 11 acres, it has a beautiful bamboo forest and a footbridge leading to a Japanese teahouse. The dwarf pines with gnarled limbs amid the splendor of the gardens are reminiscent of Kyoto, the ancient capital of Japan. Mon–Fri 10 am–4 pm, Sat 9–11:30 am. Closed from December 15 to March 15.

Thomas Massey House, Lawrence Rd. at Springhouse Rd., Broomall; 353-3644. NCH. One of the oldest English Quaker houses in Pennsylvania, this was the home of Thomas Massey, an indentured servant who arrived in Chester in 1683. The home was about to be torn down in 1964 when a descendant bought it and gave it to Marple Township for restoration. It is now furnished with 17th- and 18th-century furniture from the Chester County Historical Society. Tue–Sat 10 am–4:30 pm, Sun 2–5 pm. After Labor Day by appointment only. For group tours call in advance.

Tinicum National Environmental Center, 86th St. and Lindbergh Blvd.; 365-3118. NCH. Offering some of the final true marshland in Pennsylvania and home to more than 275 species of birds, 11 kinds of turtles, and an abundance of wildlife, Tinicum is an outdoor delight. There are walking trails, an observation tower, and a 500-foot boardwalk through the marsh. It all goes back to the 17th-century, when the Swedes, Dutch, and English diked and drained part of the marsh for grazing. Now migratory birds use the area as a resting and feeding spot during their flights in the spring and fall. Daily 8 am–4:30 pm, guided walks from the Visitors Center Sat–Sun at 9 am from April through November, Sun only from December through March. Guided walks for groups with advance reservations.

The Tyler Arboretum, 515 Painter Rd., Lima; 566-5431. *NCH.* Covering 700 acres of woodlands near Ridley Creek State Park, this is an outdoor museum of plants, flowers, and trees with 20 miles of hiking trails. It's a superior birding spot too, especially in the autumn, and the historic Lachford Hall is an 18th-century building filled with period decorative art and furnishings. Daily 8 am–7 pm, Lachford Hall Sun 2–5 pm.

University Museum, 33rd and Spruce Sts.; 898-4000. *CH.* There's a wealth of archaeology and anthropology here, including artifacts from every continent. Hundreds of excavations have brought the museum just about everything from biblical inscriptions to gold of the Incas, and one of its galleries—funded by the Nevil Foundation for the Blind—features more than 30 objects that you're encouraged to touch. Tue–Sun 10 am–4:30 pm.

Wagner Free Institute of Science, Montgomery Ave. and 17th St.; 763-6529. *NCH.* This is one of the best-kept secrets in Philadelphia, featuring dinosaur bones, mounted birds and mammals, and a Children's Discovery Room. Its enormous exhibition hall, which dates back to 1865, has more than 21,000 specimens on display. Mon–Fri 10 am–5 pm except holidays.

The Wanamaker Museum, 13th and Market Sts.; 422-2737. *NCH.* It was at this location in 1876 that John Wanamaker founded America's first department store, and the museum of the current store is a most fitting tribute to him. Behind the glass is Wanamaker's office, untouched since the day he died at the age of 84 in 1922. Everything, including his Bible, bowler hat, and the rolled-top desk is precisely as he left it. The nearby museum contains a host of information and memorabilia about retailing and includes such period items as silk stockings and high buttoned shoes. Daily noon–3 pm.

War Library and Museum, 1805 Pine St.; 735-8196. *CH.* This is a recognized national research center for the Civil War. Among its highlights are 2 life masks of Lincoln, a dress uniform and presentation sword of General Ulysses S. Grant, flags, guns, uniforms, and relics from the war between the states. Mon–Fri 10 am–4 pm, weekends by appointment.

Welcome Park, 2nd St. north of Walnut. This attractive park is located on the same site as the Slate Roof House, where William Penn lived with his second wife, Hannah, and where their son, John, was born. It was here in 1701 that Penn granted the famous Charter of Privileges, and the park is now designed in the form of a giant map of Philadelphia—as originally planned by Penn.

Wistar Museum, 36th and Spruce Sts.; 898-3708. *NCH.* This famous biomedical research facility houses a museum that contains an interesting anatomical exhibit. One exhibit demonstrates the development and evolution of the first skulls of fish up to the skulls of man. Also on display are historical and anatomical specimens with exhibits and graphs comparing the growth of people from birth to age 20. Mon–Fri 10 am–4 pm.

HISTORIC GERMANTOWN

Germantown, which recently celebrated its 300th birthday, was founded by Francis Daniel Pastorious, a German lawyer and scholar who became interested in the Society of Friends, or Quakers, about the time William Penn founded Pennsylvania. As a close friend of Penn's, Pastorious, with the help of surveyor Thomas Fairman, laid out the 5700 acres of beautiful land in large lots that eventually were split up as new settlers arrived.

Until the American Revolution, the residents of Germantown, which included Germans, Dutch, Swedes, English, and French Huguenots, enjoyed a rather quiet lifestyle. They were industrious, ethical, private folk. Within 5 years of the founding of Germantown, the Quakers, including Pastorious, became the first to protest the Colonial practice of using blacks as slaves.

When the British army captured and occupied Philadelphia, a major part of Sir William Howe's forces were quartered in some of the old stone houses you see today. On October 4, 1777, Germantown was attacked by George Washington's Continental Army. Although the patriots were repelled, they left the British stunned and shaken. This ultimately influenced France to join the colonial war effort, turning a military defeat into a diplomatic victory.

In 1793, the disastrous outbreak of yellow fever in Philadelphia forced many, including President Washington, to flee to the higher ground of Germantown. Some of the wealthiest stayed, built summer homes, and commuted from the green, airy atmosphere to their jobs in the city. Before long, Germantown was a bustling industrial city with a road, now Germantown Avenue, that served travelers between Philadelphia and points west. (Listed in the order of a walking tour)

Cliveden, 6401 Germantown Ave.; 848-1777. CH. This elaborate 18th-century home, built in 1763–67 for then-Pennsylvania Attorney General Benjamin Chew, was being used as a fort by the British when they were attacked by the Continental Army. It was the focal point of the fighting during the Battle of Germantown, sustained heavy damage as a result, and some of the cannon ball and bullet marks from October 1777 are still evident today. April–December Tue–Sat 10 am–4 pm, Sun 1:30–4:30 pm. Other times by appointment.

Upsala, 6450 Germantown Ave.; 247-6113. CH. Built in 1798-1801, this Federal-style home is highlighted by exquisite detail, authentic furnishings, and a detached, shady setting. April-December Tue–Thu 1-4 pm. Other times by appointment.

Concord Schoolhouse, 6313 Germantown Ave.; 438-6328. *NCH.* This is an excellent example of an 18th-century schoolhouse that is now an historical museum. The original bell hangs in the belfry and the schoolhouse is adjacent to the Upper Burying Ground, where early settlers and soldiers from the Revolutionary War are buried. By appointment. April–October Tue–Thu 1–4 pm.

Wyck, 6026 Germantown Ave.; 848-1690. *CH.* This Greek Revival house, part of which dates back to the 1690s, was owned and occupied for 283 years by 9 generations of the Haines family. Revolutionary soldiers were hospitalized here in 1777, and the Marquis de Lafayette was an honored guest in 1825. April–December Tue, Thu, Sat 1–4 pm. Other times by appointment.

Ebenezer Maxwell Mansion, Greene and Tulpehocken Sts.; 438-1861. *CH.* Built in 1859 for the Philadelphia merchant for which it has been named, this Norman Gothic structure is the city's only mid-19th-century house museum. April–December Wed–Sat 11 am–4 pm, Sun 1–5 pm. For special group tours, call in advance.

Deshler-Morris House, 5542 Germantown Ave.; 596-1748. *CH.* Built in 1772-73 by David Deshler, this house served as Sir William Howe's headquarters following the Battle of Germantown, and later was the residence of George Washington during the 1793 yellow fever epidemic in Philadelphia. Washington returned the following summer with his wife Martha and their two children. It is part of the Independence National Historic Park. April–December Tue–Sun 1–4 pm. Other times by appointment.

Grumblethorpe, 5267 Germantown Ave.; 843-4820. *CH.* This was Germantown's first summer home, built by John Wister in 1744 and modernized in 1808. It served as headquarters for British officers during the Battle of Germantown and Brigadier General James Agnew was wounded and died here. He is buried in the Lower Burying Ground. By appointment.

Germantown Historical Society Complex, 5 locations between 5208 and 5277 Germantown Ave.; 844-0514. *CH.* These houses, built between 1742 and 1790, hold the headquarters and library as well as the costume, textile, and furnishings museums of the Germantown Historical Society. The Baynton House (library), Coyningham-Hacker House (furnishings), and the Howell House (needlework and toys) are open to the public. Tue, Thu 10 am–4 pm, Sun 1–5 pm. Other times by appointment.

Loudoun, 4650 Germantown Ave.; 324-2877. *CH.* Built in 1796–1801 by Thomas Arnat, this is the most imposing of Germantown's Federal-style homes, overlooking Germantown Avenue from the top of Neglee's Hill. It was willed to the city of Philadelphia in 1939. By appointment.

Stenton, Windrim and 18th Sts.; 329-7312. *CH.* Built in 1723-30 for James Logan, Penn's secretary, agent, and chief justice of the Supreme Court, Stenton is reminiscent of Penn's manor home at Pennsbury. It served as George

Washington's headquarters while en route to Chadds Ford and the Battle of Brandywine. February-December Tue–Sat 1–5 pm or by appointment.

Mennonite Church and Graveyard, 6121 Germantown Ave.; 843-0943. In 1708, the German Mennonites built a log cabin for worship here, and almost 60 years later it was replaced by the stone meetinghouse you see now. The oldest stones in the graveyard date from the 1730s. For tours of the church and graveyard, please contact the Germantown Mennonite Church, 6117 Germantown Ave., Philadelphia 19144; 843-0943.

Rittenhouse Homestead, 207 Lincoln Dr.; 843-0943. CH. Built in 1707, this house was later added to by William Rittenhouse, the first Mennonite minister and first papermaker in the colonies. It is also the birthplace of the early American scientist and patriot, David Rittenhouse. Sat 10 am–4 pm. Otherwise by appointment.

Johnson House, 6306 Germantown Ave.; 438-9366. CH. This fine example of German architecture features a variety of furnishings that reflect Quaker life in the early years of Germantown. By appointment.

HISTORIC CHURCHES

Arch Street Meeting House, 4th and Arch Sts.; 627-2667. (see DOWNTOWN WALKING TOUR).

Christ Church, 2nd and Market Sts.; 922-1695 (see DOWNTOWN WALKING TOUR).

Gloria Dei Church, Swanson and Christian Sts.; 389-1513 (see SIGHTS Queen Village).

Historic St. George's United Methodist Church, 235 N. 4th St.; 925-7788. This is the oldest Methodist Church in the United States, and except for the winter of 1777–1778, it has been in constant use since 1769.

Mennonite Church and Graveyard, 6121 Germantown Ave.; 843-0943 (see SIGHTS Historic Germantown).

Mikveh Israel Synagogue, 44 N. 4th St.; 922-5446. This is the oldest synagogue in Philadelphia and the second oldest in America, founded in 1740 by Nathan Levy.

Mother Bethel A.M.E. Church, 419 S. 6th St.; 925-0616. This National Historic Landmark, founded in 1782 by Richard Allen, stands on the oldest property continuously owned by blacks in the United States. Allen was America's first black to be named a bishop, and his tomb is in the basement.

Old First Reformed Church, 4th and Race Sts.; 922-4566. The First Reformed Church was organized in 1727 by refugees seeking religious freedom in Philadelphia, and this church, originally built in the mid-1830s, has been authentically restored.

Old Pine Presbyterian Church, 4th and Pine Sts.; 925-8051. After this lot was donated to the First Presbyterian Church by William Penn's sons in 1764, this structure was built in the latter part of that decade. John Adams was among those who attended services here, and numerous famous colonists are buried in its churchyard.

St. Joseph's Church, Willing's Alley, near 4th and Walnut Sts.; 923-1733. Established in 1733 as the first Roman Catholic Church in Philadelphia, this church was built in 1838. It is part of Independence National Historic Park.

St. Mary's Church, 252 South St.; 923-7930. (see DOWNTOWN WALKING TOUR Society Hill).

St. Paul's Church, 225 S. 3rd St.; 924-9910 (see DOWNTOWN WALKING TOUR Society Hill).

St. Peter's Church, 3rd and Pine Sts.; 925-5968 (see DOWNTOWN WALKING TOUR Society Hill).

VISUAL ARTS

A stroll down Benjamin Franklin Parkway is certainly indicative of Philadelphia's reputation as one of the foremost cultural centers in the nation. Four museums—the Philadelphia Museum of Art, the Franklin Institute, the Academy of Arts and Sciences, and the Rodin Museum—rank among the finest in the world. More than 100 museums are scattered throughout the Philadelphia area. You'll also find more statues in Philadelphia than in any other city in America, and galleries featuring every art in every medium by national and local artists.

VISUAL ARTS BY AREA

CENTER CITY

AIA Gallery
Charles Sessler
Frank S. Schwarz and Son
Gallery of the Art Institute of
    Philadelphia
Gilbert Luber Gallery
Gross McCleaf Gallery
Helen Drutt Gallery
Janet Fleisher Gallery
Jeffrey Fuller Fine Art
Jun Gallery
Makler & Eric Makler Gallery
Marian Locks Gallery
The Martin Lawrence Galleries of
    Fine Art
Moore College of Art Gallery
Newman Galleries
Noel Butcher
Norman Rockwell Museum
Peale House
Pennsylvania Academy of Fine Arts
Philadelphia College of Art
The Print Club
The Swan Gallery

CENTER CITY–FAIRMOUNT PARK AREA

The Philadelphia Museum of Art
Rodin Museum

CHESTER COUNTY

The Wharton Esherick Museum

DELAWARE COUNTY

Brandywine River Museum
Chadds Ford Gallery

MONTGOMERY COUNTY

Barnes Foundation
Buten Museum of Wedgwood
Fine Arts Gallery
Frank Schwarz and Son
The Gencairn Museum
Langman Galleries

NORTH PHILADELPHIA

Stephen Girard Collection

NORTHWEST PHILADELPHIA

Goldie Paley Design Center
Hahn Gallery
Ile Ife Museum of Afro-American
   Culture
LaSalle College of Art Gallery
Philadelphia Print Shop
Woodmere Art Gallery

OLD CITY

Rosenfeld Galleries

SOUTH PHILADELPHIA

Fleisher Art Memorial

SOUTH STREET

The Custom Frame Shop Gallery
The Works Gallery

UNIVERSITY CITY

Arthur Ross Gallery
Civic Center Museum
Drexel Museum Collection
Institute of Contemporary Art

MUSEUMS AND INSTITUTIONAL GALLERIES

AIA Gallery, 17th and Sansom Sts.; 569-3186. *NCH*. This gallery of the American Institute of Architects features the work of established and promising artists, craftsmen, and designers. Mon–Fri 10 am–5 pm, Sat 11 am–4pm.

Arthur Ross Gallery, 212 S. 34th St.; 898-1479. *NCH*. Housed in the 19th-century Furness Building on the Penn campus, the opening of this gallery represented a turning point in the university's history; never before did it have an official gallery to display the 4000 art treasures it has accumulated in almost two centuries of existence.

Barnes Foundation, 300 Latches Lane, Merion; 667-0290. *CH*. Housing the late Albert Coombs Barnes collection of some 1000 paintings, this is the finest private collection of early modern art in the world, including 200 Renoirs, 100 Cezannes, and works by Rousseau, Picasso, Matisse, and others. Also, hundreds of pieces of furniture, medieval ironware, and objets d'art. Fri–Sat 9:30 am–4:30 pm, Sun 1–4:30 pm. Reservations recommended.

Brandywine River Museum, Route 1, Chadds Ford; 388-7601 and 459-1900. *CH*. Located on the peaceful Brandywine River, this museum is a century-old grist mill whose charm has been carefully preserved through the years. With its dramatic tower of glass, and brick terraces overlooking the surrounding countryside, it houses the works of Andrew Wyeth, his father N.C. Wyeth, and his son James. Included are the works of Howard Pyle, "the father of American illustration," who began teaching here in 1898 and developed the tradition in American art known as the "Brandywine Heritage." Daily 9:30 am–4:30 pm.

Buten Museum of Wedgwood, 246 N. Bowman Ave., Merion; 664-6601. *CH*. Founded in 1957 by Mr. and Mrs. Harry M. Buten, this is the only museum in America devoted to the study and exhibition of Wedgwood artistry and craftsmanship. Featured are more than 10,000 examples of the work of Josiah Wedgwood and his successors, including the largest piece of Wedgwood ever made, the five-foot tall "Alexander" vase painted by Emile Lessore (1805-1875). Tue–Fri 2–5 pm, Sat 10 am–1 pm.

Civic Center Museum, 34th St. and Civic Center Blvd.; 823-7327. NCH. This museum features everchanging regional, national, and international shows in fine arts, crafts, industrial design, and architecture. It also offers arts and crafts shows, concerts, educational programs, and international festivals. Call for information and hours.

Drexel Museum Collection, 32nd and Chestnut Sts.; 895-2424. NCH. Contains portraits of the Drexel family, as well as 18th- and 19th-century furniture, antique toys, pewter, a service of Sevres china that was made for Napoleon II, America's most historic timepieces (the David Rittenhouse clock, made in 1773), and the Rincliffe Gallery, featuring Philadelphia's largest collection of Edward Marshall Boehm porcelains. Mon–Fri 9 am–5 pm by reservation only.

Fleisher Art Memorial, 719 Catharine St.; 922-3456. NCH. Founded in 1898 as the Graphic Sketch Club, the memorial still maintains the same policy of free classes for people throughout the city. The building contains the art school, two galleries, and a collection of medieval art. In the Romanesque sanctuary are icons, medieval sculpture, primitive painting under glass, and an 18th-century Portugese chapel. Mon–Fri Noon–5 pm and 7–9:30 pm, Sat 1–3 pm, closed August and September.

Gallery of the Art Institute of Philadelphia, 1622 Chestnut St.; 567-7080. NCH. Operated by the Art Institute of Philadelphia, this gallery offers changing exhibits by faculty, students, and leading designers. Mon–Fri 9 am–5 pm, Sat 9 am–noon.

The Gencairn Museum, 1001 Papermill Rd., Bryn Athyn; 947-9919 and 947-4200. CH. This sprawling home built in the Gothic style houses one of the finest collections of medieval art in the world. The collection of 12th- and 13th-century stained glass and sculpture of the late Raymond Pitcairn is one of the finest still in private hands. Beyond the "Great Hall," which houses many items of the collection, is an exquisite retreat, the "Cloister." By appointment Mon–Fri 9 am–5 pm.

Goldie Paley Design Center, 4200 Henry Ave.; 951-2860. NCH. Built in 1954 as the private home of the late artist, Goldie Paley, the center now houses the Philadelphia College of Textiles and Science's valuable fabric collection and exhibit gallery. Its "study" collection features more than 200,000 fabric samples from throughout America and Europe; its "historical" collection features pieces dating from before the 4th century to the present. Mon–Sat 10 am–4 pm.

Ile Ife Museum of Afro-American Culture, 2544 Germantown Ave.; 225-7565. CH. This museum traces the history of black people in the United States and contains many facets of black art from America, the Caribbean, and Western Africa. There are five galleries, including a Fine Arts gallery featuring graphics, sculpture, oils, and watercolors. A 1-hour tour, by reservation only, concludes with a performance by Arthur Hall's Dance Ensemble. Tours Mon–Sat 10 and 11 am, 1 and 2 pm.

Institute of Contemporary Art, 34th and Walnut Sts.; 898-7108. NCH. Located on the University of Pennsylvania campus, the institute features exhibitions of new art via individual shows and timely themes. This is Philadelphia's major institution devoted to contemporary art. One hour of each Saturday during each exhibit is geared to children's activities, during which children have the chance to display their own talents. Mon, Wed–Fri, 10 am–5 pm, Tue 10 am–7:30 pm, Sat–Sun 11 am–5 pm.

LaSalle College of Art Gallery, 20th St. and Olney Ave.; 951-1221. NCH. This gallery, which opened in 1976, is making a concerted effort to develop a comprehensive collection that will document the major styles and themes of religion, mythology, landscape, still-life, portraiture, and abstract expression. The Susan Dunleavy collection features ancient illuminated manuscripts from the Judeo-Christian traditions. Mon–Fri 11 am–3 pm, Sun 2–4 pm.

Moore College of Art Gallery, 20th and Race Sts.; 568-4515. NCH. Founded in 1844, the college is the only art college exclusively for women in the United States. The gallery features 20th-century art as well as art of former students. An annual student exhibition is held each spring, and the college's Tyler School of Art offers lectures by well-known historians, artists, and critics. Mon–Fri 9 am–4:30 pm, Sat 11 am–4 pm.

Norman Rockwell Museum, 601 Walnut St.; 922-4345. CH. Housed in the historic Curtis Publishing Building, where the *Saturday Evening Post* was published until 1969, the museum offers the world's largest and most complete representation of the work of one of America's most beloved artists. There are more than 600 pieces of Rockwell's original work, including more than 300 *Saturday Evening Post* covers. Rockwell's studio has been replicated and a film and slide presentation highlights his career. Daily 10 am–4 pm.

Peale House, 1820 Chestnut St.; 972-7635. NCH. As part of the Pennsylvania Academy of the Fine Arts, this gallery features exhibitions of American paintings, sculpture, and graphics that change every six weeks. Tuesday through Saturday 10 am–5 pm, Sun 1–5 pm.

Pennsylvania Academy of the Fine Arts, Broad and Cherry Sts.; 972-7633. CH. The oldest art museum and art school in the United States, the Academy contains more than 4000 works covering three centuries of American art. It includes the original "Penn's Treaty With The Indians" by

Benjamin West, the "Landsdowne Portrait of George Washington" by Charles Wilson Peale, "The Cello Prayer" and "Walt Whitman" by Thomas Eakins, and "The Fox Hunt" by Winslow Homer. Founded in 1805, the Academy is housed in a magnificent Victorian building designed by the famed Philadelphia architect, Frank Furness. Tue–Sat 10 am–5 pm, Sun 1–5 pm.

Philadelphia Art Alliance, 251 S. 18th St.; 545-4302. *NCH.* Founded in 1915, the Alliance has had a profound creative influence on artists and on the cultural life of Philadelphia. Its seven galleries include numerous exhibitions of sculpture, prints, industrial design, architecture, and paintings. Free lectures are held on a wide range of topics, as well as technical demonstrations in various arts and crafts. The Alliance's Performing Arts committees present without cost internationally-known composers, authors, musicians, dancers, and theater personalities. Tue–Sat 10:30 am–5 pm.

Philadelphia College of Art, Broad and Pine Sts.; 875-4800. *NCH.* This gallery offers exhibits of contemporary art, crafts, graphics, sculptures, and mobiles. The exhibits change every five weeks. Mon–Tue, Thu–Fri 9 am–5 pm, Wed 9 am–9 pm, Sat 12–5 pm.

The Philadelphia Museum of Art, 26th St. and Benjamin Franklin Parkway; 763-8100, for a recording of the day's schedule; 765-3800. *CH.* One of Philadelphia's most famous and recognizable landmarks, this massive Greek Revival building occupies 10 acres and contains more than 200 galleries. Today the museum, which first opened in 1928, contains more than 600,000 objects spanning 2000 years of man's creativity, including paintings, carpets, silver porringers, cast-iron stove plates, and every conceivable variety of art object from every corner of the globe. The second floor is devoted to paintings and architectural installations from continental Europe, including French and English period rooms and paintings by such greats as Renoir, Cezanne, Monet, and Van Gogh. There is an Indian temple, a Chinese Palace Hall, and a Japanese Ceremonial Tea House. One of the largest exhibitions is the Kretzchmar von Kienbusch Collection of Armor and Arms. Among the services and programs available daily are gallery talks, guest lectures, traveling exhibitions, films, concerts, and workshops. Tue–Sun 10 am–5 pm. Admission is free Sun 10 am–1 pm.

The Print Club, 1614 Latimer St.; 735-6090. *NCH.* Founded in 1915 and located in an intimate townhouse, the club's emphasis is on contemporary printmaking. Its gallery presents monthly exhibitions which include theme shows, regional exhibits, and cooperative exhibitions. There is also a prestigious international competitive exhibition every year. Tue–Sat 10 am–5:30 pm.

Rodin Museum, 22nd St. and Benjamin Franklin Parkway; 763-8100. *Donations requested.* Named for the French sculptor Auguste Rodin (1840–1917), this museum contains the largest collection of his work outside France.

The Grand Staircase, Pennsylvania Academy
of the Fine Arts

Pennsylvania Academy of the Fine Arts

Among the 200 magnificent bronze, plaster, and marble sculptures are "The Thinker," "The Burghers of Calais," and "Gates of Hell." Wed–Sun 10 am–5 pm.

Stephen Girard Collection, Founder's Hall, Girard College, Girard and Corinthian Aves.; 787-2626. *NCH*. Accumulated between 1780 and 1830, the Girard collection of furniture, plate, china, and other effects is virtually unique. Among the Philadelphia artists represented here are Daniel Trotter, Ephraim Haines, Henry Connelly, William Cox, and J.B. Ackley. Thu only 2–4 pm.

The Wharton Esherick Museum, Paoli; 644-5822. *CH*. Included in the artist's studio, which is set high on a wooded hillside overlooking the Great Valley, are more than 200 pieces by Mr. Esherick covering 40 years of work. Featured are paintings, woodcuts, prints, furniture, utensils, and sculpture in wood, stone, and ceramic. Sat–Sun only, reservations required.

Woodmere Art Gallery, 9201 Germantown Ave., Chestnut Hill; 247-0476. *NCH*. Woodmere features a permanent collection of paintings, sculpture, tapestry, and objets d'art accumulated by the late Charles Knox Smith. Six exhibitions are hosted throughout the year and art classes are offered for adults and children. Mon–Sat 10 am–5 pm, Sun 2–5 pm.

ART IN PUBLIC PLACES

Philadelphia has more public art than any other city in the United States. This is due to an ordinance stipulating that one percent of the cost of all new buildings, and buildings erected on redevelopment land, must be devoted to the fine arts. All artwork must be approved by the Fine Arts Commission prior to its installment inside or outside a structure.

With such an abundance, we cannot mention all the glorious public art in Philadelphia; just in the last two decades no less than 400 new pieces have been added. Therefore, we list a blend of new art with some that has blessed the city for many years.

For your convenience, we have arranged Philadelphia's public art by region. We suggest a tour beginning in Fairmount Park on East River Drive. Fairmount Park features more than 200 pieces of sculpture, and a program was launched to conserve the sculpture within its borders. For further reference, please consult "Philadelphia's Treasure in Bronze and Stone," published by the Fairmount Park Art Association.

East River Drive ───────────────

General Ulysses S. Grant, East River Drive and Fountain Green Drive, 1897, a bronze by Daniel Chester French and Edward C. Potter.

Playing Angels, East River Drive at Fountain Green Drive, date uncertain (dedicated April 26, 1972), a bronze by Carl Milles (1875–1955).

Cowboy, East River Drive, 1908, a bronze by Frederic Remington, located just northwest of the Penn Central Railroad Bridge.

The Pilgrim, East River Drive, 1904, a bronze by Saint Augustus Gaudens, located near Boat House Row.

The Ellen Phillips Samuel Memorial, East River Drive. This series of statues symbolizing the history of America is the work of 16 sculptures working within a span of 20 years.

Abraham Lincoln, East River Drive and Lemon Hill Drive, 1871, a bronze by Randolph Rogers.

Washington Monument, in front of the Art Museum, 1897, a bronze and granite by Rudolph Siemering.

The Benjamin Franklin Parkway ———

Joan of Arc, East River Drive at the Philadelphia Museum of Art, 1890, a bronze by Emmanuel Fremiet.

Prometheus Strangling the Vulture, east entrance of the Philadelphia Museum of Art, 1952, a bronze by Jacques Lipschitz.

The Lion Fighter, east entrance of the Philadelphia Museum of Art, 1858, is a bronze by Albert Wolfe.

Atmosphere and Environment, west entrance of the Philadelphia Museum of Art, 1970, is a steel sculpture by Louise Nevelson.

The Thinker, Rodin Museum, 22nd Street and the Parkway, 1880 (enlarged 1902–04), a bronze by Auguste Rodin.

Benjamin Franklin, Franklin Institute, 20th Street and the Parkway, 1938, a marble by James Earle Frazer.

Civil War Soldiers and Sailors Memorial, 20th Street and the Parkway, 1921, is a marble by Herman Atkins MacNeil.

The Fountain of Three Rivers, Logan Circle, 19th Street and the Parkway, 1924, is a bronze by Alexander Stirling Calder.

Jesus Breaking Bread, Saints Peter and Paul Cathedral, 18th Street and the Parkway, 1978, is a bronze by Walter Erlebacher.

Heroic Figure of Man, the Bell Telephone Company, 16th Street and the Parkway, 1963, is a bronze by Joseph J. Greenberg, Jr.

City Hall and Market Street East Area ———

Three Discs One Lacking, Penn Center Plaza, 17th Street and John F. Kennedy Boulevard, 1964, is a painted steel by Alexander Stirling Calder.

The Fountain of Three Rivers, Logan Circle   *City of Philadelphia*

Leviathan, Penn Center Plaza, 17th Street and John F. Kennedy Boulevard, 1963, is nickel silver on monel metal by Seymour Lipton.

Love, 15th Street and John F. Kennedy Boulevard, 1976, is the popular painted aluminum work by Robert Indiana.

Government of the People, Plaza Municipal Services Building, Broad Street and John F. Kennedy Boulevard, 1976, is a bronze by Jacques Lipschitz.

Clothespin, Center Square, 1500 Market Street, 1976, is a steel pop sculpture by Claes Oldenburg.

William Penn, top of clocktower, City Hall, Broad and Market Streets, 1894, is a bronze by Alexander Milne Calder.

Burst of Joy, The Gallery at Market East, 9th and Market Streets, 1977, is of stainless steel by Harold Kimmelman.

Independence National Historic Park

Phaedrus, the Federal Reserve Bank, 6th Street between Market and Arch Streets, 1977, is painted steel by Beverly Pepper.

Voyage of Ulysses, Plaza between 600 Arch Street and 601 Market Street, 1977, is a stainless steel by David Von Schlegell.

Milkweed Pod, Rohm and Haas Building, 6th and Market Streets, 1966, is a bronze by Clark Fitz-Gerald.

White Water, 5th Street between Market and Arch Streets, 1978, is a carbon steel frame by Robinson Fredenthal.

Commodore John Barry, Independence Square, 1907, is a bronze by Samuel Murray.

Franklin Court, 314-322 Market Street, 1977, is of brick, flagstone, and marble by Venturi and Rauch.

Chinatown

Gateway to Chinatown, This gateway into Chinatown, at 10th and Arch Streets, stands 40 feet high, and was created by 12 master artisans from China. They used 142 cases of tiles. It is magnificent.

Benjamin Franklin Bridge

A Bolt of Lightning, Plaza of the Benjamin Franklin Bridge. This ten-story stainless steel structure is a memorial to Benjamin Franklin and was created by Isamu Noguchi. It was installed in 1984, and is still very controversial.

Society Hill

Unity, 4th Street and Willings Alley, 1970, is a metal piece by Richard Lieberman.

Floating Figure, Locust Street between 2nd and 3rd Streets, 1963, is a bronze by Gaston Lachaise.

Young Man, Old Man, The Future, Society Hill Towers, 2nd and Locust Streets, 1966, is a bronze by Leonard Baskin.

Kangaroos, 4th and 5th Streets between Spruce and Pine Streets, 1923, is of welded stainless steel by Harold Kimmelman.

Butterfly, 2nd and Delancey Streets, 1971, is of stainless steel by Harold Kimmelman.

Mustang at Play, Head House Square Corporation, 2nd and Pine Streets, instated in 1969, is a bronze by Margaret Wasserman Levy.

Rittenhouse Square

Lion Crushing a Serpent, 1832, is a bronze by Antoine Louis Barye.

Billy, 1914, is a bronze by Albert Laessle.

University City

Jerusalem Stable, Locust Walk near 34th Street, 1979, is a painted steel by Alexander Stirling Calder.

We lost, 36th Street and Locust Walk, is painted steel by Tony Smith.

Covenant, 39th Street and Locust Walk, 1975, is a painted cor-ten steel by Alexander Liberman.

Dream of Sky, 37th Street Walk and Market Street, 1976, is of fiberglass by Timothy Duffield.

Untitled, 3624 Market Street, 1974, is a fiberglass work by James Lloyd.

Face Fragment, 3500 Market Street, 1975, is of bronze, fiberglass, and polyester by Arlene Love.

GALLERIES

Chadds Ford Gallery, US 1 and 100, Chadds Ford; 459-5510. Located in the quaint Chadds Ford Barn Shops, this gallery presents the largest collection of Wyeth reproductions anywhere. It supports quality artists producing original work in all media and holds three major shows a year, including the popular Christmas miniature exhibit. Mon–Sat 10:30 am–5 pm, Sun 1–5 pm.

Charles Sessler, 1308 Walnut St.; 735-1086. Located on the second floor of one of Philadelphia's oldest bookstores, this is now known as the W. Graham Rader Gallery. Known for its prints of historical significance, it features botanical and nautical prints, as well as rare books and autographs. Restorations, appraisals, and framing are available. Mon–Fri 9 am–6 pm, Sat 10 am–5 pm.

The Custom Frame Shop & Gallery, 404½ South St.; 922-5708. This two-story gallery houses the largest selection of contemporary graphics on the East Coast, everything from original signed and numbered graphics by Picasso, Miro, and Calder to those of the new masters. Expert framing. Mon–Thu 10 am–6 pm, Fri–Sat 10 am–9 pm, closed July and August.

Fine Arts Gallery, 2 Lancaster Ave., Ardmore; 896-8161. One of the largest galleries on the East Coast, this gallery offers more than 1000 pieces of work in seven showrooms, each of which represents a different art medium. Well-known artists and new names are both represented. Periodic one-man/woman shows. Mon–Sat 9 am–5 pm, Wed 9 am–9 pm.

Frank S. Schwarz and Son, 1806 Chestnut St.; 563-4887; Suburban Shopping Center, Ardmore; 642-1500. This reputable antique shop features an excellent selection of 19th-century American paintings. Mon–Sat 10 am–5 pm.

Gilbert Luber Gallery, 1220 Walnut St.; 732-2996. This is Philadelphia's only gallery specializing in Japanese art, including a fine collection of antique woodblock prints and contemporary prints. Luber's collection is constantly updated by his annual trips to Japan. Appraisals, custom framing, and print conservation available. Mon–Sat 11 am–5 pm, Wed until 6 pm.

Gross McCleaf Gallery, 1713 Walnut St.; 665-8138. The gallery has three floors of international art and graphics and has a reputation for representing top Philadelphia artists in paintings, prints, and sculptures. Professional appraisals available. Mon–Sat 10 am–5 pm, evenings by appointment.

Hahn Gallery, 8439 Germantown Ave.; 247-8439. This gallery offers 20th-century prints by international, national, and local artists, including Benton Spruance and Earl Horter. Also, an impressive collection of 17th- and 18th-century Japanese woodblock prints and glass paper weights. Custom framing and restoration available. Mon–Sat 10 am–5:30 pm.

Helen Drutt Gallery, 1721 Walnut St.; 735-1625. Operated by Ms. Drutt, the dean of the local crafts scene, this gallery features splendid 20th-century crafts in fiber, metal, clay, and paper by internationally-known artists. Member of the Philadelphia Art Dealers Association. Tue–Sat 11:30 am–5 pm, and by appointment.

Janet Fleisher Gallery, 211 S. 17th St.; 545-7562. This gallery specializes in American Indian and American Folk art, has a comprehensive collection of prints and photographs, and presents ten major shows annually. Member of the Philadelphia Art Dealers Association. Mon–Fri 10 am–5 pm, Sat 11:30 am–5 pm.

Jeffrey Fuller Fine Art, 2108 Spruce St.; 545-8154. Located in a 19th-century Victorian brownstone, contemporary art, sculpture, drawing, and photography are displayed in the large room and hallways. Among some of the fine artists this gallery represents are Buckminster Fuller, Maurie Kerrigan, Barbara Morgan, Robert Natkin, Emlen Etting, and Richard Diebenkorn. Member of the Philadelphia Art Dealers Association. Tue–Sat 11 am–5 pm, evenings by appointment.

Jun Gallery, 1131 Walnut St.; 627-5020. Located near Washington Square, this small gallery offers lithographs, silkscreens, woodcut prints, and custom frames made from exotic woods. Mon–Sat 11 am–6 pm, Wed until 7 pm.

Langman Galleries, 218 Old York Rd., Jenkintown; 887-3500 and Willow Grove Park Mall, Willow Grove; 657-8333. The Jenkintown gallery has the area's largest showroom, featuring quality contemporary paintings, sculpture, and art objects in clay, fiber, glass, and metal. The one in Willow Grove Mall is more craft-oriented, offering sculpture to wear, paintings, prints, and contemporary multimedia objects. Tue–Sat noon–5 pm, Wed and Fri 7–9 pm, July and August by appointment only.

Marian Locks Gallery, 122 Arch St.; 592-7755. Known for her exciting shows, Marian Locks is perhaps the area's best discoverer and promoter of local talent. Outstanding examples of contemporary art. Mon–Sat 10 am–6 pm.

Martin Lawrence Galleries of Fine Art, two locations including 21 South Fifth St., The Bourse Building; 627-0794. The Lawrence Gallery and its well-known Hallowell Gallery in Conshohocken both present a wide range of internationally-known artists as well as the talents of local artists. Mon–Thu 10 am–5 pm, Fri 10 am–9 pm, Sat 11 am–6 pm, Sun noon–5 pm.

Newman Galleries, 1625 Walnut St.; 563-1779; 850 W. Lancaster Ave., Bryn Mawr; 525-0625. With a tradition of fine art since 1865, this is Philadelphia's oldest gallery. It specializes in 19th- and 20th-century American and European oil paintings, watercolors, lithographs, silkscreens, and graphics. Member of the Philadelphia Art Dealers Association. Mon–Fri 9 am–5:30 pm, Sat 10 am–4:30 pm, closed Sat in July and August.

Noel Butcher, 132 S. 17th St.; 569-1236. Established in 1982, this gallery represents a select group of contemporary painters specializing in abstract, realist, and representational work. Tue–Sat 10 am–5:30 pm.

The Philadelphia Print Shop, 8405 Germantown Ave.; 242-4750. Located in what was once a men's store, this relatively new gallery features lovely century-old original prints and watercolors. Also, old Pennsylvania maps and others from throughout the world. Seminars, lectures, and exhibitions are held throughout the year. Mon–Sat 10 am–5 pm.

Rosenfeld Galleries, 113 Arch St.; 922-1376. The Rosenfeld Galleries specialize in young, up-and-coming artists producing contemporary work in all media. Every July and August the gallery holds an intriguing humor and fantasy show. Member of the Philadelphia Art Dealers Association. Wed–Sat 10 am–6 pm, Sun noon–5 pm.

The Swan Gallery, 132 S. 18th St.; 568-9898. This gallery specializes in contemporary American crafts, including clay, fiber, metal, and glass. Member of the Philadelphia Art Dealers Association. Mon–Sat 10 am–6 pm.

The Works Gallery, 319 South St.; 922-7775. One of the oldest galleries of its kind in the United States, this features 250 artists in all forms of media and crafts. Permanent exhibition area is shown during winter months. No shows in July and August. Mon–Fri 11 am–7 pm, Sat 10:30–noon, Sun 2–6 pm.

The Great Hall of The Bourse

The Bourse

SHOPPING

Philadelphia and its suburban areas can satisfy a shopper's every whim, from small boutiques and specialty shops to the country's largest urban retail center, The Gallery I and II, as well as the largest shopping mall, King of Prussia Mall, in the nation. Philadelphia is the third-largest clothing manufacturing center in the United States. In addition, bargain hunters from throughout the East come to take advantage of the area's famed factory outlets and antique shops.

SHOPPING DISTRICTS

Center City

Center City is the name for downtown Philadelphia and the headquarters of the retail trade industry in the area. Philadelphia's oldest department stores, John Wanamaker and Strawbridge & Clothier, have been local household words since they were founded in the 1860s. Both are still located on their original sites, though Strawbridge's is now linked to The Gallery at Market Street East.

From the 1880s to the early 1900s, when it was redesigned by the famed Chicago architect William H. Burnham, John Wanamaker was the largest department store in the country. The building is now a registered federal landmark with its open balconies and huge bronze eagle. Free concerts on the world's largest pipe organ in the Grand Court of Wanamaker's have long been favorite events for Philadelphians. (see PERFORMING ARTS).

Strawbridge & Clothier, founded by two Quaker merchants, is a family-operated department store with many national firsts to its credit. Among them, the first promotional sale (Clover Day, which started in 1906), and the first department store to open a branch in the suburbs (1930) and open a store in a covered-mall shopping center (1961). Strawbridge's was also the first department store to enter the discount-store field with Clover Stores in 1971, and the first to build in a downtown shopping mall, The Gallery, in 1977.

For several years, Market Street East has been the site of Philadelphia's largest urban development project, and the expanded Gallery complex, The

Gallery I and II, already includes more than 230 shops, restaurants, J.C. Penney's, Gimbel's, and of course, Strawbridge & Clothier.

The Market Street East shopping area is now integrated with the city's transit system, making it one of the most intensive concentrations of retail stores in the nation.

At Independence Mall is The Bourse (French for "place of trade"), which during the early 1900s was the largest and grandest merchant's exchange in America. Now restored to its former grandeur, with international flags and wood-carved upper levels overlooking its main floor, The Bourse is an opulent, cosmopolitan marketplace once again. It is highlighted by a multitude of stores, some of Philadelphia's most elegant shops, and more than 20 eateries and restaurants, with those on the upper levels serving gourmet fast foods from around the world.

Society Hill

In Society Hill is New Market, which dates back to 1769 and is today a masterful blend of the colonial with the contemporary. Surrounding and overlooking a brick courtyard filled with plants, trees, and a waterfall are several levels of restaurants and specialty shops that feature everything from candies and toys to crafts and furniture. All are housed in a glass-enclosed structure which complements the Federal, Georgian, and Victorian architecture of Head House Square. The Square itself has more unique shops, cafes, and restaurants.

Rittenhouse Square

Rittenhouse Square has been a popular meeting place and market for more than 200 years. Today, among its stately brownstones and intimate restaurants, you'll find expensive boutiques, salons, and art galleries, as well as flower, jewelry, and gourmet shops.

Chestnut Street

Still more specialty shops and clothing stores are to be found on Chestnut Street, specifically, the "Chestnut Street Transitway" which is closed to automobile traffic between 6th and 18th Streets.

South Street

Then there's South Street, more popularly known as Philadelphia's Greenwich Village, where storefronts have been restored and trees line the cobbled

Chestnut Street Shopping   *City of Philadelphia*

streets. Here you'll find a host of boutiques, vintage, and punk shops that sell the latest styles in fashion.

City Line Avenue

City Line Avenue, known as "The Golden Mile," is located on Philadelphia's western boundary, a short drive from Center City. Here can be found Lord & Taylor, Saks Fifth Avenue, and many more inviting specialty shops.

Chestnut Hill

Chestnut Hill, at Philadelphia's extreme northwestern boundary, ten miles from Center City, offers fine shopping along historic Germantown Avenue with more than 100 shops specializing in designer fashions and antiques and with charming restaurants nestled among them.

An oasis within the city limits, Chestnut Hill is also a place to gawk at enormous houses, to stop for a snack at some street cafes, to pick up fresh foods at the weekly farmers market—and yes, very much to shop. Check out the Little Nook, 8005 Germantown Ave., for some of the most unusual jewelry in town, or Paperia, 8521 Germantown Ave., for funky stationery, greeting cards, and paper goods. Periodic sales sponsored by neighborhood vendors association.

Manayunk

Anyone who's made an investment in this Philadelphia area is reaping the benefits now. Formerly a lower-middle class neighborhood nestled along the hills by the Schuylkill River, sections of Manayunk—especially its commercial district along Main Street—have "yuppified" and are infusing an exciting new life here. A variety of restaurants and shops selling wonderfully impractical and decorative goods are attracting new visitors here daily. And if you get tired of all the hoopla, just stroll the hilly, windy streets for a taste of Philadelphia that is reminiscent of Europe.

SUBURBAN MALLS

Philadelphia's surrounding counties offer magnificent shopping malls and unique mini-centers, each with its own distinctive flavor. The Court and The Plaza at King of Prussia, America's largest suburban mall, feature seven major department stores and 300 shops and restaurants. The Court has elegant boutiques and Bloomingdale's first store in the Philadelphia area. The Plaza, only 100 yards from The Court, has been transformed from an open-air center into an upbeat, contemporary closed mall.

Exton Square Mall, Routes 30 and 100, Exton; 363-2860.

Granite Run Mall, Routes 1 and 352, Media; 565-1650.

King of Prussia Shopping Plaza, Routes 363 and 202; (Plaza) 265-5727; (Court) 337-1210.

Montgomery Mall, Routes 202 and 309, North Wales; 362-1600.

Neshaminy Mall, Route 1 North, Cornwells Heights; 357-6100.

Oxford Valley Mall, I-95 North, exit at Langhorne; 725-0220.

Plymouth Meeting Mall, 500 Germantown Pike, Plymouth Meeting; 828-5638.

Springfield Mall, Route 1 South and Sproul Rd., Springfield; 328-1200.

Willow Grove Park, Easton Rd. and Moreland Rd., Willow Grove; 657-6000.

MINI-CENTERS

Smaller shopping centers are prevalent throughout the Philadelphia area. Because it would be impossible to list them all, we have presented some that are intriguing or offer a particular service.

☆ **Chadds Ford Barn Shops,** Routes 1 and 100, Chadds Ford. This expanded shopping village includes merchandise the malls don't have.

Devon Shopping Center, Route 202, Devon. A mini-mall featuring a wide variety of shops.

Fox Croft Square, Route 611, Jenkintown. This shopping center has a branch of Bonwit Teller and other fine shops.

Haverford Square, Lancaster Avenue, Haverford. A courtyard of fine shops.

Olde Ridge Village Shoppes, Route 202 one mile south of Route 1, Chadds Ford. Now has 35 shops, but when completed will have 60. Features everything from gourmet food to craft shops, Indian clothing to ski wear and furniture.

Peddler's Village, Routes 202 and 263, Bucks County. Over 40 shops and several restaurants in a quaint colonial setting.

Pilgrim Gardens, Loehmann's Plaza, Township Line Rd., Drexel Hill. Pilgrim Gardens presents discount fashion shops, including Loehmann's.

Rosemont Village, 1149 W. Lancaster Ave., Rosemont. A small, enclosed mall with a skylight and featuring 20 specialty shops.

St. Peter's Village, Route 23 in Chester County, about 15 miles northwest of Valley Forge. A charming village of shops restored to original Victorian style at the Falls of French Creek.

Skippack Village, Route 113 just north of Route 73 in Montgomery County. An 18th-century street village with more than 40 shops and boutiques.

Spread Eagle Village, Lancaster Ave., Wayne. The first relay station in colonial times, this center has 27 specialty and boutique shops.

Springfield Park, 420 Baltimore Pike, Springfield. A complex that offers specialty shopping and Strawbridge & Clothier.

Spring House Village Center, Sumneytown and other locations. Built around an old barn, this center offers 40 shops in a country atmosphere.

Suburban Square, Lancaster Ave., Ardmore. The oldest shopping center in the country, it presents specialty shopping on the Main Line with elegant boutiques and the first suburban branch of Strawbridge & Clothier.

Wynnewood Shopping Center, Lancaster Ave., Wynnewood. Features a series of small specialty shops and a branch of John Wanamaker.

SHOPPING BY AREA

BUCKS COUNTY

Booktenders, Books
Country Antiques At The Church, Antiques
The Cricket Box, Crafts
Crown & Eagle Antiques, Inc., Antiques
The Great American Flea Market, Flea Markets
Jones Antiques, Antiques
Katy Kane, Antiques
Lahaska Antique Center and Flea Market, Flea Markets
Lahaska Antique Court, Antiques
Lion House, Antiques
Oaklawn Metal Craft & Antiques, Antiques
The Pontypool Shop, Crafts
Robertson & Thornton, Antiques
The Rocker Shop, Furniture
Stephen Von Hohen, Furniture

CENTER CITY

Alfred Bullard, Antiques
Alfred of Philadelphia, Florists
Allure, Clothing
American Institute of Architecture Bookstore, Books
Archway Bookstore, Books
Artie's, Discount Stores and Factory Outlets
Bailey, Banks, & Biddle, Jewelry
Beige, Shoes
Betsey's Place, Gift Shops and Accessories
Bon Appetite, Food, and Gift Shops and Accessories
Book Mark, Books
Born Yesterday, Clothing
Boyd's, Clothing

Bread & Company, Bakeries
Brownie's, Discount Stores and Factory Outlets
The Camera Shop, Photographic Supplies
Center Foods, Food
Chelsea Silverplating, Antiques
Children's Boutique, Clothing
Christine Valmy Skin Care Salons, Skin Care
Dandelion, Crafts
Earl P.L. Apfelbaum, Inc., Coins
Elder Craftsmen Shop, Crafts
Encore Books, Books
E.N. Lodge Toys, Toys
Florsheim, Thayer, McNeil, Shoes
The Flower Market, Florists
The Food Hall, Food
Franklin Mint, Gift Shops and Accessories
Frank S. Schwarz & Son, Antiques
Grace Book Store, Books
Gucci Boutique, Leather
Holt's Harry A. Tint & Sons, Tobacco
How To Do It Book Store, Books
I. Goldberg, Clothing
Jack's Camera, Photographic Supplies
Jack Kellmer Co., Jewelry
J.E. Caldwell, Jewelry
Jeweler's Row, Jewelry
John Wanamaker, Coins and Stamps
Joseph Fox Book Store, Books
J.R. Cigars, Tobacco
Judith Finkel, Antiques
Katz's Cheesecake, Food
Kenneth and Cooper, Clothing
Lou's Shoe Bazaar, Discount Stores and Factory Outlets
The Market, Food
The Market at the Commissary, Food

The Market at Wanamaker's, Food
Maternity Factory Outlet, Discount
Stores and Factory Outlets
M. Finkel and Daughter, Antiques
Mr. Pickwick & Bakery, Food
Nan Duskin, Clothing
Old City Antiques, Flea Markets
Past, Present, and Future Toys, Toys
Pearson Sporting Goods, Sports
Equipment
Philadelphia Art Supply Company,
Art Supplies
Philadelphia Diamond Exchange,
Jewelry
Philly Stamp & Coin, Inc. Coins
and Stamps
The Photo Cine Shop, Photographic
Supplies
Post Horn, Discount Stores and
Factory Outlets
Reading Terminal, Food
Reese's, Antiques
Replique Fashion Jewelry, Jewelry
Rindelaub's, Food
Robinson Luggage, Leather
Sabel Shoes, Shoes
Samuel T. Freeman, Antiques
Schaffer's, Antiques
Stock and Wares, Gift Shops and
Accessories
Strega Ltd., Shoes
Swiss Pastry Shop, Food
Taws Artist Materials, Art Supplies
Touches, Gifts and Accessories
Tucker's Pen Hospital, Antiques
Urban Outfitters, Gift Shops and
Accessories
Wayne Edwards, Clothing
Whitman Book Shop, Books
WhoDunIt, Books
The Workbench, Furniture

CENTER CITY–
FAIRMOUNT PARK AREA

Foodstuffs, Food
The Museum Shop, Gift Shops and
Accessories

Philadelphia Zoo Shop, Gift Shops
and Accessories

CHESTER COUNTY

All in One Linen, Fabrics and Linens
Ball & Ball, Antiques
Barns & Barns Antiques, Antiques
The Blue Ribbon, Crafts
Chalfont & Chalfont Antiques,
Antiques
Chester County Book Company,
Books
Children's Factory Outlet, Discount
Stores and Factory Outlets
Corner House, Discount Stores and
Factory Outlets
The Creative Hand, Crafts
Decoy Book Shop, Books
Dilworthtown Country Store, Crafts
Downingtown Farmer's Market,
Food
Dress 'n Drape, Fabrics
Dungaree Outlet, Discount Stores and
Factory Outlets
Elizabeth L. Matlat, Antiques
Entenmann's, Food
French Creek Decoy Shop, Crafts
Herbert Schiffer, Inc., Antiques
Louis Irion III, Furniture
Monroe Coldren & Sons, Antiques
Philip H. Bradley, Antiques
Stacey's, Discount Stores and Factory
Outlets
Windsor Shirt Factory, Discount
Stores and Factory Outlets

DELAWARE COUNTY

Antique Mall, Flea Markets
Arrow Root Natural Foods, Food
Bryn Mawr Stereo, Photographic
Supplies
Calico Corner, Fabrics and Linens
Cameracraft, Photographic Supplies
Eberth and Smith-Durham, Florist
Gently Country, Gift Shops and
Accessories
Hit or Miss, Discount Stores and
Factory Outlets

House of Bargains, Discount Stores and Factory Outlets
Lancaster County Farmer's Market, Food
La Sportique, Sports Equipment
Loehmann's, Discount Stores and Factory Outlets
Pembroke Shop, Antiques
Porcelain Products, Gift Shops and Accessories
T.H. Mandy's, Discount Stores and Factory Outlets
Villanova Cheese Shop, Food
Wayne Toy Town, Toys
Wilburger's Ski Shop, Sports Equipment
Women's Exchange, Clothing

LANCASTER COUNTY

ABC Linen Outlet, Fabrics and Linens
Carter's Outlet Store, Discount Stores and Factory Outlets
Child Stride, Discount Stores and Factory Outlets
David Crystal, Discount Stores and Factory Outlets
Everfast Mill Store, Fabrics and Linens
Renninger's Antiques and Collectors' Market, Flea Markets
Rock Bottom, Discount Stores and Factory Outlets
VF Outlet Store, Discount Stores and Factory Outlets

MONTGOMERY COUNTY

Albrecht's, Florists
Ardmore Farmer's Market, Food
Ashborne Market, Food
The Bookhouse of Suburban Square, Books
The Brookstone Company, Gift Shops and Accessories
Cucci Institute De Beaute, Skin Care
Eastern Mountain Sports, Sports Equipment
Edelman's Stamps, Coins and Stamps

Elysee Boulangerie, Food
Flourtown Farmer's Market, Food
General Nutrition Center, Food
Gladwyne Village Gourmet, Food
Happy Viking, Furniture
Herman's World of Sporting Goods, Sports Equipment
Her Royal Highness, Clothing
Ilona, Skin Care
Joseph A. Bank & Clothiers, Discount Stores and Factory Outlets
Kiddie City, Toys
La Bouttica, Clothing
Larmond's, Photographic Supplies
Liberty of London, Gift Shops and Accessories
Linens Unlimited, Inc., Fabrics and Linens
Marshall's, Discount Stores and Factory Outlets
Montgomeryville Farmer's Market, Food
Pappagallo, Shoes
Philadelphia Sports Specialties, Sports Equipment
Sugar Plum, Crafts
The Tinder Box, Tobacco
This End Up Furniture, Furniture
Viking Pastries, Food
Wall to Wall Sound, Photographic Supplies
Wynn Hancock, Gift Shops and Accessories

NORTH PHILADELPHIA

Howarth's Imports, Food
Lisbon Bakery, Food

NORTHEAST PHILADELPHIA

Bauer's Pastry Shop, Food
Brownie's, Discount Stores and Factory Outlets
Marlo Book Store, Books
Stein Florist, Florists

NORTHWEST PHILADELPHIA

The Antique Gallery, Antiques
Axelrod Florists, Florists

Bikes & Books, Books
Bird in Hand, Antiques
Blum's, Antiques
The Brass Boudoir, Furniture
Bredenbeck's Bakery, Food
Chandlee & Bewick, Antiques
The Chestnut Hill Cheese Shop, Food
Chestnut Hill Farmer's Market, Food
Chestnut Hill Spice Shop, Food
Concept Natural Foods Mini-Cafe, Food
The Craft Store, Crafts
The Eagle's Eye, Discount Stores and Factory Outlets
Fireside Books, Books
Fireside Toys, Toys
Gilbert Stuart Studio, Art Supplies
Helen Siki, Clothing
John de Palma, Furniture
The Leather Bucket, Antiques
Mayor Antiques, Antiques
Noodles, Food
Propper Brothers, Furniture
Robertson of Chestnut Hill, Florists
Rushlight Antiques, Antiques
Victoria and Company, Gift Shops and Accessories
Video Vision, Records, Tapes, and Video Equipment
William H. Fredrick, Furniture
The Wooden Train, Toys

OLD CITY–SOCIETY HILL

Artisan's Cooperative, Crafts
Dickens Inn Bakery, Food
Gargoyle's Ltd., Antiques
The Key & Quill Shop, Furniture

Koffmeyer's Cookies, Food
Third Street Jazz, Records, Tapes and Video Equipment

QUEEN VILLAGE AND SOUTH STREET

Aero, Clothing
Bare Essentials, Skin Care
Bitar's Middle Eastern Groceries and Pastries, Food
Fabric Row, Fabrics and Linens
Garland of Letters, Books
The General Store, Gift Shops and Accessories
The Kidd, Leather
Knit Wit, Clothing
Lily Silk, Inc., Discount Stores and Factory Outlets
Meriden Books, Books
My Jewel Shop, Jewelry
The Parlour, Clothing
Philadelphia T-Shirt Museum, Gift Shops and Accessories
Plage Tahiti, Clothing
Shoes to Boot, Discount Stores and Factory Outlets
Sophy Curson, Clothing
Toby Lerner, Clothing
Tower Records, Records, Tapes and Video Equipment

SOUTH PHILADELPHIA

Claudio's, Food
DiBruno's, Food
The Italian Market, Food
The Pink Rose Pastry Shop, Food
Sarcone & Son, Food
The Spice Corner, Food
Swiss Pastry Shop, Food

ANTIQUES

Few areas of the country can match Philadelphia and its surrounding counties for the wide variety and prices of antiques. Antique shops can be found virtually everywhere, from the colonial atmosphere of Pine Street to the rolling hills of the Pennsylvania countryside.

Center City

Alfred Bullard, 1604 Pine St.; 735-1879. Late 18th- and early 19th-century furniture beautifully displayed in an old three-story house.

Antiques, 13th and Market Sts.; 422-2000. This new department on the ninth floor of John Wanamaker's carries the largest selection of English and continental case pieces, as well as chests, secretaries and cupboards, French clocks, and accessories.

Chelsea Silverplating, 920 Pine St.; 925-1132. You can learn the details on the fine art of silverplating. The store features antique lamps and bronze items.

Frank S. Schwarz & Son, 1806 Chestnut St.; 563-4887. Also Suburban Square, Ardmore; 642-1500. Established in 1930, this well-known family specializes in 18th- and 19th-century American paintings, watercolors, and fine antiques.

Gargoyle's, Ltd., 512 12th St., 629-1700. Carries everything from architectural embellishments to soda fountains.

Judith Finkel, 1030 Pine St.; 923-3094. A small shop with the reputation for the area's finest metals, including early tin, copper, iron, and fire tools.

M. Finkel and Daughter, 936 Pine St.; 627-7797. Amy and her father are well-known for period furniture, fine quilts, and folk art.

Reese's, 928 Pine St.; 922-0796. The oldest store on "Antique Row," this one features 17th-, 18th- and 19th-century American and Oriental antiques.

Samuel T. Freeman, 1808 Chestnut St.; 563-9275. A family business since 1805, holding many sales annually of rare items that have been acquired from Philadelphia estates. Wide variety of antiques, jewelry, paintings, and Oriental rugs.

Schaffer's, 1032 Pine St.; 923-2949. Known for their stained glass and accessories.

Tucker's Pen Hospital, 728 Chestnut St.; 922-5575. Marie and Art Russell restore and sell antique pens. Theirs is the only shop of its kind in the Philadelphia area.

Chestnut Hill

The Antique Gallery, 8523 Germantown Ave.; 248-1700. A Madison Avenue shop specializing in art glass, pottery, cloisonne, bronzes, and 19th-century furniture.

Bird in Hand, 8419 Germantown Ave.; 248-2473. Great buys here in china, glass, pewter, and silver.

Blum's, 45 E. Chestnut Hill Ave.; 242-8877. Carries a general line of antiques, quilts, brass items, and accessories.

Chandlee & Bewick, 7811 Germantown Ave.; 242-0375. Features 18th- and 19th-century furniture and some accessories.

The Leather Bucket, 8520 Germantown Ave.; 242-1140. Very fine 18th- and 19th-century English and American antiques.

Mayor Antiques, 8419 Germantown Ave.; 247-7337. Primitive and American antiques, furniture, quilts, and folk art.

Rushlight Antiques, 8705 Germantown Ave., 247-1740. Fine 18th- and 19th-century American antiques and accessories. Also paintings and mirrors.

New Hope

Country Antiques At The Church, Route 202 and Upper Mountain Rd.; 794-5009. Primitive and American furniture displayed in an 1840 Baptist church.

Crown & Eagle Antiques, Inc., Route 202 three miles south of New Hope, across from Winery; 794-7972. Specializes in finest American Indian art, rugs, basketry, beadwork, and pottery. Also china and weapons.

Jones Antiques, Route 202 in New Hope; 862-2466. American and primitive antiques at very reasonable prices.

Katy Kane, 34 W. Ferry St.; 862-5873. Brides and debs come here for the selection of white lace antique dresses and accessories.

Lahaska Antique Court, Route 202 in Lahaska; 794-7884. Six antique shops selling everything from country furniture to pottery, blown glass and paintings.

Lion House, Route 202 in Lahaska; 794-5622. An exquisite shop featuring antique and estate jewelry, oriental objets d'art.

Oaklawn Metal Craft & Antiques, Route 202 in Lahaska; 794-7387. Known for its custom metal work, including lanterns, tools, and hardware. Also reproductions and restorations.

Robertson & Thornton Antiques, Route 202 between Doylestown and Buckingham; 794-3109. American antiques sold in a unique 1853 country store.

Other Antique Shops ─────────────────

Ball & Ball, 463 W. Lincoln Highway, Exton; 363-7330. Known for its 17th- and 18th-century brass, iron, and cabinet hardware reproductions.

Barns & Barns Antiques, 558 Lancaster Ave., Frazer; 647-9279. Members of International Society of Appraisers, they carry a general line of pine and oak furniture.

Chalfont & Chalfont Antiques, 1352 Paoli Pike, West Chester; 696-1862. Fine 17th-, 18th- and early 19th-century American antiques.

Elizabeth L. Matlat, 134 Wilmington Pike, Chadds Ford; 358-0359. Known for her 18th- and 19th-century antiques, crafted lighting, and books for the collector.

Herbert Schiffer Antiques, Inc., 609 W. Lincoln Highway, Exton; 363-6889. A fine collection of Chippendale furniture, handpainted country furniture, decoys, and Oriental porcelain.

Monroe Coldren & Sons, E. Virginia Ave., West Chester; 692-6551. Fifty years in the business, this family offers 18th- and 19th-century metals and hardware, antique doors, and mantels. Also authentic restorations.

Pembroke Shop, 167 W. Lancaster Ave., Wayne; 688-8185. Carries 1870–1890 Centennial furniture, as well as a line of country furniture and accessories.

Phillip H. Bradley, E. Lincoln Highway, Downingtown; 269-0427. The largest collection of American antiques and accessories in the area.

ART SUPPLIES

Any and every art supply needed by the commercial and amateur artist can be found at the centers below.

Gilbert Stuart Studio, 8407 Germantown Ave., Chestnut Hill; 247-2052.

Philadelphia Art Supply Co., 25 S. 8th St.; 627-6655.

Taws Artists Materials, 1527 Walnut St.; 563-8742.

BOOKS

There are so many excellent bookstores in the Philadelphia area that it is impossible to list them all here. Instead, we have selected those that are unique for one reason or another. Among America's most popular bookstores, B. *Dalton*, *Doubleday*, and *Waldenbooks* stores can be found throughout Center City and in suburban malls. Also, major department stores have extensive book sections with wide selections on varied subjects.

American Institute of Architects' Bookstore, 17th and Sansom Sts.; 569-3180. This store has one of the finest selections of architectural writing to be found anywhere, including books on everything from interior design, theory, and history to landscaping and gardening. It also has a wide range of books on Philadelphia travel, a children's section, and array of cards and stationery.

Archway Bookstore, 725 Walnut St.; 922-0665. A technical book center specializing in trade, industries, and sciences. A general line of books is also available.

Bikes & Books, 5952 Germantown Ave.; 843-6071. Mr. Gardner has 40,000 books covering almost any topic and subject, including American history, politics, and cooking. And while you're here, take a long look at his large array of bikes, some of which are antiques.

Bookhouse of Suburban Square, 45 Colter Ave., Ardmore; 642-4915. More than a quarter-century in the business, this knowledgeable store presents a large selection of hardbacks and paperbacks, as well as personal service that includes gift-wrapping and recommendations for all ages. Also a wide selection of cards.

Book Mark, 2049 West Rittenhouse Square; 735-5546. A reputable bookstore that carries a large stock of out of print, used, and rare books on almost any subject. They specialize in books on architecture.

Booktenders, 62 W. State St., Doylestown; 348-7160. Children up to age 16 love to read their wide range of books on almost any topic or subject. They also carry a large selection of reference books.

Liquorius Book Store, Cheltenham Shopping Center, Cheltenham; 886-3675. Three locations. This lovely bookstore features a complete selection of softcover and hardcover books.

Chester County Book Company, 929 S. High St., West Chester; 696-1661. They offer a wide range of books in many categories and all are well-stocked. There is also an extensive selection of magazines and greeting cards.

Decoy Book Shop, 107 S. Broad St., Kennett Square; 444-3032. This unique bookstore presents a full line of books for adults and children in hardback and paperback. As you might gather from its name, it also features decoys made by local craftsmen.

Encore Books, 735-8043. Twenty-five locations. David Schlessinger continues to expand his popular discount bookstores throughout Center City and the surrounding counties.

Fireside Books, 8009 Germantown Ave., 242-1442. This good, old-fashioned toy and bookstore offers personal service to those choosing from the broad selection of books on almost any topic. They take great pride in their children's books.

Garland of Letters, 527 South St.; 923-5946. Feeling tense? This is the store to visit. Their specialty is self-improvement books for relaxation and meditation and records come with them, too.

Grace Book Store, 730 Chestnut St.; 922-6868. Religious books are featured here.

How To Do It Book Store, 1608 Sansom St.; 563-1516. Everything from gardening tips to setting up your own business. If you don't know how to do it, the books in this shop will show you how.

Joseph Fox Book Store, 1724 Sansom St.; 563-4186. Knowledgeable service is always offered when selecting any of their books. Prominent in art and architectural literature.

Marlo Book Store, Roosevelt Mall Shopping Center, Cottman and Roosevelt Blvd.; 331-4469. If anybody will have it, Marlo will. They sell up-to-date books on almost any subject, including one of the largest selections of computer books. They also have a section on used books and carry the largest selection of magazines in the area.

Meriden Books, 635 South St.; 592-0545. This popular bookstore specializes in works on quality living. Paperbacks, children's books, literature on astrology, cooking, nature, and much more.

Robin's Book Store, 1837 Chestnut St.; 567-2615. Three locations. More than 30,000 titles on all subjects. They also back-date items. Poetry readings are held several times a month.

Whitman Book Shop, 1012 Chestnut St.; 923-3166. In addition to its wide range of selections, this shop makes special orders, wraps, and even delivers upon request.

Whodunit, 1931 Chestnut St.; 567-1478. This shop solves the mysteries of locating your favorite mystery and spy books.

CLOTHING

As one of the top clothing centers in America, Philadelphia offers every conceivable style and fashion in its department stores and specialty shops. This section lists some very special shops from which one can choose everything from sportswear to designer labels.

Women's Clothing

The exclusive shops carrying fashions from around the world include Nan Duskin, Toby Lerner, Saint Laurent rive gauche, Cazou and Rodier Paris (at The Bourse), Kenneth and Cooper, Sophy Curson, Knit Wit, and Plage Tahiti.

In the suburbs are Ann Pakradooni, La Bouttica, Helen Siki, and Dorothy Bullit (at Haverford Square and in Chestnut Hill).

For maternity clothes, we recommend Lady Madonna, and for the large woman, Lane Bryant. Fine quality and formal wear for day and night is offered in Center City and malls throughout the area by Casual Corner, Talbot's, Ann Taylor, Lady Bug, and Laura Ashley.

For camping and outdoor attire visit Eddie Bauer, Country Outfitters and I. Goldberg in Center City and suburban malls.

Listed below are the shops mentioned in the text that are not located in designated shopping malls:

Ann Pakradooni, 375 Lancaster Ave., Haverford; 649-4430.

Helen Siki, 18 E. Highland Ave., Chestnut Hill; 248-2887.

I. Goldberg, 902 Chestnut St.; 925-9393.

Kenneth and Cooper, 1728 Chestnut St.; 563-5266.

Knit Wit, 208 S. 17th St.; 735-3642.

La Bouttica, 18 Summit Grove Rd., Bryn Mawr; 527-5292.

Nan Duskin, 1729 Walnut St.; 563-1406.

Plage Tahiti, 128 S. 17th St.; 569-9140.

Sophy Curson, 122 South St.; 567-4662.

Toby Lerner, 1177 S. 17th St.; 568-5768.

Men's Clothing

Depending upon the event or occasion, men's dress in Philadelphia can vary from the "preppy" look to the European. You can be sure of finding stores to accommodate these two particular looks, as well as everything in between.

Smaller stores for men in Center City include Boyd's, Aero, Dimensions, Allure, Morville, Brooks Brothers, and Wayne Edwards.

In the surrounding counties, Bloomingdale's, Bamberger's Abraham & Strauss (in King of Prussia Mall), and B. Altman (in St. David's and Willow Grove) are always up-to-date in men's fashions.

For the heavy-set man, visit Jack Lang, found in Center City and suburban malls; for outdoor wear, see Eddie Bauer, Country Outfitters, and I. Goldberg.

Listed below are the shops mentioned in the text which are not located in shopping malls.

Aero, 325 South St.; 922-4340.

Allure, 1509 Walnut St.; 562-4242.
Boyd's, 1217 Market St.; 564-5851.
I. Goldberg, 902 Chestnut St.; 925-9393.
Wayne Edwards, 1517 Walnut St.; 563-6801.

Children's Clothing

Philadelphia's oldest department stores, Wanamaker's and Strawbridge's have been popular clothiers for children for more than a century. For further high quality, there is Bonwit & Teller, Saks Fifth Avenue, and Lord & Taylor. Among the smaller shops featuring fine children's attire are Born Yesterday, Children's Boutique, Her Royal Highness, and the Women's Exchange, which carries lovely homemade items.

Born Yesterday, 1901 Walnut St.; 568-6556.
Children's Boutique, three locations, including 18th and Sansom Sts.; 563-3881.
Her Royal Highness, Suburban Square, Ardmore; 642-0456.
Women's Exchange, 185 E. Lancaster Ave., Wayne; 688-1431.

COINS AND STAMPS

Trading, gift giving, collecting, investing? Philadelphia is a superb market in which to do all four.

Earl P. L. Apfelbaum, Inc., 2006 Walnut St.; 567-5200. Has given area stamp collectors more than 50 years of superb service.

Edelman's Stamps, 301 Old York Rd., Jenkintown; 572-6480. Established in 1926, this store has one of the best stocks of U.S. and foreign stamps to be found anywhere.

John Wanamaker, 1300 Market St.; 422-2830. Buying and selling stamps since 1934.

Philly Stamp & Coin Co., Inc., 1804 Chestnut St.; 563-7341. Rare stamps and coins bought, sold, and appraised. Also deals in scrap gold and silver.

CRAFTS

Artisan's Cooperative, 419 S. 2nd St.; 928-1532. A collection of handmade quilts, pottery, candles, toys, and other items crafted by skilled artisans throughout America.

The Blue Ribbon, Ludwig's Corner, Routes 100 and 401, Elverson; 458-5066. A Victorian home filled with handcrafted items, folk art, pottery, and a variety of Chester County crafts.

The Craft Store, 8229 Germantown Ave.; 247-8444. More than 120 craftsmen from throughout the nation are represented in this lovely shop. Along with a fine collection of stoneware and pottery, you'll find wooden boxes, pillows, leather goods, and quilts.

The Creative Hand, Exton Square Mall, Routes 30 and 100, Exton; 363-1677. A cooperative of local artists and craftsmen selling their wares in an 18th-century home.

The Cricket Box in the Grist Mill, 10 N. Main St., Yardley; 493-1553. The walls of this shop are adorned with stencils, wreaths, thermo painting, quilted blankets, and pillows.

Dandelion, 1700 Locust St.; 546-7655, and Exton Square, Exton; 363-6602. These unique craft shops feature hand-crafted jewelry, pottery, and clothing, as well as calendars, greeting cards, and novelty items.

Dilworthtown Country Store, 275 Brinton's Bridge Rd., West Chester; 399-0560. Built in 1758, this is one of the oldest general stores in Pennsylvania. Features 18th-century crafts, folk art, and herbs.

Elder Craftsmen Shop, 1628 Walnut St.; 545-7888. Beautiful handwork and collection of crafts by individuals over 60.

French Creek Decoy Shop, St. Peter's Village; 469-0190. Handcrafted decoys by local craftsmen and Eastern shore artists. Chris Murray, who owns this shop, specializes in waterfowl sculpture, and also carries antiques and collectibles.

Helen Druitt Gallery, 305 Cherry St.; 735-1625. (see VISUAL ARTS Galleries).

The Pontypool Shop, 9 N. State St., Newtown; 968-3004. More than 230 artists and craftsmen are represented in this shop which features tin items, unique stained glass, knitted specialties, and handmade pillows.

Sugar Plum, Gwynned Center, 832 N. Bethlehem Pike; 646-0461. Over 375 artists are represented in this shop, which is filled with pottery, bowls and vases from New England, folk art handcrafted decoys, and decorative figurines, animals, and lamps.

The Work's Craft Gallery, 319 South St.; 922-7775. (see VISUAL ARTS Galleries).

FACTORY OUTLETS
AND DISCOUNT STORES

Pennsylvania is renowned for its factory outlets, and they are abundant in Philadelphia and its nearby counties as well. At the top of the list, of course, is Reading—a scant 56 miles from Philadelphia—which is the capital of outlet shopping in America with over 100 stores from which to choose. Among the newer outlets is Lancaster Outlet City, which has 16 shops offering truly unusual savings.

Women's Clothing Outlets

Corner House, Fifteen locations, including Exton Square Mall, Routes 30 and 100, Exton; 363-6102. Discounted prices on such favorites as Villager and Lady Bug.

Hit Or Miss, Twelve locations, including 375 Lancaster Ave., Stafford Shopping; 687-9998. Popular labels at discount prices.

Lily Silk, Inc., 716 4th St.; 922-2368. Designer fashions at surprising savings.

Loehmann's, Pontiac Rd., Drexel; 789-9100. Designer and fine clothing discounted.

Maternity Factory Outlet, Four locations, including 1714 Walnut St.; 545-8061.

Post Horn, 2130 Arch St.; 567-0363. Offers 30 percent discount on J.G. Hook clothing under the Post Horn label.

Stacey's, two locations, including Gateway Shopping Center, Route 202 and Valley Forge Road, Wayne; 688-9980.

T.H. Mandy's, two locations, including 1149 Lancaster Ave., Rosemont; 527-2557.

Men's Clothing

David Crystal, three locations, including 13th St. and Rosemont Ave., Reading; 921-0201. Designer apparel for men discounted.

Women and Men's Clothing

Artie's, 15 locations, including 1714 Walnut St.; 545-6855. Since 1939, these stores have been luring customers with their remarkable low prices for labels that include Christian Dior, Calvin Klein, John Meyer, and Bobbie Brooks.

Brownie's, 6722 Bustleton Ave.; 333-0220. This store is more than 30 years old and is still discounting prices by 40 and 50 percent on famous brands.

The Eagle's Eye Sportswear Outlet, two locations, including 8620 Germantown Ave., Chestnut Hill; 248-5055. Classic sportswear for men, women, and children at healthy savings.

Joseph A. Bank Clothiers, Inc. two locations, including 379 Lancaster Ave., Haverford Square; 896-8500. Traditional clothing at excellent savings.

Marshall's, five locations, including Route 202 at DeKalb Pike, King of Prussia; 337-2346. A fine selection of discounted clothes for men, women, and children.

Windsor Shirt Factory, 11 locations, including Frazer Shopping Center, Route 30, Frazer; 647-2332. Shirts, sweaters, blouses, and accessories at remarkably low prices.

Children's Outlets

Carter's Outlet Store, 2353 Lincoln Highway, Lancaster; 644-9536. Children's clothing from toddler to age 14 at 20 to 60 percent off. Clothing for men and women, also.

Children's Factory Outlet, nine locations, including 232 E. Lancaster Ave., Malvern; 644-9536.

House of Bargains, Springfield Shopping Center, Sproul Rd. and Route 1, Springfield; 487-1652.

Jeans for Men and Women

Dungaree Outlet, Ludwig's Corner, Routes 100 and 401; 458-8527.

Rock Bottom, Lancaster Outlet City, Lancaster; 291-9462.

VF Outlet Store, Mill Ave. and Park Rd., Reading; 378-0408.

Shoes

Child Stride, Lemon St. and Center Ave., Ephrata; 733-2215.

Lou's Shoe Bazaar, 1715 Chestnut St.; 564-4637.

Shoes to Boot, 736 4th St.; 625-0731.

FABRICS AND LINENS

ABC Linen Outlet, 916 Windsor St., Reading; 373-7321. Savings of more than 30 percent on quality famous-brand domestic linens, sheets, towels, blankets, bedspreads, and tablecloths.

All In One Linen, several locations, including Lancaster Ave., Frazer; 647-2555. Brand-name sheets, bedspreads, towels, napkins, and tablecloths discounted up to 50 percent.

Calico Corner, 745 Lancaster Ave., Strafford-Wayne; 688-1505. Choice seconds on the finest imported and domestic decorative fabrics for drapery, slipcovers, and upholstery. Also, savings of up to 50 percent on bolt material and remnants.

Dress 'n Drape Fabrics, five locations, including Frazer Shopping Center, Lancaster Ave., Frazer; 644-5007. Large selection of drapery fabrics, patterns, notions, trimmings, yarn, and art needlework. Also custom-made drapes from a large selection of fabrics.

Everfast Mill Store, 601 E. Lancaster Ave., Shillington; 777-1331. A wide variety of Schumacher remnants at low prices.

Fabric Row, South 4th St., Queen Village. A row of shops dealing with every kind of fabric imaginable at extraordinary prices.

Linens Unlimited, Inc., three locations, including 323-31 Old York Rd., Jenkintown; 572-6777. A large selection of linens, sheets, towels, comforters, and tablecloths—among many other items—discounted from 30 to 50 percent on current goods, from 70 to 75 percent on discontinued items.

FLEA MARKETS

Antique Mall, south side of Route 1, Chadds Ford; 388-1174. Open Saturday and Sunday, 11 am–6 pm. Indoor market featuring 50 antique dealers.

The Great American Flea Market, Route 13 and Levittown Parkway; 946-1154. Open Friday and Saturday, 11 am–4 pm; Sunday 8 am–4 pm. Indoor market that has just about everything.

Lahaska Antique Center and Flea Market, Route 202 in Lahaska; 794-5000. Almost 50 indoor shops featuring a host of antiques and collectibles.

Old City Antiques, 306 Cherry St.; 592-0989. Open Saturday and Sunday, 10:30 am–5 pm. More than 55 antique dealers.

Renninger's Antique and Collectors' Market, Exit 21 of the Pennsylvania Turnpike, then about 1.2 miles north on Route 272, Adamstown; 1-267-2177. Sunday 7:30 am–5:30 pm. Five hundred dealers selling everything from baseball cards to fine antique furniture.

FLORISTS

Whether it's flowers for a friend, a wedding, or your own pleasure, try one of these noted shops.

Albrecht's, Flowers & Greenhouses, Montgomery Ave. and Meeting House Lane, Narberth; 667-2800. Since 1882, three generations of the Albrecht family have supplied the Philadelphia area with beautifully designed floral arrangements. They carry everything from exotic flowers to cut orchids and imported tulips.

Alfred of Philadelphia, 259 S. 21st St.; 985-1198. These florists carry flowers, plants, dried material, and gifts. They specialize in gourmet fruit baskets. Plant rental is available.

Axelrod Florists, 921 Cheltenham Ave.; 843-3904. More than 75 years of excellence and floral decorations.

Eberth and Smith-Durham, Sheraton Society Hill Hotel; 238-6000. Settled into their new location and still creating beautiful flower arrangements. They also carry imported French fabrics, and super gifts, too.

The Flower Market, 117 S. 16th St.; 569-0889. The world's finest flowers by the stem at popular prices. Also, floral arrangements for large conventions and plant rentals.

Robertson of Chestnut Hill, 8501 Germantown Ave.; 242-6000. Creative florists, known for imported tulips and unusual novelty and gift items.

Stein Florist, 7059 Frankford Ave.; 338-7100, and 2223 N. Front St.; 338-7100. Mr. Stein has the largest volume of flowers of any retail store in the city.

FOOD

Philadelphia's ethnic mix has produced a rich variety of international foods and American "firsts," such as ice cream, the Philadelphia cheese steak sandwich, and the Hoagie. Shopping for food is fun in this special city.

Bakeries

Bauer's Pastry Shop, 9825 Bustleton Ave.; 673-6560. Fifty years old now, this bakery continues to serve up delightful renditions of butter cake, forest cake, and cinnamon buns. But these are only a sampling of the many German specialties that also include super wedding and birthday delicacies.

Bredenbeck's Bakery, 8126 Germantown Ave., Chestnut Hill; 247-7374. Its English tea scones are considered the best in Philadelphia.

Dickens Inn Bakery, Head House Square; 928-9307. Watch through the bay window as they make pastries for the restaurant; then step inside, where homemade croissants, quiches, Danish pastries, English pies, gateaux, and eclairs fill the shelves.

New Market   *New Market Association*

Elysee Boulangerie, five locations, including Montgomery Mall, Routes 202 and 309 in Montgomeryville; 362-2418. Known for its wide range of breads, from French rye to raisin, pumpernickel, and sourdough.

Entenmann's, Lancaster Ave., Exton; 363-2290. Cakes, cookies, and doughnuts at discount prices. Thursdays, half price.

Katz's Cheesecake, three locations in Philadelphia, including The Bourse; 265-6088. Cheesecake in numerous flavors, including Fudge Swirl, Walnut Praline, Peach Melba, and Blueberry.

Koffmeyer's Cookies, New Market; 922-0717. All-natural cookies speckled with chocolate bits and nuts.

Lisbon Bakery, 5220 N. 5th St.; 457-5907. This, the only Portuguese bakery in Philadelphia, is noted for its traditional breads, rolls, and pastries, including delicious custard cups.

Mr. Pickwick & Bakery, 1519 Walnut St.; 569-8884. Mrs. Bardell offers a wide range of delicious English cakes and pastries.

The Pink Rose Pastry Shop, 734 S. 9th St.; 592-0565. This small, intimate cafe serves espresso coffee, tea from China, and a wide variety of French, Italian, German, and American pastries—including spectacular homemade tarts, cookies, and cakes.

Rindelaub's, 128 S. 18th St.; 563-3993. Fifty years old, the upstairs bakery continues to turn out famous German chocolate cake, peerless cinnamon buns, decorated gold cakes, and all-butter sponge cake. The breads and rolls are outstanding, too.

Sarcone & Son, 758 S. 9th St.; 922-0445. Since 1918, has specialized in traditional Italian breads, rolls, bread sticks, pizza shells, and pepperoni bread (its center is a piece of thinly sliced pepperoni in tomato sauce).

Swiss Pastry Shop, 35 S. 19th St.; 563-0759. Since 1925, delightful Swiss cakes including dobash, a seven-layered vanilla cake with chocolate buttercream filling. Also, Viennese crescent rolls and unique salt sticks.

Viking Pastries, 39 Cricket Ave.; 642-9227. This established Scandinavian bakery specializes in breads, croissants, Viking onion rolls, Swedish fruit tarts, rum balls, and cookies.

International & Gourmet Foods

Ashbourne Market, 7904 High School Rd., Elkins Park; 635-1442. Hard-to-find items include a large selection of imported and domestic cheeses, coffees and teas from around the world, caviar, fresh baked goods, and much more.

Bitar's Middle Eastern Groceries & Pastries, 616 S. 2nd St.; 925-4950. Lebanese specialties baked in the heart of Queen Village. Great pita bread, spinach pies, cheese pies, and a unique strudel-like pastry made with heavy cream.

Bon Appetite, 213 S. 17th St.; 546-8059. Known for its beautiful cookware, this shop also has a fine line of gourmet delicacies, including a large selection of teas and coffees from around the world.

The Chestnut Hill Cheese Shop, 8507 Germantown Ave., Chestnut Hill; 242-2211. This little shop brims with all kinds of cheeses and gourmet foods.

The Chestnut Hill Spice Shop, 8123 Germantown Ave., Chestnut Hill; 242-5449. Eat-in restaurant that sells spices, teas, and sauces served there.

Claudio's, on 9th St. between Carpenter and Christian; 627-1873. A 19th-century shop featuring imported and domestic cheeses, 40 different oils, and Italian, French, and Greek groceries.

DiBruno, 930 S. 9th St.; 922-2876. For 57 years, Mr. DiBruno has operated this popular deli and gourmet food shop in South Philly. Not only is he well known for his cheeses from around the world, but also for his own homemade cheese spreads and popular wine vinegars. Customers still come in every day for his delicious gourmet salads and large selection of Italian cold cuts.

The Food Hall, Strawbridge & Clothier, The Gallery at Market East; 629-6000. An English kitchen offering fresh breads and pastas, deli meats, a selection of gourmet foods, Godiva chocolates, and a fine line of cookware.

Foodstuffs, 533 N. 22nd St.; 665-8410. This full-line grocery store carries select cuts of meat and poultry along with fresh fish. Baked goods are available every day along with herbs when in season.

Gladwyne Village Gourmet, 385 Righters Mill Rd., Gladwyne; 642-6022. Two locations. Shelves stocked with gourmet goodies; cheese sculptured into whatever shape you desire.

Howarth's Imports, 3216 N. Front St.; 739-1264. Owner Frank Donovan specializes in English, Scottish, and Irish delicacies.

The Market, The Gallery at Market East; 925-7162. A collection of fresh-food specialty grocers in a lively market atmosphere.

The Market at the Commissary, 130 S. 17th St.; 568-8055. Much of the great food served in the restaurant is available here.

The Market at Wanamaker's, John Wanamaker, 13th and Market Sts.; 422-2000. A series of little shops where you'll find baked goods, traditional deli items, fresh produce, and a fine selection of gourmet foods.

Noodles, 8341 Germantown Ave., Chestnut Hill; 247-7715. Not only can you buy fresh pasta and sun-dried tomatoes here, but you can also come for breakfast or an ice cream cone.

The Spice Corner, 9th and Christian; 925-1661. Carries a large selection of spices, teas, fresh-ground coffee, and dried and glazed fruits.

Villanova Cheese Shop, 779 Lancaster Ave., Villanova; 525-5034. There are so many items to choose from that many customers like to view this as their food hardware store. Carries everything from imported truffles and pates to a large selection of teas, coffees, jams, and mustards.

Markets

Ardmore Farmer's Market, Suburban Square, Ardmore; 896-7560. Open 6 am–10 pm Thursday; noon–10 pm Saturday; 11 am–6 pm Sunday. One of the newer markets on the Main Line, this one features 18 merchants selling everything from fresh produce and meat to Dutch delicacies.

Chestnut Hill Farmer's Market, 8229 Germantown Ave., Chestnut Hill; 242-5905. Located behind the Chestnut Hill Hotel, this group of individual stalls features fresh produce and a large assortment of cheeses, pastas, salads, pastries, candies, and cut flowers.

Downingtown Farmer's Market, Lancaster Ave., Downingtown; 269-4050. A large complex that offers fresh produce, cheeses, pastries, and meats. Many shops in the complex also have various items and considerable savings. Open 10 am–10 pm Friday and Saturday; 10 am–6 pm Sunday.

Flourtown Farmer's Market, Bethlehem Pike, Flourtown near Hall's Lane. Open Thursday through Saturday, this new market combines chichi food stands from nearby Chestnut Hill with the more organic foods of Amish purveyors. Great baked goods and produce.

Italian Market, 9th St., from Wharton to Christian Sts., South Philadelphia. This vibrant, bustling marketplace is a magnificent and energetic place to shop. With neighborhood merchants' stores filled to overflowing, and even more to be found on the sidewalk tables and pushcarts, you'll find everything from fresh fruits and vegetables to a full range of meats, poultry, seafood, pastas, cheeses, and baked goods. Not only is it all fresh, but it's also reasonably priced, too.

Lancaster County Farmer's Market, Lancaster Ave. and Eagle Rd., Wayne; 688-9856. Open Wednesday, Friday, and Saturday, 6 am–4 pm. Popular Main Line spot that offers fine produce, a large selection of meat and fish, herbs, and Pennsylvania Dutch cooking. Some merchants sell craft items and antiques.

Montgomeryville Farmer's Market, Horsham Rd. near the intersection of Routes 309 and 202. Several food stalls, one of which has existed for 31 years; specializes in German foods. Clothing and merchandise items also available Thursday, 6 pm–10 pm, Saturday, noon–10 pm, Sunday 11 am–6 pm.

Reading Terminal Market, 12th and Filberts Sts.; 922-2317. Open Monday through Saturday, 8 am–6 pm. Now redecorated, the Market is a fun place to shop and eat around a beer garden and courtyard. More than 60 merchants sell everything from caviar to wild rabbit, sausages, breads, and olives; Amish farmers sell poultry, produce and baked goods on Thursday, Friday, and Saturday.

Natural Foods ────────────────────────

Arrow Root Natural Foods, 834 W. Lancaster Ave., Bryn Mawr; 527-3393. More than 100 bins of natural bulk items, and a large selection of discounted vitamins.

Center Foods, Broad and Pine Sts.; 735-5673. One of the largest selections of organic and natural foods; now carries a full line of macrobiotic items.

Concept Natural Foods Mini-Cafe, 8617 Germantown Ave.; 247-3215. Serves homemade soups and sandwiches for lunch, with two other rooms offering vitamins, health foods, and cosmetics.

General Nutrition Center, the Court at King of Prussia; 768-9913. A full range of vitamin supplements, natural diet aids, body care products, and physical fitness equipment.

FURNITURE

If you are furniture shopping, take advantage of the varied offerings below.

The Brass Boudoir, 8000 Germantown Ave., Chestnut Hill; 247-3815. Handcrafted, custom-made beds and accessories by local craftsmen.

Happy Viking, Route 309, six miles north of Montgomeryville; 362-1900. A small world of Scandinavian furnishings.

John de Palma, 8528 Germantown Ave., Chestnut Hill; 247-3538. Established in 1836, specializes in 18th-century reproductions.

The Key & Quill Shop, 129 S. Second St.; 923-8522. Housed in the historic 1769 Bond House, one will find authentic reproductions of antiques found in Independence Mall.

Louis Irion III, 44 N. Valley Rd., Paoli; 644-7516. Specializes in fine English and American reproductions from the 18th and 19th century.

Propper Brothers, Cresson and Levering Sts., near Green Lane Bridge, Manayunk; 483-0544. Since 1888, fine quality furniture at everyday discount prices.

The Rocker Shop, 1776 Easton Rd., Doylestown; 348-0170. Famous brand furniture in every style and period; quality woods.

Stephen Von Hohen Furniture, Inc., 174 Keystone Dr., Telford; 257-1135. Collection of antique furniture reproductions. Each piece is signed, dated, and numbered, and an authenticated certificate accompanies each when purchased.

This End Up Furniture, six locations, including The Court at King of Prussia; 265-0468. Durable furniture that's both handsome and affordable.

William H. Frederick, two locations, including 8705 Germantown Ave.; 247-1668. Indoor and outdoor furniture as well as a full line of gift and accessory items. Free interior consultation.

The Workbench, 1610 Chestnut St.; 563-9393. With its main furniture store based in New York, this spot offers European Bauhaus contemporary furniture with a simple look and contemporary lines.

GIFT SHOPS
AND ACCESSORIES

There are many unique gift shops throughout the Philadelphia area. These are among the best.

Betsey's Place, 323 Arch St.; 922-3536. Among the large selection of souvenirs are brass and pewter reproductions, handcrafted wooden banks, and replicas of historic row houses. The miniatures and annual Christmas ornaments are popular collectibles.

Bon Appetit, 213 S. 17th St.; 546-8059. This cutlery and gourmet specialty food shop features handpainted trivets and a line of high quality kitchen utensils.

The Brookstone Company, The Court at King of Prussia; 337-0774. Also, Willow Grove Shopping Center, Jenkintown; 657-8787. Everything you need but can't find, featuring all kinds of tools and household and personal items.

Franklin Mint, Wanamaker's Department Store, 13th and Market Sts.; 422-2000. Also, Willow Grove Park, Jenkintown; 659-2368. A fine line of collectible items, including pewter, bronze, crystal, sculptures, lithographs, and jewelry.

The General Store, 260 S. 20th St., Philadelphia; 732-6858. Everything you can imagine, from penny candy to Tiffany lamp shades and lots in between.

Liberty of London, Suburban Square; Ardmore; 649-0813. Founded in England by Sir Liberty, this shop carries on the British tradition by supplying its customers with imported fabrics, including prints designed by William Morris. They also carry a fine line of ready-to-wear clothing for men and women along with silk scarfs, hats, and bow ties.

The Museum Shop, Philadelphia Museum of Art, 26th St. and Benjamin Franklin Parkway; 787-5452. Also, the Franklin Plaza Hotel, 16th and Vine Sts.; 448-2000. The finest collection of art books to be found anywhere, along with a fabulous collection of contemporary jewelry that changes to reflect the different exhibitions at the Museum. They also carry a nice selection of pottery and lithographs.

Philadelphia T-Shirt Museum, 118 South 18th St.; 665-0185. This fun shop carries the largest selection of screened prints in Philadelphia.

Philadelphia Zoo Shop, 34th St. and Girard Ave.; 387-6400. This shop is only six years old and is housed in a replica of an old carriage house built in 1876. Caters to children as well as adults with its fine line of zoo-related gift items, games, books, stuffed animals, mugs, figurines, ceramics, and jewelry.

Porcelain Products, Spread Eagle Village, 503 W. Lancaster Ave., Wayne; 687-4220. Special emphasis on Hummel figurines, Liardo, Boehm, and national brands of china.

Stock and Wares, Suburban Square, Ardmore; 896-0537. Also, 1610 Chestnut St.; 563-3933. Full line of kitchen gadgets, including flatware and glassware. Also, pillows and frames.

Touches, 225 S. 15th St.; 546-1221. This shop helps accessorize your outfits with beautiful handbags, shawls, and belts. Also carries an unusual collection of handmade jewelry.

Urban Outfitters, 1801 Walnut St.; 569-3131. Also, **The Warehouse,** 4040 Locust St.; 222-3358. A contemporary department store with an urban attitude, carries trendy high-style clothing and home furnishings. Also a wide variety of housewares and toys. Sportswear is a specialty.

Victoria and Company, 8229 Germantown Ave., Chestnut Hill; 248-4040. This lovely gift shop is located behind the Chestnut Hill Hotel and carries Sodahl, Swedish dishes, Fukagawa, Japanese porcelain, and Louisville, Kentucky stoneware. Also American art, placemats, cards, and wrapping paper.

Wynn Hannock, 42 Suburban Square, Ardmore; 649-6271. Often referred to as a mini-Bloomingdale's, carries a wide range of gift items that include crystal, pottery, imported Italian furniture, stationery, and place mats.

JEWELRY

Bailey, Banks & Biddle, 16th and Chestnut Sts.; 564-6200. Outstanding since 1832. Diamonds and gold, famous brand watches, fine china, and crystal. Also, international gift department.

Jack Kellmer Co., 717 Chestnut St.; 627-8350. Diamond importers and gemologists specializing in precious stones and estate jewelry, plus objets d'art.

J.E. Caldwell, Chestnut and Juniper Sts.; 864-8829. With its fine jewelry and gifts, this has been a Philadelphia landmark for 150 years.

Jeweler's Row, Sansom St., between 7th and 9th, and 8th St., between Chestnut and Walnut. More than 300 wholesale and retail jewelers make this the largest jewelers' district in the nation, except for New York.

My Jewel Shop, 202 S. 17th St.; 732-3880. Some of the finest designers of jewelry are represented here, with original works incorporating precious stones, gems, pearls, and 14-carat gold.

Philadelphia Diamond Exchange, The Bourse; 627-7462. A large selection of high-quality diamond jewelry.

Replique Fashion Jewelry, Warwick Hotel, 17th and Locust Sts.; 546-1170. Among the most authentic reproductions to be found anywhere.

LEATHER

The Gucci Boutique, John Wanamaker, 13th and Market Sts.; 422-2000. Exclusive Italian leather handbags, shoes, and accessories for men and women.

The Kidd, 650 South St.; 627-3285. Owner George Hatzakorzian and his family design all the clothes featured here and in their Manhattan showroom. Suede knit sweaters, suede long- and short-sleeved sweaters, suede and leather ties for men.

Robinson Luggage, 101 S. Juniper St.; 735-9859. Among the widest arrays of luggage in the area.

PHOTOGRAPHIC SUPPLIES

The following retail stores provide full customer service, including equipment sales, repairs, and developing for both amateur and professional photographers.

The Camera Shop, Inc., 19 locations throughout the area; 572-0300.

Jack's Camera, 26 locations throughout the area; 642-9517.

Photo Cine Shop, 129 S. 18th St.; 567-7410.

For quick, guaranteed, one-day film development, see the following:

Cameracraft, 29 S. State St., Newtown; 968-2833.

The Camera Shop, Inc., 19 locations; 572-0300.

Jack's Camera, 26 locations; 642-9517.

Larmond's, Easton and Moreland Rds., Willow Grove; 659-3310. Promises to develop and print your 35mm color negative film in one hour.

RECORDS, TAPES, AND VIDEO EQUIPMENT

Bryn Mawr Stereo, Lancaster Ave., Bryn Mawr; 525-6300. Large selection of quality tapes, records, and equipment.

Third Street Jazz, 10 N. 3rd St.; 627-3366. This is considered one of the best, if not the best, record shops in the city. It carries everything.

Tower Records, 537–39 South St.; 925-0422, and 608–10 South St.; 574-9888. This new addition to the South Street scene is impressive. One store is devoted to classical music, while the other caters to the contemporary sound—right across the street from one another. Together, they should be able to meet any of your musical needs, and with an enormous sign, you can't miss Tower.

Video Vision, 8919 Ridge Ave.; 487-3410. One of Philadelphia's largest video and computer showrooms.

Wall to Wall Sound, the Plaza at King of Prussia; 624-1690. 18 locations throughout the area. These stores carry one of the largest selections of home entertainment equipment. Prices are competitive.

SHOES

Beige, 1715 Walnut St.; 564-2394. Catering to the woman's needs in fine shoes in a wide range of colors and styles.

Florsheim Thayer McNeil, 11 locations throughout the area; 825-9976. High quality shoes for men and women.

Pappagallo, the Court at King of Prussia; 337-9054. Fashionable shoes for women in an assortment of colors and trim.

Sabel Shoes, Inc., 1707 Walnut St.; 567-3516. Stylish, quality shoes sold in an elegant townhouse setting.

Strega, Ltd., 1505 Walnut St.; 564-5932. Distinctive shop specializing in European footwear for men and women.

SKIN CARE

Bare Essentials, 4th and South Sts.; 922-0677. Along with one-hour makeup consultations, offers a full range of its own brand of cosmetics.

Christine Valmy Skin Care Salon, Rittenhouse Regency, 225 S. 18th St.; 546-5660. Presents a wide array of facial products and treatments, with everything custom-blended and personally designed for individual needs. Also, makeup lessons and depilatory waxing.

Cucchi Institut de Beaute, Suburban Square, Ardmore; 642-2772. Specializes in skin care analysis, facials, makeups, body waxing, and cellulite treatments.

Ilona, 411 E. Lancaster Ave., Wayne; 687-4444. Face and skin care offered in a relaxing, nurturing environment.

SPORTS EQUIPMENT

Eastern Mountain Sports, Suburban Square, Ardmore; 896-0627. Features cross-country and downhill skiing equipment, plus backpacking and climbing supplies.

Herman's World of Sporting Goods, the Plaza at King of Prussia; 265-8514. A chain of sporting goods shops that carries a large selection of name-brand sports clothing and equipment.

La Sportique, Radnor Racquet Club, 175 King of Prussia Rd., Radnor; 293-1407. Features a fine line of tennis clothing and equipment.

Pearson Sporting Goods, 1128 Chestnut St.; 923-1600. If you're into sports, you'll find everything you need here—even the trophy (if you win).

Philadelphia Sports Specialties, the Court at King of Prussia; 657-8848. High quality athletic footwear, clothing, and accessories.

Wilburger's Ski Shop, 1201 Old York Rd., Abington; 885-1480. Offers a wide range of skiing equipment for the novice and champion skier.

TOBACCO

Holt's Harry A. Tint & Sons, 16th and Sansom Sts.; 563-0763. Philadelphia's oldest and largest tobacco and cigar importer.

J. R. Cigars, 1399 Sansom St.; 546-3116. This location is the largest store in the chain. Its prices may well be the lowest in Philadelphia.

The Tinder Box, the Court at King of Prussia; 265-5673. Carries a large line of tobaccos and gifts.

TOYS

E.N. Lodge Toys, 1523 Chestnut St.; 563-8697. This selective shop offers a wide range of toys and games at reasonable prices for players of all ages.

Fireside Toys, 816 E. Evergreen Ave.; 248-3122. Specializes in doll houses and imported toys.

Kiddie City, seven locations throughout the Philadelphia area; 265-7850. Carries a large volume and variety of toys.

Past, Present, and Future Toys, 24 S. 18th St.; 854-0444. Sherry Tilman, owner of this charming shop, supplies hard-to-find toys and lets you touch while looking.

Toys R Us, many locations in Philadelphia area. Best discounts and selection.

Wayne Toy Town, 163 E. Lancaster Ave., Wayne; 688-2299. Imported dolls and toys, a large selection of miniatures, educational supplies, and creative toys. A favorite for Halloween costumes.

The Wooden Train, 8437 Germantown Ave., Chestnut Hill; 242-5600. This old-fashioned toy store features original and hard-to-find toys.

SPORTS

SPORTS TO SEE

Philadelphia can certainly lay legitimate claim to being "The City of Winners." It all began in May of 1974, when the Philadelphia Flyers of the National Hockey League won their first of two consecutive Stanley Cup championships, bringing two million people into the streets of the city for the largest parade in its history. Two years later, the Philadelphia Phillies won their first of three straight National League East baseball titles, which they crowned with their first World Series championship in 97 years in October of 1980.

Not to be outdone, the Philadelphia Eagles of the National Football League soared to the top of their division and, in January of 1981, flew to the Super Bowl in New Orleans, La. At the same time, the Philadelphia 76ers were reaching the finals of the National Basketball Association playoffs for a third season. In 1983, they won the NBA world championship.

While these professional teams were attracting sellout throngs, Philadelphia continued to be the site of major professional golf and tennis tournaments, as well as a host of amateur sports events—among them rowing, track, cricket, and rugby. Horse racing at Keystone Race Track, as well as auto racing in the Pocono Mountains, also flourished.

Auto Racing

Every summer, the world's finest stock-car drivers come to the Pocono International Raceway in nearby Long Pond, Pa., for the 500 Stock Car Race, followed shortly thereafter by the best Indy-car drivers for the annual Pocono 500. In mid-September, the same track is the site of The Race of Champions, featuring modified stock cars and their daredevil drivers.

Boxing

Philadelphia has produced some of the best prizefighters in the world, including former heavyweight champion Joe ("Smokin' Joe") Frazier. Though many major bouts are held in nearby Atlantic City, N.J., some occasionally unfold at the Spectrum where, along with the Civic Center, closed-circuit telecasts of most major championship fights can be seen. For tickets and information, call: 389-5000 (Spectrum) or 686-1776 (Civic Center).

College Basketball

The Big Five Conference presents some of the most competitive collegiate basketball to be found anywhere. Conference members Temple, Pennsylvania, LaSalle, Villanova, and St. Joseph's square off against each other and the nation's top basketball powers on their home courts, as well as at the festive Palestra. The annual Big Five Tournament is an event in itself. For tickets and information, call: 898-6151.

Cricket

On Saturday afternoons from April through September, this forerunner of what we know as baseball is played in West Fairmount Park and various other fields in the Philadelphia area. Admission is free. For schedules and information, call: 878-2552 (Prior Cricket Club) or 748-0707 (Commonwealth Cricket Club).

Golf

Just ask Jack Nicklaus—the Philadelphia area has some of the most beautiful and challenging golf courses in the world, and on occasion are the sites of major Professional Golf Association tournaments. (see SPECIAL EVENTS.)

Horse Racing

Thoroughbred racing is held at Philadelphia Park in Cornwells Heights from September through May, except on Thursdays. Admission includes parking. For information, call: 639-9000.

Horse Shows

Among the nation's most prestigious equestrian events is the Devon Horse Show and Country Fair, which is staged in suburban Devon in late May and early June. Earlier in May is the Grand Prix of horse jumping at the Military Academy in Valley Forge. In September comes the annual American Gold Cup Horse Show, also in Devon. (see SPECIAL EVENTS).

Major Leagues ────────────────────

The Philadelphia Eagles, National Football League. Exhibition games in August, regular-season games from September through December at Veterans Stadium. For tickets and information, call: 463-5500.

The Philadelphia Flyers, National Hockey League. Exhibition games in September and early October, regular-season games from October through April at the Spectrum. For tickets and information, call: 465-4500.

The Philadelphia Phillies, National Baseball League. Games from April through October at Veterans Stadium. For tickets and information, call: 463-5000.

The Philadelphia 76ers, National Basketball Association. Exhibition games in September and early October, regular-season games from October through April at the Spectrum. For tickets and information, call: 339-7676.

Rowing ──────────────────────────

This is a sport whose roots run deep in Philadelphia's history, offering a perfect excuse for a family outing complete with a picnic on the banks of the beautiful Schuylkill River. Among the top events are the annual Dad Vail Regatta in May (the largest intercollegiate regatta in the world) and the Independence Day Regatta on July 4. Admission is free; depending upon the event, however, plan to arrive early for a choice spot on the river bank. Check local newspapers for details, or call the Schuylkill Navy, 232-7689.

Tennis ──────────────────────────

One of the major stops on the professional tour is the annual U.S. Indoor Tennis Championships, held at the Spectrum in January and featuring the world's top male players. In the fall, the top female players are featured at the Spectrum in the U.S. National Indoor Women's Tennis Championships. In the summer, the Pennsylvania Lawn Tennis Championships take place at the Merion Cricket Club.

Track and Field ───────────────────

Some of the world's finest athletes compete each January in the Philadelphia Track Classic at the Spectrum. The last week of April features the Penn Relays, the oldest amateur track and field meet in the nation. (see SPECIAL EVENTS.)

Wrestling ────────────────────────

Among Philadelphia's most raucous crowds are those attending the occasional wrestling matches at the Spectrum and the Civic Center. For tickets and information, call: 389-5000 (Spectrum) or 686-1776 (Civic Center).

SPORTS TO DO

Many Philadelphians lead sporting lives, and visitors and new residents are encouraged to join in the fun. Whether it's rowing on the Schuylkill River, hiking through the Wissahickon Valley, hunting in French Creek State Park, rafting on Brandywine Creek, or playing a snappy match of tennis or round of golf, the Philadelphia area offers a myriad of sports to do.

Bicycling

Municipally-sponsored events start in the early spring and continue through mid-fall, and include the Bike Safety Rodeo, the Fairmount Park Invitational Bike Race, and the Philadelphia-to-Atlantic City Bike Ride. For information, call the Department of Recreation (686-3616) or the Fairmount Park Commission (686-1776).

In the city, Fairmount Park has 23 miles of bike paths, including East and West River Drives, in the Wissahickon Valley from Ridge Avenue to Rittenhouse Street, and Forbidden Drive. Bicycles can be rented from the Philadelphia Discount Bicycle Center, 826 N. Broad St.; 765-9118. The Philadelphia-Valley Forge Bikeway runs from Independence Hall to Valley Forge National Park.

Ridley Creek State Park has trails winding among old buildings and plantations, picnic areas, and even a stocked stream. Telephone: 566-4800 (no rentals available).

Tyler State Park features more than 10 miles of paved bike trails. However, the trails on the west side of Neshaminy Creek are very hilly, so be sure to dismount and walk when weary. Telephone: 968-2021 (no rentals available).

Valley Forge National Historical Park offers 2500 historic acres, including miles of bicycle paths. Motorized vehicles and skateboards are prohibited from the bike trails. For rental information, call: 783-7700.

Bocce

This traditional European staple of the Philadelphia sports scene combines elements of bowling, horseshoes, and croquet.

Circoio Boccista Marchigiano Club is one of the oldest clubs of this type in existence, and Pete Carpani is always around to reminisce about the game's legends. Located at 5030 Lancaster Ave. Telephone: 473-9673.

Overbrook Italian American Democratic Club is the largest in the city, with more than 5000 members. Located at 638 N. 66th St. Telephone: 471-9594.

Second Ward Bocce Club has won more league championships than any other in Philadelphia. Located at 606 Washington Ave. Telephone: 339-8784.

Bowling

Though universally known as bowling, this sport is called "tenpins" by many in Philadelphia, where bowling alleys (once called "pin palaces") abound.

Boulevard Lanes offers 48 lanes at 8011 Roosevelt Blvd. Telephone: 332-9200.

Del Ennis Lanes, operated by the former Phillies slugger, presents 36 lanes at 741 Huntingdon Pike. Telephone: 379-0880.

Golf

Philadelphia and its surrounding counties have more than 100 golf courses, including private, semi-private, and public facilities. Five of those offered in the city are municipally operated:

Cobbs Creek, 72nd St. and Landsdowne Ave.; 877-9746.

Franklin D. Roosevelt, 20th St. below Pattison Ave.; 467-2418.

J.F. Byrne, Frankford Ave. and Eden St.; 637-9935.

Juniata, "M" and Cayuga Sts.; 743-4060.

Walnut Lane, Walnut Lane and Henry Ave.; 482-4484.

Among the better county-operated courses outside the city are:

Montgomeryville Golf Club, Route 202 in Montgomeryville; 855-6112.

Paxon Hollow Golf Club, Paxon Hollow Rd. in Marple Township: 353-0220.

Valley Forge Golf Club, 401 North Gulf Rd., King of Prussia; 337-1776.

Health Clubs

Health clubs are popular in the Philadelphia area. We list our recommendations.

Clark's Uptown Racquet, Swim & Health Club presents a full range of health equipment and instruction. Included are a pool, saunas, and whirlpool. In the Franklin Plaza Hotel, 17th and Vine Sts. Telephone: 864-0616.

The Fitness Source features a large array of home exercise equipment, including Universal, Tunturi, and Tredex. Located at 537 Easton Rd., Horsham. Telephone: 441-4040.

Hershey Parlors, offering a complete health spa with exercise room, saunas, and whirlpool. In the Hershey Hotel, Broad St. at Locust; 893-1600.

Living Well Fitness Salon has more than 25 salons throughout the Philadelphia area. Telephone: 667-7504.

Paoli Health & Fitness offers professional, individual instruction. Located off Route 30 in Paoli, near the train station. Telephone: 296-0433.

Philadelphia Athletic Club, now coed, offers a fully-equipped gym, jogging track, and racquetball and handball courts. Also, Olympic-size swimming pool. Located at 200 N. Broad St. Telephone: 564-2002.

Topper's Salon and Health Spa features exercise machines, diet consultation, fitness evaluation, aerobic dancing, sauna, whirlpool, massage, and juice bar. In the Bourse Building, Independence Mall East. Telephone: 627-3545.

YMCA, with 17 branches throughout Philadelphia and its surrounding counties, offers a wide variety of recreation programs and facilities for men and women. Located at 1421 Arch St.; 557-0082.

Hiking

With the abundance of parks and open, rolling hills in the Philadelphia area, hiking is both popular and historically stimulating.

The **Batona Hiking Club** is your ticket if you like company, especially that of fellow hiking enthusiasts. These people spend their weekends hiking throughout Pennsylvania and New Jersey. Telephone: 352-1961.

Fort Washington State Park gives one a chance to hike and step back into history at the same time. Located on Militia Rd. off Bethlehem Pike, Whitemarsh. Telephone: 646-2942.

Horseshoe Trail is for the professional hiker. It features a 120-mile trail that starts at Routes 23 and 252 in Valley Forge State Park and, marked by yellow horseshoes along the way, courses west until it meets the Appalachian Trail, which covers 2000 miles from Maine to Georgia. If you're up to it, call the Horseshoe Trail Club at 664-0719 for further information.

Nature Center of Charleston winds through acres of ponds and fields. There's even a springhouse. Afterward, be sure to check out the exhibits, bookstore, and gift shop. On Route 29 at Hollow Rd. in Phoenixville. Telephone: 935-9777.

Peace Valley Park is not only a hiking trail but also a nature center of 1500 acres. There's also Lake Galena and a children's area. In Doylestown. Telephone: 345-7860.

The Tyler Arboretum has acres of plants, blossoms in season, and rare trees. Located at 515 Painter Rd., Lima. Telephone: 566-5431.

Schuylkill Valley Nature Center offers trails, including one for the handicapped. Also, educational and nature-hike programs. Located at 8480 Haggy's Mill Rd., Roxborough. Telephone: 482-7300.

Wissahickon Valley is a magnificent part of Fairmount Park, and has trails that were traveled by the Lenni Lenape Indians. Telephone: 686-3616.

Horseback Riding

The Philadelphia municipal area has 80 paths of riding trails in Fairmount Park, the Wissahickon, and Pennypack Park. In the surrounding counties, horseback riding ranks high on the popularity list because of the miles of hills, dales, and trails that meander through thick stands of trees. Much of the best areas are, of course, also historical.

In Philadelphia rentals are available at **Chat's Riding Stables,** 8089 Rowland Ave., 624-8118. Western riding only, through Pennypack Park. Cost is $7 per hour for guided trail rides.

Cobbs Creek Park Riding Stables, 63rd and Catherine Sts.; 747-2300. Rides, at $8 per hour, by appointment.

Valley Forge National Historical Park has miles of trails, including the famed 120-mile Horseshoe Trail. Rentals are available at **Great Valley Farm and Stables,** Berwyn; 296-7492. Non-guided tours weekdays from 9 am to dusk, $10 per hour; weekends, $12 per hour, $15 for 90 minutes, and $20 for two hours. English riding only.

More horseback riding in Chester County is available at four stables. They are:

Chelsea Hill Farm, Route 322 and Chichester Rd., Aston; 494-9884. Guided and non-guided trail rides seven days a week, 9 am–5 pm, for $8 per hour.

Gateway Stables, Merrybell Lane, Kennett Sq.; 444-9928. Guided trail tours for $8 per hour and lessons for $10 per hour. Mostly English riding, but some western. Reservations must be made the previous day.

Kimberton Riding Stables, Egypt and Longford Rds., Phoenixville; 933-9889. Guided and non-guided rides for $10 per hour, Mon 3 pm–dusk, Tue–Sun, 8:30 am–dusk, Western riding only.

Sheeder Mill Farm, Pughtown Rd., Spring City; 469-9382. Non-guided rides for $10 per hour, trail instruction is $7 per hour. Reservations required at least one hour in advance.

In Delaware County:

Ridley Creek State Park, two and one-half miles west of Newton Square on Route 3 offers more excellent trails. Rentals are available at **Keen Stables,** Media; 566-0942. Guided trail rides are $10.60 per hour, 10 am–6 pm daily. Reservations necessary.

Four more stables offer horseback riding in Bucks County. They are:

Merrymount Farms, 374 Worthington Mill Rd., Richboro; 968-0524. English riding only, $10 per hour, by appointment only.

Pony Riding Circle, Ridge Rd., Perkasie; 795-2504. Trail rides along Nockamixon Lake daily from 9 am–6:30 pm, at $5 per hour.

Sunnyfield Stables, Twining Bridge Rd., Newtown; 968-9925. Guided and non-guided rides daily from 9:30 am–6 pm at $8 per hour.

Tohickon Valley Park and **Ralph Stover Park** join at Tohickon Creek in Bucks County and feature a spectacular view at High Rocks Cliffs. Tohickon is one mile north of Point Pleasant on Cafferty Rd.; Stover, on Dark Hollow Rd. one mile east of Piperville. Telephone: 757-0571. Rentals are available from a number of stables in the area; please check Yellow Pages.

In Montgomery County, horseback riding is available at **Ashford Farms,** River Rd., Miquon; 825-9838. English saddles only, Tues–Sun 9 am–5 pm, at $10 per hour.

Hunting

Hunting is a major sport in Pennsylvania. So major, in fact, that hunters annually spend $315 million pursuing this sport throughout the state. No less than six state game lands are located near Philadelphia—four in Bucks County, one in Chester, and one in Berks.

Hunting seasons in Pennsylvania are (approximately):

Small game, October 29–November 26; Deer (archery), October 1–28; Buck, November 28–December 10; and Doe, December 12–13.

French Creek State Park has 5000 acres available for hunting and trapping through March 31 of the following year. Located seven miles northeast of the Pennsylvania Turnpike Interchange (Exit 22) on Route 345. Telephone: 582-1514.

Nockamixon State Park offers 3000 acres for hunting and trapping from the fall archery season through March 31 of the following year. Located five miles east of Quakertown on Route 313. Telephone: 847-2785.

For further information, call the Pennsylvania Game Commission in Philadelphia. The telephone number is 671-0440. Licenses required if over 17 ($8.25 per year for Pennsylvania resident; $60.50 annually for non-resident). They are available at the Municipal Services Building in Philadelphia and local sporting goods stores throughout the five counties.

Ice Skating

When it's cold enough in the winter, ice skaters flock to the creeks and ponds of the Philadelphia area. Otherwise, they're skating on the ice of numerous artificial rinks in and around the city. Four of them are operated by the Department of Recreation:

Rizzo Recreation Center, Washington Ave. at Interstate 95; 686-2925.

Scanlon Recreation Center, "J" and Tioga Sts.; 739-5515.

Simons Recreation Center, Walnut Lane and Woolston St.; 424-9857.

Tarken Recreation Center, Frontenac and Levick Sts.; 743-3266.

Other popular rinks in the city are:

Penn Center Ice Skating Rink, 17th and JFK Blvd; 564-4430.

University of Pennsylvania Class of '23 Rink, 3130 Walnut St.; 387-9223.

Among those outside the city are:

Old York Road Ice Skating Rink, Church and York Rds., Elkins Park; 635-0331.

Skatium, Darby and Manoa Rds., Havertown; 853-2225.

Wintersport Ice Skating Arena, 515 York Rd., Willow Grove; 659-4253.

Racquetball

As is true throughout the country, Philadelphians have found racquetball to be an excellent way to get fit and stay that way.

Center City Sports Club, 1818 Market St.; 963-0963.

Clark's Uptown, in the Franklin Plaza Hotel; 17th and Vine Sts.; 864-0616.

Club la Maison, 219 Sugartown Rd., Wayne; 964-8800.

Pier 30 Tennis-Racquet Ball Club, Delaware and Bainbridge Aves.; 985-1234.

Roller Skating

Carman Gardens Roller Skating Rink, 3226 Germantown Ave.; 223-2200.

Cornwells Roller Skating Center, 2350 Bristol Pike, Cornwells Heights; 638-7766.

Lancaster Roller Skating Rink, 4061 Lancaster Ave.; 387-8372.

Radnor Rolls, 789 Lancaster Ave., Villanova; 527-1230.

Valley Forge Sports Garden, Route 202 and Swedesford Rd., King of Prussia; 296-8131.

Running

Among other jogging activities, Philadelphia is the annual site of two of the most formidable events of their kind in the nation. One is the **Broad Street Run** every May; the other, the **Greater Independence Marathon** on the last Sunday of November. If you want to practice for these events or just get in shape, **Fairmount Park** has a half-dozen trails complete with distance markers. There's also a Perrier Parcourse Fitness Circuit along Forbidden Drive in Fairmount Park, with 18 exercise stations along the course.

Valley Forge National Historical Park is also a superior area (2500 historical acres) to jog. Telephone: 783-7700.

Tennis

Fairmount Park operates more than 100 all-weather tennis courts, as well as offering free instruction for children. The park also sponsors the Fairmount Fall Festival Championship, an annual amateur event. Another 150 courts, operated by the Department of Recreation, are scattered throughout the city. Telephone: 686-1776.

Among the popular indoor courts in Philadelphia are:

Pier 30 Tennis Club, Pier 30 of Penn's Landing near Delaware Ave. and Bainbridge St. Telephone: 985-1234.

Robert P. Levy Tennis Pavilion, 3130 Walnut St. Telephone: 898-4741.

Among the popular indoor courts in surrounding counties are:

Downingtown Inn Sports Palace and Spa, Route 30, Downingtown. Telephone: 269-2000.

High Point Racquet Club, Upper State and County Line Rds., Chalfont. Telephone: 822-1951.

Pickering Racquet Club, Pickering Creek Industrial Park, off Route 100, Lionville. Telephone: 363-1052.

Radnor Racquet Club, 175 King of Prussia Rd., Radnor. Telephone: 293-1407.

Valley Forge Sports Garden, Swedesford Rd. and Route 202, Berwyn. Telephone: 296-8131.

Water Sports

Fishing

Rivers, streams, creeks, and the lakes in the Philadelphia area are fished primarily for trout, though many other species can be hooked, too. Licenses are required if over 16 ($12.25 for Pennsylvania residents; $20.25 for out-of-staters, and $2.25 for senior citizens). These are available at the Municipal Services Building in Philadelphia and sporting goods stores throughout the five counties. For specific information about fishing in Pennsylvania, consult the summary book that accompanies your license.

French Creek State Park, (582-1514) with Scott Lake and Hopewell Lake, features warm-water species, including pike, chain pickerel, tiger muskie, perch, bass, blue gill, catfish, and of course, trout.

Hibernia Park (384-0290) features Brandywine Creek, which is stocked with three kinds of trout, and also has a small pond where children can fish for its stocked trout.

Newlin Mill Park (459-2359) is bordered on the west by Chester Creek, which also has the three species of trout, a few palominos, small— and large-mouth bass, and carp.

Nockamixon State Park (847-2785) is fed by three creeks (Tohickon, Maycock, and Three-Mile Run), which are filled with muskie, walleye, small-and large-mouth bass, yellow perch, and channel cat fish. Some say this is absolutely the best fishing in the area.

Ridley Creek State Park (566-4800) and its namesake, Ridley Creek, are also known for trout.

The Schuylkill River, which features rainbow, brook, and brown trout, as well as muskie, can be fished from Manayunk to Fairmount Park; five miles of the Wissahickon from Germantown Pike to the Walnut Lane Bridge, and Pennypack Creek from State to Pine Rd. F.D. Roosevelt Lake is located at 20th St. and Pattison Ave.

Valley Forge National Park (783-7700) is bordered on the west by Valley Creek and on the north by the Schuylkill, both of which have rainbow, brook, brown trout, and muskie.

Rafting

Point Pleasant, Route 32, seven miles north of New Hope/Yardley exit on Interstate 95, Point Pleasant. Rentals available. Telephone: 297-8400.

Rowing and Sailing

The Philadelphia area is replete with water sports, and with the Schuylkill River winding through the heart of the city, rowing is at the top of its list. (Those stately boat houses of Boat House Row are sufficient testimony to that.) If you're broad of back and would like further information about participating, call **The Schuylkill Navy** at 232-7689.

If you'd rather canoe or sail the placid Schuylkill, the **East Park Canoe House** has rowboats, canoes, and sailboats available for rent by the hour from spring through fall. It's located on East River Dr., south of the Strawberry Mansion Bridge. Telephone: 225-3560.

Among the popular canoeing and sailing sites outside the city where rentals are also available, are:

Brandywine Creek, where canoeing is offered by the Northbrook Canoe Co., Northbrook Rd., north of Route 842 in Northbrook. These people are *very* popular, however, and reservations are a must. Telephone: 793-2279.

French Creek State Park, about seven miles northeast of the Pennsylvania Turnpike's Morgantown interchange (Exit 22). Telephone: 582-1514.

Marsh Creek, west of the town of Eagle on Route 100 in Downingtown. Telephone: 458-8515.

Point Pleasant, Route 32, seven miles north of the New Hope/Yardley exit on Interstate 95, Point Pleasant; 297-8400. This is one of the largest and finest river recreation facilities in the East with five locations offering canoeing, inner-tubing, and whitewater and quiet rafting on the scenic Delaware River.

Swimming

Philadelphia has 86 municipal swimming pools, more than any other city in the country. **Fairmount Park** offers five outdoor pools and one indoor pool, all fully-staffed with lifeguards. Locker rooms are available, and admission is free. The indoor pool is located in Memorial Hall, 42nd St. and Parkside Ave. in West Fairmount Park, and is open from October through May. Telephone: 686-1776.

Many hotels, motels, and private clubs in and around the city have swimming facilities, and the four counties surrounding Philadelphia offer them as well. Among the most popular outdoor sites outside the city are:

French Creek State Park, about seven miles northeast of the Pennsylvania Turnpike's Morgantown interchange (Exit 22). Telephone: 582-1514.

Sailing on the Schuylkill River in Downtown Philadelphia

City of Philadelphia

Marsh Creek State Park, west of the town of Eagle on Route 100 in Downingtown. Telephone: 458-8515.

Tohickon Valley, one mile north of Point Pleasant on Cafferty Rd. Telephone: 757-0571.

Skiing

The Philadelphia area offers a number of slopes from which to choose, all within easy driving. For really superb skiing, try going a little further to the Pocono Mountains. (see RESORTS).

Chadds Peak, four miles west of Route 202 on Route 1, Chadds Ford. Telephone: 388-6476 or 388-7421.

Spring Mountain, off Route 19 and 73 near Schwenksville. Telephone: 287-7900.

Among the better skiing areas within 75 miles are:

Doe Mountain, 15 miles southwest of Allentown off Routes 29 and 100. Telephone: 682-7109.

Hahn Mountain, off Route 22 at Lenhartsville. Telephone: 756-6351.

Little Gap, five miles east of Palmerton, 30 miles north of Allentown. Telephone: 826-7700.

Mount Heidelberg, one-half mile south of Bernville on Route 183. Telephone: 488-1035.

Cross-country Skiing

French Creek State Park, seven miles northeast of the Pennsylvania Turnpike's Exit 22 on Route 345. Telephone: 582-1514.

Ridley Creek State Park, two and one-half miles west of Newton Square on Route 3. Telephone: 566-4800.

Valley Forge National Historical Park, Valley Forge. Telephone: 783-7700.

SPECIAL EVENTS

Through the years, Philadelphia has developed a host of events to satisfy every whim. Indeed, there is so much going on in and around Philadelphia that something—be it a fair, tour, festival, concert, or sporting event—is unfolding every day of the year.

Nevertheless, there are some annual events that have become synonymous with the seasons in which they occur; unique experiences that, in view of the crowds they attract year after year, clearly have a hold on Philadelphians and their friends.

This is the nature of the events we have listed below. Some are traditional, some are cultural; some are inspirational, while others are educational and informative; still others are held strictly for the sheer fun and joy that they produce. Regardless of their purpose, however, these are the kinds of events that are sure to appeal to visitors as much as they do to Philadelphians themselves.

Please be aware that although these events are held in the same season of every year, the month in which they take place may vary slightly.

January

Benjamin Franklin's Birthday, Poor Richard's Club, 251 S. 18th St.; 466-4109. The day begins with a continental breakfast at a different place every year. Following it is a pilgrimage through the historic sites commemorating Franklin, such as the Franklin Institute, Franklin Court, and the place of his burial. This culminates with a luncheon at which the Benjamin Franklin medal is presented. *CH.*

The city also holds free special events and activities.

Chinese New Year, Chinese Cultural Center, 125 N. 10th St.; 923-6767. The celebration begins with a 10-course banquet at the Cultural Center, and continues for two months. *CH.* Reservations required.

Mummers Parade, Broad Street past the judging stand at City Hall. This world famous New Year's Day parade, known as Philadelphia's Mardi Gras, features 25,000 costumed Mummers, including string bands, fancies, and comics performing the traditional "Mummers Strut" before adoring crowds of more than 400,000 people.

New Year's Day Mummers Parade

Philadelphia Convention & Visitors Bureau

Philadelphia Sport, Camping, Vacation and Travel Show, Civic Center, 34th St. and Civic Center Blvd.; 823-7350. In anticipation of summer, the Civic Center comes alive with warm-weather displays, exhibits, and entertainment. *CH.*

Philadelphia Track Classic, the Spectrum, Broad St. and Pattison Ave.; 686-3616 and 389-5000. This event attracts the nation's top track stars to Philadelphia every January. *CH.*

U.S. Indoor Pro Tennis Tournament, the Spectrum, Broad St. and Pattison Ave.; 947-2530 or 389-5000. This tournament brings the best players from the men's professional tour to the Spectrum for one of the circuit's outstanding events. *CH.*

February

Black History Month, Afro-American Historical and Cultural Museum, 7th and Arch Sts.; 574-0380. In commemoration of black American contributions to the nation's history, the museum hosts numerous free lectures, exhibitions, and musical presentations. Philadelphia churches, museums, colleges, schools, community centers, libraries, and theaters also offer unusual and entertaining opportunities to learn about black culture.

Ice Capades, the Spectrum, Broad St. and Pattison Ave.; 389-5000. Spectators of all ages are thrilled by these lavish shows on ice. *CH.*

Mummers String Band Show of Shows, Civic Center, 34th St. and Civic Center Blvd.; 823-7280 and 568-1976. Extravagantly costumed bands perform, drill, and strut before large crowds at the Civic Center. *CH.*

Philadelphia Boat Show, Civic Center, 34th St. and Civic Center Blvd.; 823-7350. An annual display that features more than 400 yachts, sailboats, and power boats. Also sophisticated marine gear and even boat homes. *CH.*

Washington's Birthday Weekend, Valley Forge National Park, Route 202, King of Prussia; 278-3558. Special events include an actual reenactment of the Continental Army's hard winter here more than two centuries ago.

March

The Book and the Cook, various Philadelphia-area locations; 636-1666. A restaurant and cookbook event, you have the opportunity to wine and dine at fine restaurants in the company of major food and wine book authors. *CH varies.*

Philadelphia Flower and Garden Show, Civic Center, 34th St. and Civic Center Blvd.; 625-8250. This, the largest and most varied flower show in the nation, covers more than four acres of the Civic Center with flowers, landscapes, nurseries, garden clubs, and competitive exhibits. It includes more than 170 major exhibits and at least as many minor ones. Sponsored by the Pennsylvania Horticultural Society. *CH.*

St. Patrick's Day Parade, numerous locations throughout the Philadelphia area. The city and its environs celebrate this traditionally festive day with bands, banners, and lots of green beer.

April

Easter Promenade. This stroll down Walnut Street features music, entertainment, and celebrity guests, and is highlighted by the fashion contest at Rittenhouse Square.

Ethnic Folklife Festival, International House, 3701 Chestnut St.; 387-5125. The folklife traditions of Philadelphia's myriad ethnic groups are featured in music, food, crafts, and dancing. *CH nominal.*

Historic Yellow Springs Art Show, Route 113, Chester Springs; 827-7911. This historic Inn is the site of fine art by local and national artists. *CH.*

National Dance Week, 546-7240. The Philadelphia Dance Alliance sponsors a series of programs throughout the city oriented to the local dance scene.

Penn Relays, Franklin Field, 33rd St. near South St. World's oldest and largest track meet. Bill Cosby used a scene from the relays in one of his shows. *CH.*

Pennsylvania Crafts Fair Day, Brandywine River Museum, Route 1, Chadds Ford; 388-8601. Crafts from area-wide artists are on display in the courtyard of the museum.

University Hospital Antique Show, 33rd St. Armory; 687-6441 or (week of show) 387-3500. Reputed to be the finest antique show in the nation, this event features guided tours, lectures, and gourmet luncheons— all for the benefit of the Hospital of the University of Pennsylvania. *CH.*

Valborgsmassoafton, American Swedish Historical Museum, 1900 Pattison Ave.; 389-1776. The Swedish tradition of welcoming the arrival of spring features food, fun, dancing, and a bonfire at night. *CH Nominal.*

May

Architect's Week, AIA Gallery, 17th and Sansom Sts.; 569-3186. Lectures and tours sponsored by Philadelphia's finest architects culminate in civic, environmental, and designer awards. *CH.*

Brandywine Battlefield, Route 1, Chadds Ford; 459-3342. An authentic reenactment of the historic 18th-century battle is staged every May.

Devon Horse Show, Devon Fairgrounds, Route 30, Devon; 964-0550. The nation's finest riders compete for more than $80,000 in prize money in one of America's most prestigious horse shows. Up to 150,000 turn out to enjoy the country fair atmosphere of this week-long event, begun in 1896. *CH.*

Jambalaya Jam, The Great Plaza at Penn's Landing. A weekend event packed with all the excitement of New Orleans, including Creole and Cajun cooking and jazz. Check newspapers for specific events. *CH varies.*

Mozart on the Square (see PERFORMING ARTS Summer Concerts).

The Old City Street Festival and Block Party, Society Hill. Each May, dozens of Center City riverfront-area restaurants participate in this old-fashioned block party with lots of food, drink, and fun.

Philadelphia Open House, various locations. One of many events sponsored by the 1600 Friends of Independence National Historic Park, this series of walking and bus tours gives people a chance to enjoy private homes, gardens, and historic buildings usually closed to the public. Homes included are in Society Hill, Rittenhouse Square, Independence National Historic Park, Chestnut Hill, Germantown, and on the Main Line. *CH.*

Rittenhouse Square Flower Market, Rittenhouse Square. This annual event attracts large crowds buying flowers, plants, and all kinds of food. Contributions go to children's charities.

June

Corestates Pro Cycling Championship, start/finish line on Benjamin Franklin Parkway, near the Philadelphia Museum of Art. Top cyclists compete for prize money in the nation's only professional race. Course is 156 miles long.

Elfreth's Alley Fete Days, Elfreth's Alley; 574-0560. Private homes on this, the longest continuously-occupied street in America, are opened to the public on the first weekend in June. *CH.*

Flag Day, Betsy Ross House, 239 Arch St.; 627-5343. Special activities in honor of the red, white, and blue include music, arts, and crafts—and (while they last) cookies.

Great Teddy Bear Rally, Philadelphia Zoo, 34th St. and Girard Ave. Cuddly teddy bears and their owners participate in parades, talent shows and hilarious contests. A free clinic for ailing teddy bears is also available. *CH.*

Head House Crafts Fair, Head House Square, 2nd and Pine Sts. Some 50 craftsmen demonstrate their skills and display their wares on the square every Saturday and Sunday through August.

Mann Music Center, 52nd St. and Parkside Ave., 567-0707. The Philadelphia Orchestra and guest stars perform in the pastoral setting of Fairmount Park. Free tickets available on the day of each show at the Visitors Center, 16th St. and John F. Kennedy Blvd. Through July. *CH/NCH.*

Mellon Jazz Festival (see PERFORMING ARTS Summer Concerts).

Ringling Brothers Barnum & Bailey Circus, the Spectrum, Broad and Pattison Sts.; 389-5000. The "Greatest Show on Earth" wows young and old alike. *CH.*

Rittenhouse Square Clothesline Exhibit, Rittenhouse Square; 423-7254. This is the oldest outdoor exhibit of fine art in the country, and it unfolds every June with more than 20,000 works in oil, watercolor, and acrylic. Prints, graphics, silk-screens, and etchings also are on display—and for sale.

Swedish Summer Festival, American Swedish Historical Museum, 1900 Pattison Ave.; 389-1776. This "Midsommar" holiday includes folk music, food, children's games, and dancing. *CH Nominal.*

Yellow Springs State Craft Festival, Route 113, Chester Springs; 827-7911. Select craft dealers from throughout the state have been chosen to display the finest of their work here. *CH.*

July

Independence Day Regatta, on the Schuylkill in Fairmount Park; 769-2068. In an area in which rowing is among the most traditional sports, this is one of the highlights of the season. Thousands line the banks of the river with picnic blankets, tents, tables of food, and coolers while enjoying the races.

Philadelphia Freedom Festival, various locations. The city's July 4 celebration is one of the biggest, brightest and noisiest to be found anywhere—

and understandably so. Special events leading up to and including Independence Day include parades, fireworks, a Mummers' strut, concerts, an official ceremony at Independence Hall, a hot-air balloon race, and an Old City restaurant festival.

Port Indian Regatta, Schuylkill River, two miles west of Norristown. The fastest boats on the East Coast show up for these races. There's also water skiing demonstrations and water skiing kite fliers. Check newspapers. CH *(parking)*.

Robin Hood Dell East, East Fairmount Park; 567-0707. Top stars from the popular entertainment world of music and dance featured in a series of low-cost summertime concerts. Through August. CH.

August

Philadelphia Folk Festival (see PERFORMING ARTS Summer Concerts).

September

American Gold Cup, Devon Fairgrounds, Route 30, Devon; 438-8383. Outstanding horse-jumping for prize money at the Fairgrounds. CH.

Fairmount Park Fall Festival, Fairmount Park and on the Benjamin Franklin Parkway; 568-6599. Activities and special events—some free—are held to welcome the arrival of fall. Also, the Harvest Show, featuring beautiful displays of fall flowers in Memorial Hall. Call for free brochure.

International In-Water Boat Show, Penn's Landing, Delaware and Spruce Sts.; 449-9910. Yachts and boats of all kinds sail to the landing for five days of display and fun. CH.

Labor Day Weekend Festival, Front St. to 3rd St. and Walnut St. to Market St.; 925-6999. Old City restaurants and taverns join in festivities highlighted by bands, dancing, even a flea market.

Von Steuben Day Parade, Benjamin Franklin Parkway from 20th St. to Independence Hall. A colorful tribute to the German general who trained the soldiers of the Continental Army at Valley Forge.

October

Battle of Germantown, 6401 Germantown Ave., Cliveden; 848-1777. A reenactment of the battle in which the Continental Army suffered its devastating defeat. NCH.

Chadds Ford Days, Route 100, Chadds Ford; 388-7376. Country rides and knee-slapping music are just part of the fun. There's also artisans in colonial garb at workbenches and selling their wares, and the traditional Art Show hosted by well-known Brandywine Valley artists. The Country Antiques Fair is highlighted by more than 20 notable dealers. CH *(parking)*.

Chester County Day, various sites in Chester County; 431-6365. Tours highlighting the historic homes and locations of Chester County. CH.

Columbus Day Parade, Broad St. to Marconi Plaza. In commemoration of the famous explorer's birthday, with official ceremonies at the Plaza.

Museum Showcase, various locations; 627-1770. Sponsored by the Women of Greater Philadelphia, these two weeks of special exhibits and programs—some free—bring the spotlight to more than 120 museums in the city and its environs.

Pulaski Day Parade, up Broad St. Presented each year by the Polish American Congress, this parade is highlighted by ethnic bands and costumes and commemorates the contributions of General Casimir Pulaski during the Revolutionary War.

Radnor Hunt Three-Day Event, Radnor Hunt Club, Providence Rd., Malvern; 644-5107. This annual event for the benefit of Paoli Memorial Hospital presents competition in a wide range of equestrian divisions that include dressage, cross country, road and track, and steeplechase. Their country fair features specialty foods, crafts, antiques, jewelry, and clothing. CH.

Scandinavian Festival, American Swedish Historical Museum, 1900 Pattison Ave.; 389-1776. Swedish, Danish, Finnish, and Norwegian traditions are celebrated with three days of exhibits, singing, dancing, and such culinary delights as Icelandic pancakes and sailor's storm soup. CH *Nominal.*

Super Sunday, Benjamin Franklin Parkway. This huge block party, started in 1970, provides a great opportunity for friends and families to enjoy exhibits, games, rides, and a wide variety of foods. From noon to 6 pm on the second Sunday of October.

November

Giant Tinkertoy Extravaganza, Franklin Institute, 20th St. and Benjamin Franklin Parkway. Kids and the young-at-heart let their imaginations run wild, creating the most extraordinary configurations from giant Tinkertoys.

Greater Philadelphia Independence Marathon, this 26.2 mile race, Philadelphia's reply to those in Boston and New York, starts in Fort Washington. By the time it concludes at Independence Hall, participants, including some of the finest runners in the world, have covered a course that truly captures the breadth and character of Philadelphia.

Philadelphia Craft Show, Memorial Hall, Fairmount Park; 787-5431. Some of the finest artists and artisans in the country present outstanding works in glass, ceramics, fiber, wood, jewelry, quilts, clothing, weaving, and mixed media. CH.

Thanksgiving Day Parade, up Broad St. Started in 1919 and sponsored by Gimbel's, this is the second-largest parade of its kind in the nation and features more than 5000 participants that include national and local celebrities. You'll enjoy floats, bands, clowns, balloons, the Philly Phanatic— and even Santa Claus.

December

Army-Navy Football Classic, Veterans Stadium, Broad St. and Pattison Ave. The most colorful gridiron game of all.

Christmas at Brandywine Museum, Brandywine River Museum, Route 1, Chadds Ford; 459-1900. Lavish Christmas exhibits include model trains, antique porcelain dolls, and courtyard shops in winter dress. CH.

Christmas Tours of Historic Houses, Fairmount Park; sponsored by the Philadelphia Museum of Art, 787-5431. Also, the houses of historic Germantown; sponsored by the Germantown Historical Society, 848-1777. The historic houses of Fairmount Park and Germantown come alive with lights and authentic 18th-century Christmas decorations. CH.

Disney World on Ice, the Spectrum, Broad St. and Pattison Ave.; 389-5000. The world famous characters of Walt Disney make their annual appearance at the Spectrum. CH.

Kennel Club of Philadelphia Dog Show, Civic Center, 34th St. and Civic Center Blvd.; 387-8333. This is a glimpse back at what dog shows used to be, featuring some of the finest canine specimens in America. CH.

Longwood Gardens, Route 1, Kennett Square; 388-6741. This spectacular display of poinsettias (four acres of them in heated indoor gardens) and Christmas trees is a must. So, too, is the sparkling Christmas Tree Lane (from 5–9 pm). There are also more than 100 organ and choral concerts in the conservatory. CH.

Lucia Fest & Julmarknad, American Swedish Historical Museum, 1900 Pattison Ave.; 389-1776. Swedish Christmas traditions come alive in music, pageantry, and foods of the season. *CH.*

"The Nutcracker," Academy of Music, Broad and Locust Sts.; 893-1935. The Pennsylvania Ballet delights young and old alike with this traditional presentation every Christmas season. *CH.*

Washington Crosses the Delaware, Washington Crossing Historic Park; 493-4076. An authentic reenactment of Washington leading his troops across the Delaware River on Christmas Day, 1776, before surprising the British at Trenton.

SELF-GUIDED CITY TOURS

Included in this chapter are three tours that will enable you to discover Philadelphia on your own. The first tour covers the downtown area of the city from Independence National Historic Park through many exciting areas and concluding at the Powel House. It is a walking tour, the best way to explore this section of Philadelphia. The remaining two tours are driving tours. One travels a scenic route through Valley Forge and Brandywine Valley. The other is a Metro tour beginning at Fairmount Park and following an exciting course that ends at Philadelphia's famous waterfront area.

For all tours, a companion to read directions or to walk with will almost certainly increase your enjoyment and fun. We recommend that you take your time and set your own pace. Philadelphia has too much to see and do to rush through its marvelous attractions!

DOWNTOWN WALKING TOUR

Philadelphia has an unmistakable reverence for the old, the traditional, and the historic. To fully grasp this appreciation, certain areas of Philadelphia must be explored on foot, and you find that to do so is a joy.

Our downtown walking tour is keyed to Independence National Historic Park— "America's most historic square mile"—and the bordering areas of Old City and Society Hill. Since there is so much to see, we suggest you tailor this tour to the time you can afford. At a brisk pace, stopping at only a few sites along the way, you can make it in one day. But should you wish to spend time at the points of interest and pause for lunch, we strongly recommend you divide the tour into two days. In the first section, explore Independence National Historic Park and Old City, which will require between four and five hours, depending upon the lines outside Independence Hall. In the second section, enjoy Society Hill, for a three to four hour tour.

Independence National Historic Park ———

Begin at the Visitors Center, Independence National Historic Park, 3rd and Chestnut Streets. If you have driven into the area, you'll

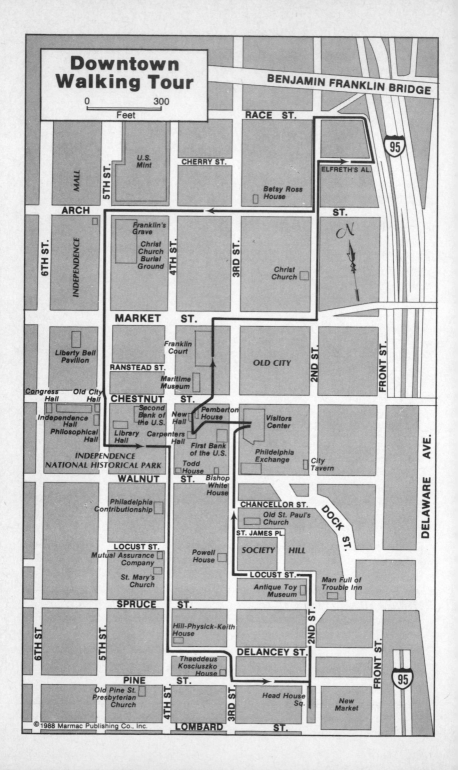

find convenient parking in the underground garage at 2nd and Sansom Streets. The brick walkway between the garage and the Visitors' Center is a nice convenience.

At the Visitors' Center

In the center you'll find exhibits and information about regular events and special activities of the day. Here you sign up for the free guided tours of the *Bishop White House* and the *Todd House*, which are open by guided tour only. At *Independence Hall*, tours are on a first-come, first-served basis.

Most park buildings are open daily from 9 am–5 pm, and the hours of some are extended during the summer. The hours are subject to change, so check at the Visitors' Center for the latest information.

At the Center we strongly recommend *A Promise of Permanency*, an interactive computer exhibit dealing with a variety of constitutional issues. To properly set the mood for the tour, take in the 20-minute film, "Independence," directed by the famed John Huston.

From the front entrance of the Visitors' Center, cross 3rd Street. To your left is the *First Bank of the United States*, which is probably the nation's oldest bank (built between 1795 and 1797). The building, though not open to the public, is an outstanding example of neoclassical architecture.

Carpenters' Hall

Also, on your left, facing the First Bank is *Carpenters' Hall*, where delegates gathered to air their grievances against King George III during the First Continental Congress in September of 1774. The following spring, the Second Continental Congress met in the State House, now Independence Hall. Carpenters' Hall later served as a hospital and an arsenal for American forces during the Revolutionary War.

To the right of Carpenters' Hall is *New Hall*, which served as the Office of the War Department in 1791 and 1792. It is now a museum of United States Marine Crops history.

Upon leaving New Hall, you will see *Pemberton House*, a replica of the 18th-century home of Joseph Pemberton, a wealthy Quaker merchant. It is now a museum depicting the development of the United States Army and Navy from 1775 to 1800.

Cross Chestnut Street; to the left on the corner with Orianna is the *Maritime Museum*, which depicts the history of Philadelphia as a port city. The United States Navy was founded here.

On to Franklin Court

Now follow the sign to Franklin Court, which is located on Market Street between 3rd and 4th Streets. The ramp will take you to the underground museum, a tribute to the genius and inventiveness of one of Philadelphia's most famous citizens, Benjamin Franklin. In addition to an original music stand and stove, which were among his many inventions, enjoy the multimedia salute to Franklin's wit and diplomatic accomplishments. A bank of telephones will "connect" you with many of his contemporaries, providing a verbal portrait of Franklin the man. There is a marionette theater extolling his success and a film, "Portrait of a Family," depicting the life of Franklin and his family.

Leave the movie theater and enter the Franklin courtyard, where the only house he ever owned once stood. Built between 1763 and 1765, it was 34 feet square and three stories high, with the kitchen in the cellar. It was, he once said, "a good House contrived to my Mind."

Also in the courtyard are three of the five Market Street buildings Franklin designed. They are the *Franklin Tenant House,* which contains artifacts from the site of his home; the *Aurora Print Shop,* which was once operated by his grandson; and the *Postal Museum,* now an 18th-century United States Post Office where every piece of mail is cancelled with the signature, "B. Free Franklin." As postmaster of the new nation, Franklin used "Free" as his middle name because the country had freed itself of English rule.

Now turn right on Market Street, then left on 2nd Street to *Christ Church.* Built in 1727, the church was attended by 15 signers of the Declaration of Independence, including Benjamin Franklin and George Washington.

Elfreth's Alley ——————————————————————

Continue north on 2nd Street, cross Arch Street to Elfreth's Alley. Turn right on the Alley. Dating back to 1690, this is the oldest, continuously-occupied street in the nation. Thirty homes which line the alley were built in the 1720s and 1730s. Numbers 120 and 122 are the oldest, built between 1724 and 1728; they are private homes and open to the public only on the first Saturday in June.

You may tour Number 126, however. Built around 1750, it is named "The Mantua Maker's House" because it was the home for two mantua makers, or dressmakers, between 1762 and 1794. The period furnishings and original woodwork on the interior are more than two centuries old. The best time to visit Elfreth's Alley is the first weekend in June, when "Fete Days," a tradition since 1935, bring a host of colonial demonstrations to the street.

The Alley ends at Front Street. Turn left (north) on Front Street and walk one block to Quarry Street, turn left, and, on your right, you'll see an authentic 1876 fire house that now houses the *Fire Museum.*

Return to Arch Street ——————————————————

From there, turn left (south) on 2nd Street, return to Arch Street, and turn right (west) on Arch Street. Mid-block on your right at 234

Arch Street is the *Betsy Ross House*, where legend has it, the seamstress stitched the first American flag at the personal request of George Washington. This is an outstanding example of the 18th-century Philadelphia home.

Continue on Arch Street across 3rd Street to *Loxley Court*, which was owned by the Loxley family from the 1740s to 1901. This is a quaint courtyard that's worth a peek through the iron fence; some of these row houses were built between 1775 and 1827.

Continue on Arch Street to Franklin Statue, a bust 16 feet high and covered with 80,000 pennies symbolizing his slogan, "A penny saved is a penny earned." Across the street is the *Arch Street Friend's Meeting House,* built on land that William Penn gave to the Quakers in 1693.

In the next block, on the north side of the street, at 5th Street and Arch, is the largest of the nation's three *United States Mints*. An audio-visual tour explaining the manufacture of coins takes about 45 minutes.

Also the *Christ Church* burial ground is at **the corner of Arch and 5th Streets.** Through an opening in the brick wall, view the plain gravestones of Deborah and Benjamin Franklin. It's an old custom to toss a penny on the gravestones for good luck.

On the southwest side of Arch and 5th is the *Free Quaker Meeting House*, built in 1783 by the Quakers who supported the Revolution.

The Liberty Bell

Turn left on 5th Street, cross Market Street, and continue to the Liberty Bell Pavilion. The Liberty Bell, the symbol of American freedom, was ordered in 1751 to commemorate the anniversary of William Penn's Charter of Privileges for the State of Pennsylvania. The bell, which was cast in London, cracked while being tested. It was subsequently recast and in 1776 fulfilled the Old Testament prophecy with which it is inscribed, "Proclaim liberty throughout the land, unto all the inhabitants thereof."

Although nobody is certain when the bell cracked next, it occurred according to legend during the funeral of Chief Justice William Marshall in 1835. The last time the bell rang formally was on Washington's birthday in 1846.

When you leave the *Liberty Bell Pavilion*, **take the tree-lined sidewalk to the left, cross Chestnut Street, and go directly to the East Wing of Independence Hall,** where free guided tours of the Hall originate. The Hall is open by tour only, and all tours are conducted on a first-come, first-served basis.

While you're waiting for your tour, you may want to visit the old *City Hall* to the left at 5th and Chestnut Streets. This structure was built in 1790 as the home of Philadelphia's government, but used by the United States Supreme Court until 1800. On the right side of Independence Hall is *Congress Hall*, site of the inaugurations of Washington (his second) and John Adams.

Independence Hall ────────────────────────

Independence Hall was constructed between 1732 and 1756 as the State House of the Province of Pennsylvania, and from 1775 to 1783 (except for the time of the British occupation) was the meeting place for the Second Continental Congress. The Assembly Room was the site of five major events— the appointment of Washington as Commander in Chief of the Continental Army in 1775; the adoption of the Declaration of Independence on July 4, 1776; agreement on the design of the American flag in 1777; the adoption of the Articles of Confederation in 1781; and the writing of the Constitution in 1787.

Since most of the original furniture was destroyed during the British occupation, most of what you see are period pieces. However, the silver inkstand on the President's desk in the Assembly Room is the one used during the signing of both the Declaration and the Constitution, and the "rising sun" chair is the original used by Washington during the Constitutional Convention

Upon leaving Independence Hall, *Philosophical Hall* will be to your left. This is the only privately-owned building on Independence Square, the home of the American Philosophical Society, which was founded by Franklin in 1743. The building is not open to the public.

Pause for a Rest ────────────────────────

It might be a good idea here to pause for a rest on one of the benches in Independence Square, where the first public reading of the Declaration of Independence took place on July 8, 1776. Notice the reproductions of 18th-century street lamps; there are 56 of them, one for each signer of the Declaration of Independence.

On to Chestnut Street ──────────────────

Cross 5th Street from the square at Philosophical Hall. Facing this building is *Liberty Hall*, built in 1789-90, the oldest subscription library in the United States.

Behind the Hall is the *Second Bank of the United States*, built between 1819 and 1824 and one of the finest examples of Greek Revival architecture in America. Today it contains an extensive collection of paintings of colonial and federal leaders (most by Charles Wilson Peale) called "Faces of Independence." **Enter by Chestnut Street.**

Continue down Chestnut Street to 4th Street. Turn right on 4th Street. On the corner of 4th and Walnut Street on the left is *Todd House*, which was occupied from 1791 to 1793 by lawyer John Todd, Jr. and his wife, Dolley Payne. After her husband died during the 1793 epidemic of yellow fever, Dolley married James Madison, who later became the nation's fourth President. They subsequently moved to the Madison estate in Virginia, but the home still reflects the lifestyle of the 18th-century middle class in Philadelphia.

After leaving the Todd House, take a peek at the garden next door. Many of the plants, trees, shrubs, and flowers found here grew in the same spot before the 18th century. Next door you will come to the *Pennsylvania Horticultural Society.* The lobby features ever-changing exhibits, and in its library you will find 13,000 volumes and 200 periodicals with a full collection of seed catalogues. The Society, the oldest of its kind, sponsors the world's largest and most elaborate flower show every year at the Civic Center.

Continue walking east on Walnut Street to The Bishop White House. This lovely row house was built by the Reverend William White in 1787. He was the first Episcopal Bishop of Philadelphia and chose this location because it was midway between Christ Church and St. Peter's Church, for both of which he served as rector. The home has been magnificently restored to the way he and his family lived in the 18th century. Many of the items you see throughout the house actually belonged to the Reverend. **Walk to Walnut and Third Street and our tour of Society Hill begins.**

At this point you may wish to conclude the tour and reserve the following Walking Tour of Society Hill for another day.

Society Hill ─────────────────────────

Though it could have been so named because the wealthy lived here in colonial times, Society Hill actually traces back to the Free Society of Traders, a group of businessmen and investors persuaded by William Penn to settle here in 1683.

Continue on 4th Street, crossing Walnut Street until you come to the Philadelphia Contributorship on your right. By now you might have noticed a hand-in-hand firemark on various historical properties on your tour; this is the symbol of America's oldest fire insurance company, the Contributorship, which was founded by Franklin in 1752. The Greek Revival style headquarters were built in 1836. The charming museum inside features a wealth of fire-fighting and insurance memorabilia.

Next, on your right, are the two buildings that house the offices of the *Mutual Assurance Company.* One was occupied by Dr. William Shippen, a Pennsylvania delegate to the Continental Congress, and a man who wrote the first American treatise on anatomy. Later, this was the home of the president of the American Philosophical Society, Dr. Caspar Wistar, after whom the wisteria vine was named. A genial, scholarly man, Wistar started what became known as "Wistar Parties," inviting scientists and statesmen to his home every Saturday night; these parties are still held by the society.

The Mutual Assurance Company is also known as The Green Tree, because prior to its founding in 1784, no company would sell fire insurance to those who owned buildings and homes with trees in front of them. The Green Tree did, however, and you can see its symbol on a number of homes and buildings in the area.

See St. Mary's Churchyard

Next door at 244 S. 4th Street is St. Mary's Church, founded in 1763 and the principal Roman Catholic Church during the Revolution. Walk back to the churchyard and view the gravestones of some of the famous people buried here. Among them are Thomas Fitzsimmons, a signer of the Constitution, and Commodore John Barry, the "Father of the American Navy."

Proceed further south on 4th Street across Spruce Street. The Hill-Physick-Keith House is at 321 S. 4th Street. Built by Henry Hill five years after the Revolution, it was later occupied by Dr. Philip Syng Physick, "the father of American surgery." The house is bordered on three sides by a large 19th-century garden. For tours of ten or more, call in advance.

From the house, turn left (east) on Delancey Street between 3rd and 4th Streets. If you wish to pause and rest, there are benches in Delancey Park. Here you'll see Sherl Joseph Winter's statue of the "Three Bears." The homes around the park are splendid examples of 18th- and 19th-century federal row houses.

The Kosciuszko House

At the corner of Delancey and 3rd Streets, turn right on 3rd Street and, on the corner at Pine Street, you'll see the Thaddeus Kosciuszko House. It was here that Kosciuszko, the Polish engineer who designed America's impregnable defensive fortresses at Saratoga and West Point during the Revolution, lived during his second visit in 1797–98. In the words of Thomas Jefferson, Kosciuszko was "as pure a son of liberty as I have ever known, and of that liberty which is to go to all, and not to the few or the rich alone."

On the southwest corner of 3rd and Pine Streets is St. Peter's Church, whose tall white spire dominates the area. Built in 1760, the church still has the original white pew (Number 41) where George and Martha Washington worshipped with their good friends, the Samuel Powels. Buried in the churchyard are naval hero Stephen Decatur, artist Charles Wilson Peale, and John Nixon, who first read the Declaration to the people.

Headhouse Square

Turn left on Pine Street, continuing east to Headhouse Square, built in 1745 and the last of Philadelphia's original street-wide markets. At

Pine and 2nd Streets is the *Head House*, built in 1805 as a fire house and community center, and so named because it is located at the head of the square. Now completely restored, with numerous shops, restaurants, and cafes surrounding it, Headhouse Square is a delightful place to visit, especially in the summertime, when local entertainers, craftsmen, and artists add to the bustle.

On the east side of the square is *New Market*, a complex of offices, specialty shops, and restaurants. As an extension of the Atwater Kent Museum, the Blake House collection includes many of the artifacts retrieved from the original square, including pieces of porcelain, earthenware, and stoneware.

The Man Full of Trouble

Now walk north on 2nd to Spruce Street. To you right is *Man Full of Trouble Tavern*. This is the only remaining 18th-century tavern in Philadelphia, handsomely restored by the Knauer Foundation to look just as it did in 1759. Beyond the tavern, Spruce Street ends at *Penn's Landing* and the *U.S.S. Olympia*, Commodore George Dewey's flagship and the only survivor of the Spanish-American War fleets.

Continuing north on 2nd Street, to the left, is the *Perelman Antique Toy Museum*. This is sheer delight, with its collection of cap pistols, fire engines, stage coaches, tin and cast iron toys, and the largest collection of mechanical banks in the world.

Continue on 2nd Street and turn left (west) on Locust Street. To the right are the 30-story apartment buildings of *Society Hill Towers*, which were completed in 1964 during the major thrust of restoration in the area.

The Powel House

Proceed on Locust. At 3rd Street, turn right (north). On your left is *Powel House*. Built in 1765 by Samuel Powel, a wealthy property owner and the city's mayor in 1776, this was one of colonial Philadelphia's most fashionable houses. The Powels often entertained the Washingtons here and, in turn, visited the President and First Lady at Mount Vernon.

Continue further north on 3rd Street to St. Paul's Episcopal Church on your right. Built in 1765, it is now the headquarters of the Episcopal Diocese of Pennsylvania. Buried in the churchyard is Edwin Forrest, the great 18th-century actor for whom the Forrest Theater was named.

On the corner of 3rd and Walnut Streets is the *Philadelphia Exchange*, which was built in 1832 through 1834 and was the commercial hub of the city for half a century.

Turn right on Walnut Street. The *City Tavern* is on your left, an ideal place to conclude your walking tour. John Adams called it the "most genteel" tavern in America and it may well have been. Adams, Franklin, and members of the Continental Congress and Constitutional Convention often gathered here for discussion over mugs of ale.

MAIN LINE—VALLEY FORGE— BRANDYWINE VALLEY DRIVING TOUR

This tour begins a few blocks southwest of the Adams Mark Hotel on City Line Avenue. **At Route 23—Conshohocken State Road—turn right (northwest)** and you soon will be in the hills and dales and streams and brooks of Philadelphia's prestigious Main Line. The homes, you will discover, are magnificent.

Route 23 is our primary course to Valley Forge. If you wish to stay aboard, you will not be disappointed—especially in the fall, when the foliage is spectacular. However, for those who would rather gain a greater appreciation of the Main Line, we offer a scenic alternative.

The Scenic Route

Follow these directions. **After the intersection with Rock Hill Road, on the right, stay on Route 23 as it bears gradually to the left and watch carefully for Manayunk Road on the left. Turn left on Manayunk Road, and, very soon, right on Bryn Mawr Avenue. Follow that to Old Gulph Road. Turn right and at the fork with Hagy's Ford Road bearing right, stay to the left on Old Gulph Road. Next, turn left on Gypsy Lane. Follow that to Montgomery Avenue and turn right, but quickly you will turn right on Cherry Lane. Follow that until the dead end at Mill Creek Road, and turn right. Soon this will dead end with Gulph Mill Road, where you turn left. When it joins Youngs Ford Road, Gulph Mill winds to the left.**

Proceed straight ahead, on Youngs Ford to Williamson Avenue, which intersects from the left. Turn left, and follow that to the dead end with Morris Avenue. Follow that to Mill Road, and turn left. After that crosses Gulph Mill Road, turn right on Montgomery Avenue—Route 320—and follow the signs to U.S. 76. Take U.S 76 west to the Valley Forge exit.

Those taking the Route 23 tour will pick up U.S. 76 at Conshohocken. **Just follow the signs to U.S. 76 west and, once you're on the expressway, follow it to the Valley Forge exit.**

Washington's Headquarters at Valley Forge

National Park Service

Valley Forge Visitors' Center

At the junction of Routes 23 and 363 is the Visitors' Center for *Valley Forge National Historical Park.*

Here, an audio-visual program and various exhibits await you. Should you choose to linger in the area where George Washington and his Continental Army of 11,000 troops spent the bitter winter of 1777-78, the park's staff will help you plan your visit.

Enjoy the Park

There is much to be seen here. From the tower on Mount Joy, for example, there is a panoramic view of the 2000-acre park, which is a gripping sight any time of the year. Colonial atmosphere abounds in three furnished headquarters, and reconstructed huts, memorials, and monuments seem to be everywhere. Markers throughout the park help tell the story of one of the most important chapters in American history.

When you decide to move on, **follow Route 23 through the park.** Eventually it will intersect with North Gulph Road, and, as you turn right, will continue west as Route 23. **At the intersection of Route 252, on the left, you should turn left and follow Route 252 to Route 202. There, turn right and follow Route 202 south to U.S. 1.** This will take you about half an hour.

Brandywine Battlefield Park

At U.S. 1, turn right, and soon, on the right, will be the *Brandywine Battlefield Park.* Here, audio-visual presentations in the Visitors' Center tell the story of Washington's defeat by the British in the Battle of Brandywine on September 11, 1777. There are two historic houses in the park, the headquarters of Washington and the Marquis de LaFayette, which depict life as it was during the Revolution.

Further on U.S. 1, on the left, is the *Brandywine River Museum,* which houses three generations of Wyeth paintings (see VISUAL ARTS).

Longwood Gardens

Nearby, are the magnificent *Longwood Gardens,* one of the nation's most vital horticultural showplaces. Established by the late Pierre S. du Pont, its water gardens, conservatories, arboretum, fountain displays, and open-air theater are famous for their beauty. December is a splendid month to visit. There is nothing quite like Longwood at Christmastime.

Further on U.S. 1 in Kenneth Square is *Phillips Mushroom Place,* which houses a museum explaining the history and lore of mushrooms through various audio-visuals. You will also see mushrooms in various stages of development, and there are plenty to buy.

Should you wish to proceed directly back to Philadelphia at this point, **backtrack east on U.S. 1, cross Route 202, and continue east to Route 322, turn right, and this will take you to Interstate 95.** Here, you simply head north to Philadelphia.

Hillendale Museum ————————————————

However, if you're still in a sightseeing mood **turn right off U.S. 1 soon after you leave Phillips Mushroom Place on Route 52.** This, too, will lead you to I-95, but along the way you can visit the *Hillendale Museum* and *Winterthur Museum and Gardens.*

The Hillendale Museum focuses on the crucial role played by the mountains, oceans, major rivers, and the plains in the expansion of the North American continent by Europeans searching for rich natural resources.

A little further down on Route 52, Winterthur, a museum in Henry Francis Du Pont's 200-room mansion, features the world's finest collection of decorative arts made or used in America between 1640 and 1840.

From here, **continue on to I-95, and take it north to Philadelphia.**

METRO DRIVING TOUR

Plan a full day to take in this sweeping look at Philadelphia. This will allow time to explore some of the many fascinating sites along the way. Without stops, the drive will take about two hours. You will see Fairmount Park, drive down the magnificent Benjamin Franklin Parkway, past City Hall, and through Penn's Landing.

The tour begins in Fairmount Park, but it can easily be joined anywhere along the way.

Begin at Fairmount Park ————————————

William Penn's vision of Philadelphia as a "greene Countrie Towne" is enhanced by *Fairmount Park*, the largest city park in the world, whose 8900 acres are replete with forests, parks, gardens, and wide open spaces. It also embraces more than 400 acres of waterways and 100 miles of trails, bridle paths, and bikeways. Stretching northwest from the heart of the city, along the Ben Franklin Parkway and the Schuylkill River, the park also has some of Philadelphia's most notable historical attractions— including the *Art Museum*, the *Philadelphia Zoo*, and perhaps the finest array of original Early American homes to be found anywhere.

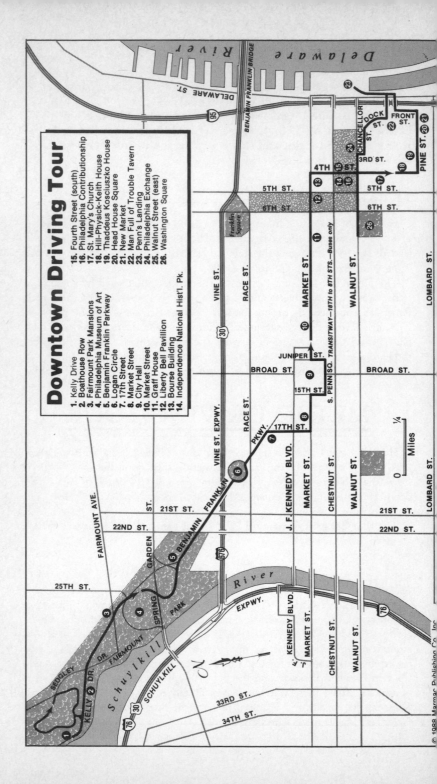

Downtown Driving Tour

1. Kelly Drive
2. Boathouse Row
3. Fairmount Park Mansions
4. Philadelphia Museum of Art
5. Benjamin Franklin Parkway
6. Logan Circle
7. 17th Street
8. Market Street
9. City Hall
10. Market Street
11. Liberty Bell Pavillion
12. Bourse Building
13. Independence National Hist'l. Pk.
14. Fourth Street (south)
15. Philadelphia Contributionship
16. St. Mary's Church
17. Hill-Physick-Keith House
18. Thaddeus Kosciuszko House
19. Head House Square
20. New Market
21. Man Full of Trouble Tavern
22. Penn's Landing
23. Philadelphia Exchange
24. Walnut Street (east)
25. Washington Square

© 1988 Marmac Publishing Co., Inc.

In 1812, the city purchased five acres along the river to build a reservoir and public gardens; eventually, even the park's magnificent mansions were brought under the city's official umbrella. In 1876, the park was the site of the Centennial Exposition honoring the nation's 100th birthday. And the area of the park along the river and Wissahickon Creek has long been listed in the National Register of Historic Places.

Certainly a delightful way to explore the park is by riding one of the replicas of trolley cars that weave through it, pausing at many locations along the way. Pay a single fare, and you will have on-and-off privileges all day, as well as discount admissions to the historic houses, zoo, and museums on the route. Tours begin and end at the Visitors Bureau, 16th Street and JFK Boulevard, but tickets can be purchased at any trolley stop. The trolleys depart to the Visitors Bureau every 20 minutes from 10 am to 4 pm Wednesday through Saturday.

Mount Pleasant

Begin in Fairmount Park at the Grant Monument on Kelly Drive. Take Fountain Drive to the first left. This is Mount Pleasant Drive. Soon you will come upon the Georgian mansion of *Mount Pleasant.* John Macpherson, a Scottish sea captain, built this mansion in 1761 with the fortune he had made by pirateering. In 1775, John Adams dined here and called it "the most elegant seat in Pennsylvania." Later, Benedict Arnold bought Mount Pleasant for his bride, Peggy Shoppen, but he was convicted of treason before they could move in.

Nearby is *Rockland,* of Philadelphia's most handsome federal homes, and *Ormiston,* which was restored by the city in 1976. Rockland is not open to the public.

Laurel Hill Mansion

Now bear left onto Randolph Drive, and soon on your left will be *Laurel Hill Mansion,* a classic brick summer house overlooking the Schuylkill. It was built by Francis and Rebecca Rawle in 1760, but the octagonal dining room was not added until after the Revolutionary War. Laurel Hill was later owned by "the father of American surgery," Dr. Philip Syng Physick, who left it to his daughter, Sally Randolph. The city paid the Randolphs $68,000 for the mansion in 1869.

At Strawberry Mansion Drive, turn left, and on your left is *Woodford,* whose ground floor was built in 1756 by Quaker judge William Coleman, a close friend of Benjamin Franklin. Later the home was owned by David Franks, who lavishly entertained Tory officers during the British occupation of Philadelphia.

Strawberry Mansion

Now turn left onto Strawberry Mansion, so named in the mid-1800s because it was a dairy farm that served strawberries and cream. The mansion had been purchased in the 1820s by Judge Joseph Hamphill, who entertained the renowned John C. Calhoun, the French Marquis de Lafayette, and Daniel Webster. While building a racetrack on the property, Hamphill's son, Coleman, started growing strawberries imported from Chile.

As you leave Strawberry Mansion, again turn left on Strawberry Mansion Drive; on your right is *Robin Hood Dell East,* in June, July and August a favorite site of thousands for its music, big bands, and ethnic programs. Beyond the Dell is *East Laurel Hill Cemetery;* the mausoleums and monuments there are of sufficient architectural interest to be named in the National Register of Historic Places.

Belmont Mansion Drive

Cross Strawberry Mansion Bridge, and as you begin to bear left, turn right on Greenland Drive, then left on Chamounix Drive. Follow this past Ford Road to Belmont Mansion Drive, turn left, and you will pass Playhouse in the Park, which is closed now, but was the nation's first municipally-owned theater.

Next, on your left, is *Belmont Plateau,* which offers a sweeping view of the river and the city. On your right is *Belmont Mansion.* During the Revolution, Judge William Peters, its owner, returned to England, leaving his patriot son here to entertain the likes of George Washington, James Madison, and Benjamin Franklin.

Now turn right, continue across Belmont Avenue and follow South Georges Drive past Ohio House to the Mann Music Center. This is the summer home of the Philadelphia Orchestra, which presents concerts Monday, Tuesday, and Thursday nights in June and July.

Horticultural Center

Continue on South Georges Drive around Catholic Fountain, then bear left onto States Drive, cross Belmont Avenue again, and follow North Horticultural Drive to the Horticultural Center. Opened in 1979, the center has numerous examples of the more than 2000 species of plants that have been identified in Fairmount Park. Many are descendants of seeds that arrived in the ballasts of ships from around the world.

Japanese House

Next, on Horticultural Drive is *Japanese House,* an authentic reconstruction of a 17th-century Japanese house, tea house, and garden. Built in 1957, it is graced in the springtime by blooming azaleas. In 1976, Japanese crafts-men refurbished Japanese House as a gift to the United States on its 200th birthday. Nearby is *Memorial Hall*; it and Ohio House are the only buildings remaining from the Centennial Exposition. A scale model of the centennial grounds is displayed in the basement.

Directly to the east of Memorial Hall is *Cedar Grove*, a Quaker farmhouse that was built in the 1740s and contains a fine collection of Jacobean, Queen Anne, Chippendale, and Federal furniture. Just down the road is *Sweetbriar*, built in 1795 by Samuel Breck so that he and his bride could escape the yel-low fever epidemic that killed thousands of Philadelphians. The Brecks lived here for 40 years—until their daughter died of "river fever."

Zoological Garden

Now backtrack out of Sweetbriar, turn left on Landsdowne Drive, and follow it across Girard Avenue to 34th and the *Philadelphia Zoolog-ical Garden*. Opened in 1874, this was America's first zoo, and its 42 acres are now home for more than 1700 animals, including rare and endangered spe-cies. Actually, the botanical garden preceded the arrival of the animals; in 1785, The Solitude—the manor of Penn's grandson—was a home surrounded by an "English garden" where Washington and Franklin were guests.

Return to Girard Avenue, turn right, and cross the Girard Ave-nue Bridge to Poplar Drive. Turn right, follow it across Sedgely Drive, and on your right will be *Lemon Hill*. This is another mansion that was built by Robert Morris, a signer of the Declaration of Independence and a close friend of Washington. Originally named "The Hills," it later was sold to Henry Pratt, who built the current house in 1800. When the lemon trees flourished, it was renamed Lemon Hill.

Boathouse Row

Continue on Poplar Drive until you turn left to Kelly Drive. On your left will be one of Philadelphia's most famous series of landmarks—*Boathouse Row*. Originally named to designate the row of fishermen's house-boats that used to anchor between the dam and the boathouses, these houses were later built by private groups. They are now occupied by nine rowing clubs, and serve as racing and social headquarters for numerous rowing events in the spring, summer, and fall.

At the end of Boathouse Row, in the middle of an intersection, you will see the Lincoln Monument, with the President holding the Emancipation Proclamation.

See the Waterworks

Bear right at the intersection and see the *Waterworks*; this is a National Historic Engineering Landmark of Greek Revival buildings currently being restored to their original grandeur. Its machines pumped water from the river to the reservoir in the 19th century. In the mid-1920s, however, the reservoir was replaced by the Art Museum.

As you backtrack, bear right on Kelly Drive and you will pass the Azalea Garden, where more than 2000 bushes explode in color every spring. Soon, on your right, looms the awesome *Philadelphia Museum of Art* (see VISUAL ARTS).

Benjamin Franklin Parkway

Now continue down Benjamin Franklin Parkway, the broad, grand boulevard that stretches all the way from *Fairmount Park* to *City Hall*. Calling this "Philadelphia's Champs-Elysees" is no exaggeration—it was the idea of architect Jacques Greber, who was born in Paris and completed it in 1918 at a cost of $22 million. Not surprisingly, most of Philadelphia's parades pass this way.

As you approach Logan Circle, to the left is the *Free Library of Philadelphia* (see SIGHTS), which is a replica of the Ministry of Marine on the Place de La Concorde in Paris. To the right is *The Franklin Institute Science Museum* and the *Fels Planetarium* (see SIGHTS), the magnificent museum that also contains the national memorial to Benjamin Franklin. Next on your right is the *Academy of Natural Sciences* (see SIGHTS), which is the oldest natural history museum in the country. Logan Circle is circular now, but it was one of the five squares that Penn originally designed in the city. Today it is an absolute delight, and its fountain figures are the work of the famed sculptor Alexander Calder.

Head out of Logan Circle and then further down the Parkway, and catch a glimpse of the *Cathedral of Saints Peter and Paul* on your left. This impressive Roman-style church is the head church of the Philadelphia archdiocese. It was completed in 1864 and six of Philadelphia's last nine bishops and archbishops are buried beneath its altar.

City Hall

As you approach the end of the Parkway, turn right on 17th Street, drive to Market Street and turn left, and *City Hall* will reappear before you.

At the laying of its cornerstone in 1874, the orator closed with these words: "Do we not say, 'Dear, dear Philadelphia,' when we leave behind us this noble building to say it for us?"

Larger than the U.S. Capitol, City Hall required 30 years to build, and is the tallest building in the world without a steel support system. The statue of Penn on top of it (37 feet high, 26 tons) is the world's largest on the top of a building. It may have cost $24 million to construct City Hall, which was a lot of money then, but $1 billion would be needed to duplicate it today. Bearing the richest array of sculpture of any public building in the nation, its architecture is French Renaissance or "Second Empire," patterned after the New Louvre in Paris. It contains more than 600 rooms, and below the statue is a breezy observation gallery with a sweeping view of Philadelphia in all directions.

If you do not choose to visit City Hall, you will still get a good idea of its imposing nature by turning right off Market, left on South Penn Square, and following that to the left. This will have taken you halfway around City Hall, and bring you again to *Market Street*; **turn right and continue east.**

Market Street East Area

For several years this area—known as Market Street East—has been the city's largest urban development project, and when completed, will rank among the most intensive concentrations of retail stores in the nation. **On your left, at the corner of 13th and Market,** looms a reminder of when it all started: *John Wanamaker's*, the first department store in America.

On 7th and Market Streets, on the right, is *Graaf House*, where Thomas Jefferson lived when he wrote the Declaration of Independence. Now reconstructed, Graaf House has a film that deals with Jefferson's contributions to American history, and displays regarding the Declaration of Independence. You can also see the actual room where it was written.

Independence Square

After driving one block further, you are facing an area that is known as "America's most historic square mile." Turn right, and on the left you will pass the *Liberty Bell Pavillion, Independence Hall,* and *Independence Square.* It was in 1948 that the federal government designated Independence Square and the blocks surrounding it as "Independence National Historic Park," pouring millions of dollars into its reconstruction, and today it is Philadelphia's greatest tourist attraction.

At Pine Street, turn left and continue east to Front. Along the way you will see quaint cobbled streets lined with colonial homes and fenced-in gardens. You will also pass some historic churches, as well as New Market and Head House square.

Penn's Landing

At Front Street, turn left and drive north to Chestnut Street, turn right, and follow Chestnut Street across Interstate 95 to Delaware Avenue. Turn left and follow the signs into Penn's Landing.

It was here on the banks of the Delaware River that William Penn's ship, "Welcome," docked more than 300 years ago; and he certainly would not recognize it now. More than $35 million has been spent on the 37 acres here, turning it into Philadelphia's latest pride and joy and one of its most popular tourist spots. Now a waterfront designed for people, its half-mile esplanade is the site of many festivals, much music, and nighttime fun.

The U.S.S. Olympia

Here you will also find some old ships, the most noteworthy being the *U.S.S. Olympia*. She is the only survivor of the Spanish-American War fleets, and as Commodore Dewey's flagship, it was from her bridge that he gave the command, "You may fire when you are ready, Gridley," that signaled the start of the Battle of Manila Bay on May 1, 1898. It was victory in that battle that informed the world that America had arrived as a world power.

The Olympia's last mission was in October of 1921, when she brought the body of the Unknown Soldier from Le Havre, France, to its resting place of honor in Arlington Cemetery.

Another vessel, the *Moshulu,* is not only the largest all-steel ship still afloat, but it also has a fulltime restaurant and a maritime exhibit aboard.

Port of History

The nearby *Port of History* is the site of many changing exhibitions and is used as a performing arts center. It features an interesting multimedia presentation on Philadelphia that is narrated by Jack Klugman. It is given six times a day, from Wednesday through Sunday every hour on the half hour from 10:30 am.

Further down the waterfront is the *World Sculpture Garden,* whose permanent outdoor exhibit of historic sculpture was developed by the Fairmount Park Art Association.

For a greater appreciation of the Port of Philadelphia—the world's largest freshwater port—Penn's Landing is also the departure point for *Rainbow River Tours.* These tours of the Delaware River operate daily from late June to early November, with two-hour cruises starting at 11 am, 1:30 and 7:30 pm, and also at 9:30 pm on Friday and Saturday. For groups of 20 or more, advance reservations are necessary (925-7640). The *Spirit of Philadelphia* will also become a part of the riverfront. This cruise ship will also offer tours along the Delaware River, and feature dining and dancing. Call Cruise International (923-4993).

Washington Square ————————————————

To finish off your tour, **leave the Port and take Dock Street to Chancellor Street. Turn left onto Chancellor, a right at 3rd Street, a left at Walnut and follow Walnut** to *Washington Square* between Walnut and Locust Streets. In 1704, this square was designated as a Potter's Field and later, hundreds of soldiers of the Revolutionary War and many victims of the great yellow fever epidemic of 1793 were buried here.

ONE-DAY EXCURSIONS

Within an hour and a half of Philadelphia you can find yourself among rolling hills and some of the most gorgeous countryside to be found anywhere. To the northwest is Lancaster County, land of Mennonite and Amish folk for generations, and which served as a setting for the film *Witness* a few years back; to the northeast is New Hope, the "Patchwork of Americana" and site of some of the most original and creative arts and crafts shops in the nation; for a change of pace, there is Atlantic City to the southeast with its casinos, boardwalk, and beaches, and the Pocono Mountains to the north, a place of beauty and non-stop fun. While we have listed the Poconos in this chapter, realistically, the trip could easily be extended.

Lancaster County and New Hope are both accented by Pennsylvania's seasons, which furnish not only dramatic changes in the countryside, but that also bring a unique atmosphere to the individual times of the year. Compared to metropolitan Philadelphia, the pace is so slow that you'll find yourself tempted to meander down the numerous obscure roads that invariably wind through quaint towns and past pert antique shops and out-of-the-way historic sites. And the food...well, come with an appetite.

Because of the wealth of things to do, see, and appreciate in the Lancaster County and New Hope areas, we strongly suggest at least one overnight stay to relax in an inn, experience bed-and-breakfast with a local family, and simply enjoy yourself far from the hustle and bustle of the big city. If you are just out for a drive with no stops, however, you can do the entire part of either tour in one day. Or if you are a Philadelphia area resident, divide the trips into several days.

NORTHWEST TO LANCASTER COUNTY

Leave the City via the Schuylkill Expressway

Follow the Schuylkill Expressway (Route 76) west to Route 202 and, following the signs to Paoli, continue on Route 202 south past

Paoli to the Exton exit (Route 30 Lancaster Avenue). Turn right (west) and follow Route 30 through its intersection with Route 100. Within three miles, you will come to the Route 30 bypass; take this, as it will speed the rest of your trip to Lancaster.

At Route 10 (there is a Sunoco station on your right) turn right. This road is stunning, especially in the fall when the foliage is bursting with color. At the intersection with Route 340 (there is a Turkey Hill Mini Market on your left), you may want to visit *The Knittery* on the right, where some great deals on sweaters are available in this quaint red barn.

First Stop-Intercourse

Continue west on Route 340, which will take you into Intercourse, PA. Turn right on 772, and on your right is the entrance to the *Kitchen Kettle*, a neat little village where you can indulge in homemade fudge, jams, and baked goods while watching local craftsmen at work. Having parked in the Kitchen Kettle lot, you can also stroll back to Main Street (Route 340) and visit the *Old Curiosity Shop*, the *Old Country Store*, and *Nancy's Corner*. It's fun to browse through these three places, if only to admire the lovely homemade quilts and crafts.

Amish Country

The best way to familiarize yourself with the Mennonite and Amish people and their traditions is to drop by *People's Place*, which is on the same side of Main Street as Nancy's Corner. Here you'll find an *Amish Story Museum*, films, and a craft and book shop; and on the second floor, a tribute to a self-taught Amish craftsman named Aaron Zook.

Proceed west on Route 340 to the *Noah Martin Emporium*, where Amish farmers sell and trade everything from tools to old buggies. Next is the tiny town of *Bird-In-Hand* where, in the *Plain & Fancy* complex, there is another group of shops, a Gay Nineties Museum, an antique doll house, a recreation of an old order Amish house, buggy rides, and an animal barn. There is also the Plain & Fancy Farm and Dining Room, where giant portions of homemade cooking are served family-style.

Proceed north on Route 772. You'll come to a fork in the road. To the right is *J. Ebersole's Chair Shop*, where they still make children's chairs the way they did generations ago. Just beyond that is the *Phillips Lancaster County Swiss Cheese Company*. If you're there between 9 am and noon, you'll be able to watch them make the kind of cheeses you're sure to buy before leaving.

Ephrata Cloister

Now continue north on Route 772 (left at the fork in the road at Ebersole's). This will take you through a vintage stretch of Amish and

Pennsylvania Dutch family in Lancaster County

Mennonite fields and farms. **At Route 222, turn right and continue to the Ephrata exit. After exiting right, turn left on Route 322** and, after driving through the middle of town, you'll soon come to the *Ephrata Cloister* on your left.

This retreat was founded in 1732 by Conrad Beissel, who led a German Protestant sect, the Seventh-Day Baptists, which decided to withdraw from the world. Pious and celibate, they led a harsh, self-sustaining existence, eating one meal per day and sleeping on wooden benches with hard blocks for pillows. Tours of some of the buildings are available and you may explore others on your own. Members of the original settlers are buried in the graveyard.

If you can arrange it, try to be here in the evening on Saturdays and Sundays from July to September when many turn out for the Vorspiel, a one-hour musical drama that depicts the cloister people after their care for the wounded from the Battle of Brandywine had inspired a return to the world around them. For schedule and information call 717-733-4811.

Moravians Settlements

As you leave the Cloister, turn left on Route 322 and, as you approach the overpass, follow the sign which will put you on Route 772 south. Follow Route 272 south to Route 772, turn right, and follow it through Rothsville to Lititz. This magnificently quaint little town was settled by the Moravians in the mid-1700s and still has original buildings from that time.

Don't miss the *Sturgis Pretzel House*, 219 E. Main Street, which was America's first pretzel bakery and which still has the original ovens, now more than 200 years old. After you've watched the pretzels being made, you'll also know how to twist them yourself before you leave.

Continue west on Main Street to the fountain in Moravian Square, turn right on Broad Street, and on your left you'll find the *Candy Americana Museum & Wilbur Chocolate's Factory Candy Outlet.* Here you'll see a wide variety of chocolate candies in the making, and will no doubt buy some upon your departure.

To Donegal Mills Plantation

Now, continue on Route 772 west to the square in Mannheim, PA. There, take the Mannheim-Mount Joy Road to Mount Joy, cross the main street (Route 230) and continue on New Haven street to the dead end. Turn right and continue south on Route 141 exactly three miles. At the sign of Donegal Mills Plantation, turn right and follow the signs to the plantation. This is a 19th-century Georgian mansion and restoration of a community that was settled in the 1700s by a Scotch-Irish adventurer who found the area irresistible.

Guided tours include the mansion itself, where the antiques date back to the Empire and Victorian periods. Excellent dining is to be found in the mill. Another superior choice for dining is nearby, on Pinkerton Road in Mount Joy. This is an honest-to-goodness working farm where you can relish Pennsylvania Dutch cooking at its finest. It's served family-style, and the prices are as welcome as is the food.

Now take Route 141 south to Marietta, PA, turn left on Route 23, and, shortly after crossing Route 30, you'll come to Wheatland on your right. This was the home of Pennsylvania's only President, James Buchanan, and the tour is well worth the 45 minutes it requires.

Lancaster

Continue on Route 23 into Lancaster, PA, and, at 15 West King Street, join the Lancaster Walking Tour. Call ahead for schedules at 717-392-1776. This outstanding tour, which lasts 90 minutes and starts at 10 am and 1:30 pm, takes you to more than 50 points of interest in a historic city that was the capital of the United States for a day.

Afterward, consider visiting the *Rock Ford Plantation* at 881 Rock Ford Road. This magnificently preserved mansion on the banks of the Conestoga River was once the home of General Edward Hand, an Irish doctor whom George Washington named as his Adjutant General.

There's also the *Heritage Center Museum of Lancaster County.* Located on the corner of Center Square and Queen Street, the museum features works spanning generations of the country's renowned craftsmen and artists.

Since a trip to Pennsylvania's Dutch country isn't really complete without a visit to a farmer's market, stop by the *Central Market* on Penn's Square. In a huge market typical of many in the area, your mouth will water at baked goods only minutes from the oven, tantalizing meats in the butcher shop, and fruits and vegetables straight off the farm. The least you can do is pick up some shoo-fly pie for the short trip to the *Amish Homestead,* **a few miles east on Route 30 (Lancaster Avenue).**

The Amish Homestead is a 71-acre farm dating back to 1744 that is occupied and operated by an Amish family. It includes acres of crops, a tobacco shed, and animals everywhere. You can bring a picnic lunch and enjoy it on the farm.

Next is *Dutch Wonderland,* an amusement park for children with a Pennsylvania Dutch flavor. It is accented by covered bridges, an Amish farmhouse, and scenes from an Amish quilting bee. There's also an abundance of rides, including one by monorail that provides a sweeping view of the 44-acre park.

Next door at the *National Wax Museum* are reproductions of such historical figures as William Penn, Ben Franklin, and Daniel Boone.

At the *Amish Farm and House*, a little further east on Route 30, you'll see a typical Pennsylvania Dutch farm and learn in detail of Amish history, religion, and customs during a 45-minute tour of the 1805 stone house.

Then comes the *Weaverton One Room Schoolhouse* where hundreds of children from first to eighth grade were taught "The Three R's" by a single teacher. Children especially enjoy this site.

Now turn south on Route 896. Soon you'll come to the *Amish Village*, featuring another schoolhouse, a blacksmith shop and springhouse, an operating smokehouse, and more animals.

A few miles further south on Route 896, don't miss the *Strasburg Steam Railroad*. Here you'll enjoy a 4¼-mile ride on America's oldest short-line railroad (dating back more than 130 years) through the heart of Pennsylvania Dutch countryside.

Finally, drop by the *Choo Choo Barn* on nearby Route 741, where an elaborate collection of model trains course through scale-model reproductions of the surrounding countryside. Not far away is the *Toy Train Museum*, headquarters of the Train Collector's Association. It houses a host of model trains that date back to the late 1880s.

NORTH TO NEW HOPE

Follow Broad Street (Route 611) north. After you cross Cheltenham Avenue, Broad Street will become Old York Road (still Route 611), and at Willow Grove it will become Easton Avenue.

Approaching Doylestown, stay to the left as the Route 611 bypass skirts the west side of this 19th-century county seat of Bucks County. Exit at Route 313, turn left and go to the town of Dublin, PA. There, turn left on Dublin Road, which will take you to the *Pearl S. Buck House, Green Hills Farm.*

This 1835 stone farmhouse, where the famous humanitarian and winner of both the Nobel and Pulitzer prizes lived and wrote from 1935 until her death 40 years later, was declared a National Historic Landmark in 1980. She once said that the stone walls of her home symbolized, for her, strength and durability.

It's tastefully furnished in Early American and European, and because she spent so much of her life in China where her parents were missionaries, it's accented by original Oriental touches. Among the highlights of the home is the desk upon which Miss Buck wrote her famed book, *The Good Earth.*

A guided tour of the home and the Green Hills grounds, where Miss Buck is buried, takes about two hours; the tour is sometimes led by Florence, Miss Buck's housekeeper for almost 20 years.

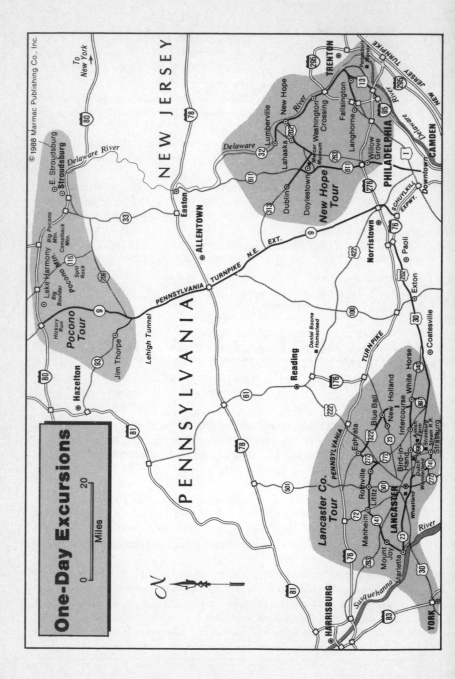

One-Day Excursions

0   20
Miles

© 1988 Marmac Publishing Co., Inc.

NEW JERSEY

PENNSYLVANIA

To New York

Stroudsburg
E. Stroudsburg
Delaware River
Big Pocono Mtn.
Camelback Mtn.
Split Rock
Lake Harmony
Big Boulder
Pocono Mtn.
Hickory Run
Pocono Tour
Jim Thorpe
Hazelton
Lehigh Tunnel

PENNSYLVANIA TURNPIKE N.E. EXT.

Easton
ALLENTOWN

Reading
Daniel Boone Homestead

Lumberville
New Hope
Delaware River
Washington Crossing
Fallsington
Langhorne
Lahaska
Doylestown Museum
Willow Grove
New Hope Tour
Dublin
TRENTON
295
Pennsbury Manor
NEW JERSEY TURNPIKE
Delaware River
PHILADELPHIA
CAMDEN
Downtown
SCHUYLKILL EXPWY.
Norristown
Paoli
Exton

TURNPIKE

Blue Ball
New Holland
White Horse
Ephrata
Bird-in-Hand
Intercourse
Amish
Dutch Wonderland
Strasburg
Strasburg Steam R.R.
Rothville
Lititz
Manheim
Wheatland
LANCASTER
Mount Joy
Marietta
Lancaster Co. Tour
Susquehanna River
HARRISBURG
YORK
Coatesville

Moravian Pottery and Tile Works ─────────

Now take Route 313 back toward Doylestown. Soon, on your right, you'll see the *Moravian Pottery and Tile Works*—the north part of the "Mercer Mile."

Henry Chapman Mercer (1856-1930) was an archaeologist, anthropologist, historian, and writer, as well as one of the most ambitious collectors and innovators of his time. He wasn't an architect, but he still designed and, using unskilled laborers from nearby farms and a dutiful horse named Lucy, built the Pottery and Tile Works, a home that looks more like a fortress, and the Mercer Museum.

All are worth seeing, and not just because they were the first buildings ever to be constructed solely of reinforced concrete. It was in the Pottery and Tile Works that Mercer developed the methods and formulas for manufacturing tiles that are still seen today in the casino in Monte Carlo, the Pennsylvania State Capital and the Bryn Mawr College Library. The factory was closed after his death and eventually turned into a museum. In 1974 it was reactivated, and now, with Mercer's original machinery, kilns, molds, and tools on display, it is once again producing tiles the way Mercer did 75 years ago.

Within walking distance is Mercer's home, *Fonthill*. Here you'll find 39 rooms in which the ceilings, walls, and floors are covered with Mercer's distinctive tiles; there are also countless engravings, prints, and artifacts that he collected on his worldwide explorations.

Now take the short drive to the *Mercer Museum*, which contains 40,000 tools, implements, and utensils from pre-industrial days. The tools represent all types of manufacturing from past times, from the making of shoes, toys, hats, and candies to boats and bathtubs. There's also a fascinating collection of caskets and gallows.

Now take Route 313 southeast to Route 202, turn left, and you'll find yourself on the course that the earliest travelers took between New York City and Philadelphia. There are still areas of beautiful countryside along the way.

Peddler's Village ─────────────

At Route 263, turn left for Lahaska (originally called "Lahaskeke" by the Indians, meaning "place of much writing"). Here, among the grass, streams, and waterfalls are herringboned bricked walkways that will lead you to the 42 shops of *Peddler's Village*. They are extraordinary shops, too; so extensive is the selection of stencils, potholders, decoys, quilts, candles, brass, and other creations that if you know someone who "has everything," you'll be able to surprise with a gift from here.

Across the street (Route 202) is *The Yard*, another group of distinctive shops. You'll also find a number of restaurants on both sides of the street.

Bucks County Vineyards & Winery ─────

Now take Route 202 toward New Hope. Dotted with old stone houses, these few miles abound with antique shops that attract collectors and dealers from throughout the nation. You will then come to the *Bucks County Vineyards & Winery.*

Located on a Pennsylvania farm granted to Jacob Holcomb by William Penn in 1717, the winery now bottles about 61,000 gallons a year. You're also invited to tour the *Wine Museum* where, on the third floor, there's a *Fashion Museum* containing an astonishing collection of original costumes from the stage and screen. Arthur Gerold, the winery's president, once owned America's largest theatrical costume company, Brooks-Van Horn. Here you'll find original costumes worn by Richard Burton and Robert Goulet in "Camelot"; Julie Andrews in "My Fair Lady"; Angela Lansbury in "Mame"; Marlon Brando in "The Godfather", and the first costume ever worn by Barry Manilow, bought for him by Bette Midler because he was short of cash.

A cheese shop has also been added, and some of what you purchase here was no doubt made by an Amish cooperative dedicated to the art.

On to New Hope ───────

Now follow Route 202 into New Hope. Originally an art colony founded in 1900 by some internationally-famous artist who had settled along the Delaware River, this is now a thriving arts center. Artists of all types live in this charming town and on nearby farms, and as you would expect, the selection of original work in New Hope's nearly 100 shops is extraordinary.

On the Corner Square is the *Parry Mansion*, a historical home that was occupied by five generations of the Parry family. Tours are available and ten of its rooms reflect the changes of lifestyle between colonial times and the early 1900s.

On the northwest corner of Cannon Square, which commemorates the Civil War dead, is the *Logan Inn.* The original structure was the Ferry Tavern, built in the 1720s. It's now a splendid example of the colonials' facility for adding on to existing buildings, and long ago was named after James Logan, William Penn's secretary and another friend of the Lenni Lenape Indians.

The tavern's interior, presided over by a huge clock, is decorated with 18th- and 19th-century antiques. Townsfolk frequent the tavern and its restaurant, and ten guest rooms are available.

Across the street is the *Bucks County Playhouse.* Once an old grist mill, it was converted into a playhouse in 1939 and is now known as the State Theater of Pennsylvania. (see PERFORMING ARTS Theater).

An absolute must is the New Hope Station, built in 1890 and now the starting point for the *New Hope Steam Railroad.* Here, an old steam locomotive is ready to take you on a trip through the country to Lahaska and back. It takes about an hour.

On New Street are the New Hope *Mule-Drawn Barge Rides*. For an hour, you can unwind beneath the awnings of a flat-bottom barge as it's pulled by a pair of mules through the canal of the town, out into the country, and back.

Phillips Mill

If you have the time, **take the lovely country drive on Route 32, along the Delaware River to Phillips Mill,** one of the many charming towns of Solebury Township. This is one of the most picturesque communities you'll find anywhere, and the restored grist mill from which the community got its name is still the home of the Phillips Mill Community Association, which has served area artists for decades.

Further north on Route 32 is Lumberville, another village of stone and frame houses, pleasantly surrounded by the canal, the river, and a ridge of mountains called "the Coppernose." It has also been the home of the *Black Bass Hotel* since 1727, (see LODGING), an outstanding spot to dine and drink in the scenery. Some of the specialties are Charleston Meeting Street Crab, New England lobster pie, and Benjamin Franklin's smoked oysters.

Washington Crossing

South of New Hope on Route 32 is *Washington Crossing,* where George Washington led his soldiers across the Delaware River on Christmas night of 1776 to defeat the Hessians in a surprise attack on Trenton. Some 500 acres of the area now comprise *Washington Crossing State Park,* including an exact replica of Emanuel Leutze's painting "Washington Crossing the Delaware," and the Old Ferry Inn, where the General ate dinner before crossing the river. Between the Inn and the Memorial Building is a boat barn containing four replicas of the boats used that historic night more than 200 years ago. (They are used every Christmas Day to re-enact the feat, beginning at 2 pm.) The northern 100 acres of the park have been devoted to an explosion of wild flowers second to none.

A little further south are three attractions—two of them historic, the other for children.

William Penn

Within five miles of each other are *Fallsington,* where William Penn worshipped, and *Pennsbury Manor,* his estate on the Delaware River. Fallsington is a lovely village where no less than two dozen 18th-century houses still stand with pride, and where the *Stagecoach Tavern,* a favorite stop for travelers between New York and Philadelphia from the 1790s to the 1920s, has been faithfully restored.

Nearby is the Manor, which Penn began building during his first visit to his colony in the early 1680s, but which he did not occupy until his second visit in 1700. Even then, due to financial problems which prompted a return to England (and the fact that his wife and daughter really preferred the city life), he lived in the Manor only two years. It is now a total recreation of what Penn so loved then (however briefly). A decade of research was invested in the Manor's reconstruction. Tours are available.

Sesame Place

Finally, there's *Sesame Place*. **Off Interstate 95 in Langhorne, PA,** this is a 21st-century play park geared to children aged 3 to 13. Here they can meet real-life Sesame Street characters, as well as enjoy televised adventures and live science shows. Make sure they bring their bathing suits; the water games are guaranteed to get them wet.

NORTH TO
THE POCONOS

How to Get There

Take the Schuylkill Expressway west to the Pennsylvania Turnpike, east on the turnpike to the Northeast Extension, and follow that north to the mountains. The Poconos are served by regular bus service from Philadelphia, and major airlines land at ABE Pocono Airport in Allentown and Wilkes-Barre/Scranton Airport in Avoca.

A Place of Beauty

Only 85 miles northwest of Philadelphia are the majestic Pocono Mountains, a 2400-square mile expanse of natural beauty highlighted by a host of outdoor and indoor recreational activities. "Pocono" is an Indian name for "a stream in the mountains." This range is blessed with countless streams, creeks, lakes, and gorgeous waterfalls. With each season defined by its own breathtaking scenery and climate, the Pocono Mountains are an exhilarating experience every month of the year.

Winter Sports

In the winter, four major ski areas—Big Boulder, Camelback, Jack Frost Mountain, and Shawnee Mountain—are among the finest in the East. Beginner, intermediate, and expert trails are available, and all facilities include fully-staffed ski schools, rentals, and lodge activities. There are 11 top ski resorts in the Poconos, each offering a variety of trails, cross-country trails, slopes, snowmaking equipment, and lifts. Snowmobiling, sledding, tobogganing, ice skating, sleigh rides, and ice fishing are also extremely popular in the Poconos in the wintertime.

Summer Recreation

Warm weather means just as much fun. As "the Myrtle Beach of the North," the Poconos have more than 30 golf courses, several of championship caliber. Indoor and outdoor tennis courts abound, with many resorts offering special packages for tennis and golf. Three state parks—Delaware Gap Recreational Area, Big Pocono State Park, and White Haven State Park— provide more than 1000 campsites, 15 of which are open year-round. You will also find exceptional areas for fishing, boating, whitewater rafting, canoeing, swimming, hiking, horseback riding, and hunting.

Among numerous other attractions are shops where pottery, baskets, and candy are handmade before your eyes. There are various museums, a wildlife park, and the Alpine Slide where, after a chair-lift ride to the top, you'll careen to the bottom over a 3600-foot, toboggan-like course in a plastic sled. There's Pocono Action Park, where you can drive Lola T-560s around a winding road course and receive your official times after doing so. The 2½-mile tri-oval high speed course of the Pocono International Raceway attracts top drivers on the NASCAR and Indy-car circuits to the mountains each summer.

Where to Stay

Lodging in the Poconos is extensive. You can stay in a charming country inn, a modern hotel or motel, or any of the fine lodges and resorts. And then there are the honeymoon resorts. It was in the Poconos that the sunken tub, the heart-shaped pool, and the in-room swimming pool were invented; as a result, the Poconos are now the Honeymoon Capital of the world, with its honeymoon resorts attracting more than 275,000 newlywed couples each year.

In view of the many types and plans of accommodations that are available in the Poconos, you may wish to order brochures in advance and study them in detail. We recommend you call or write the Pocono Mountains Vacation Bureau, Box 5, Stroudsburg, PA, 18360; 717-421-5791.

Dining Out

There are countless restaurants offering the full range of seafood and American, continental, international, French, Italian, and Chinese cuisine. The specialty, however, is the always fresh Pocono Mountain trout.

SOUTHEAST TO
ATLANTIC CITY

Leave the City via the
Benjamin Franklin Bridge ——————————

Follow the signs to the Atlantic City Expressway. This will take you straight to the New Jersey shores of Atlantic City. Since the approval of casino gambling in 1976, investors have invested $1.5 billion in this resort. There are casinos to enjoy table games, including more than 550 blackjack, 100 roulette, 150 craps, 20 baccarat, and 30 big six wheels. There are also more than 10,000 slot machines.

In addition, the casino hotels offer razzle-dazzle musical revues and a variety of entertainment in lounges. A boxing fan? Matches are scheduled regularly. There's also the world-famous Boardwalk, fine dining, and lots of fellow visitors. For more information, see LODGING Resorts.

THE INTERNATIONAL VISITOR

Philadelphia continues to grow and develop as a truly international host city. Upon landing at Philadelphia International Airport, flights from foreign countries taxi to the Overseas Terminal and there international passengers are greeted by the full complement of immigrations and customs facilities and services. Consulates and ethnic societies in the Philadelphia area stand ready to help those arriving daily from around the world, to make Philadelphia a home away from home. We have listed aids and resources for international visitors and those relocating in Philadelphia, beginning with the consulates, trade offices, and ethnic societies.

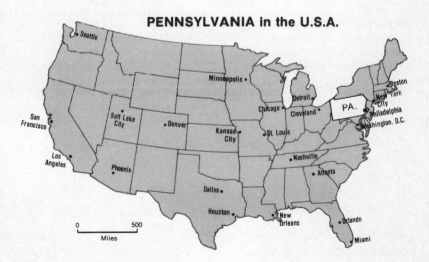

PENNSYLVANIA in the U.S.A.

Philadelphia Council for International Visitors, Museum of the Philadelphia Civic Center, Civic Center Blvd. at 34th St., Philadelphia 19104; 823-7261. Serving as Philadelphia's host for foreign guests in partnership with the Department of Commerce, the Civic Center, and community organizations, CIV offers professional appointments with United States counterparts and an emergency language bank that offers phone translations in more than 60 languages (dial TRY-5-CIV). The organization also provides home hospitality and guided tours by CIV volunteers, as well as introductions to Philadelphia's cultural, civic, and business resources. CIV serves between 3000 and 4000 visitors from more than 100 countries annually.

International House of Philadelphia, 3701 Chestnut St., Philadelphia 19104; 387-5125. This residence, program, and cultural center provides a unique living experience for 450 students form 50 countries, in addition to sponsoring nationally recognized media, arts, and folklife programs and offering services for foreign students throughout the Philadelphia area.

Consulates and Trade Offices

Argentina, 513-257-5027.

Austria, 3 Pkwy.; 563-0650.

Belgium, 1500 Market St.; 972-3770.

Canada, 3 Pkwy.; 561-1750.

Colombia, 1015 Chestnut St.; 922-1927.

Costa Rica, 355 E. Main St., Moorestown, NJ; 609-235-6772.

Denmark, 956 Public Ledger Building, Independence Sq.; 625-9900.

Dominican Republic, 422 Lafayette Building, 5th and Chestnut Sts.; 923-3006.

Ecuador, 24 Pear Tree Lane, Lafayette Hills; 825-5209.

El Salvador, 3400 Walnut St.; 642-1354.

Finland, 112 Christian Ave.; 465-5565.

France, 3 Pkwy.; 563-0650.

Germany, 1101 PNB Plaza Building, 5th and Market Sts.; 922-7415.

Great Britain, 3 Pkwy.; 563-0650.

Guatemala, 42 S. 15th St.; 563-3100.

Haiti, 1430 Land Title Building; 561-1030.

Honduras, 6825 Lindbergh Blvd.; 365-6693.

Israel, 225 S. 15th St.; 546-5556.

Italy, 2128 Locust St.; 732-7436.

Japan, 956 Public Ledger Building, Independence Sq.; 625-9900.

Losotho, 42 S. 15th St.; 563-7512.

Mexico, 21 S. 5th St.; 922-4262.

Monaco, Suburban Station Building; 665-0152.

Netherlands, 3 Girard Plaza; 567-7011.

Panama, 2019 Rittenhouse Sq.; 546-0767.

Portugal, 527 Lafayette Building; 925-3222.

Spain, 728 W. Lehigh Ave.; 225-7176.

Sweden, 112 Christian St.; 465-5565.

Switzerland, 700 Crittenden St.; 248-2424.

Uruguay, 5th and Chestnut Sts.; 925-6992.

Venezuela, 3 Penn Center Plaza; 568-0585.

Ethnic Societies

China, Cultural and Community Center; 923-6767.

France, Alliance Francaise de Philadelphia; 735-5283.

Germany, German Society of Philadelphia; 627-4365.

Ireland, Federation of United Irish-American Societies; 843-8051.

Italy, American Institute for Italian Culture; 688-4961.

Jewish, Federation of Jewish Agencies of Philadelphia; 893-5600.

Korea, Korean Association of Philadelphia; 688-8163.

Norway, Lief Ericson Society International; 565-3165.

Panama, Pan American Association; 735-4061.

Philippines, Filipino Executive Council of Greater Philadelphia; 763-5540.

Poland, Polish-American Association; 634-8472.

Russia, Russian Brotherhood Organization; 563-2537.

Scotland, American-Scottish Foundation; 563-5812 (residence).

Spain, Council of Spanish Speaking Organizations; 574-3500.

Sweden, American-Swedish Historical Foundation; 389-1776.

Wales, Welsh Society of Philadelphia; 844-0664 (residence).

Bank Hours

Philadelphia's banking hours are generally from 9 am through 5 pm Monday through Friday and many of their branch locations have Saturday hours as well.

Currency Exchange and International Banking

Always try to exchange foreign currency at a bank, where you will be offered the most competitive rate. However, the cashier in major hotels will be able to exchange foreign currency, too.

International banking services in Philadelphia include purchase and sale of foreign currencies and foreign travelers' checks, cable transfers, foreign drafts on overseas banks, foreign collections, import/export financing, and issue of commercial letters of credit. The following banks in Philadelphia are at your service, and all have numerous branch locations.

Continental Bank. 12th and Chestnut Sts.; 564-7000.

Fidelity Bank, Broad and Walnut Sts.; 985-6000.

First Pennsylvania Bank, Center Sq., 1500 Market St.; 786-5000.

Girard Bank, One Girard Plaza, Broad and Chestnut Sts.; 585-2000.

Mellon Bank, Broad and Chestnut Sts.; 553-3000.

Philadelphia National Bank, Broad and Chestnut Sts.; 629-3100.

Provident National Bank, Broad and Chestnut Sts.; 585-5000.

Customs Allowances ─────────────────────────

You are allowed to bring into the United States from overseas the following duty free:

One liter of alcoholic beverages; one hundred cigars; two hundred cigarettes. Be aware that state liquor laws supersede the national regulations.

There is a personal exemption of $300; over this amount the next $600 in goods is charged at a flat rate of 10%.

Gifts that are mailed to the United States under the value of $25 are duty free; over that amount the recipient will be charged duty.

Driving ─────────────────────────────────────

Driving in the United States is in the right lane. An international driver's license should be secured through your local automobile association before you leave home. United States gallons of gasoline are one-fifth smaller than the United Kingdom's imperial gallon. Gasoline stations along the highways are generally open on weekends or in the evenings, and some remain open 24 hours; watch for signs.

The national 55 mph (miles per hour) speed limit is observed and strictly enforced by the use of police radar observation. In Pennsylvania, you are allowed to turn right at a red traffic light except where posted and the law dictates you must call the police immediately when you have an accident.

Electricity ──────────────────────────────────

110 volts, 60 cycles A.C. Bring an adapter for your razor and/or hair dryer.

Medical Insurance ───────────────────────────

Medical insurance should be secured prior to arrival. There is no national health service in the United States.

Money ───────────────────────────────────────

The United States dollar ($) is divided into 100 cents (¢). The coins are: penny worth 1¢ (copper-colored); nickel 5¢; dime 10¢; quarter 25¢; half-dollar 50¢ (all of which are silver-colored), and the silver dollar $1. The bills or notes are all one color, green, and are in denominations of one dollar, five dollars, ten dollars, twenty dollars, fifty dollars, one hundred dollars, and one thousand dollars.

Postage ──────────────────────────────────────

Mail service is generally good and letters cross the country in one to three days. Zip codes must be used for guaranteed delivery. Express mail which guarantees next-day delivery is available. Check with the nearest post office for information on rates.

Public Holidays

The following holidays are considered legal holidays in most businesses, including government offices. Banks and businesses will not operate on these days. Some holidays are celebrated on the closest Monday to the holiday in order to give working people a long weekend. This is indicated in the listing.

January 1, New Year's Day.
January 15, Martin Luther King's Birthday.
February 22, George Washington's Birthday, celebrated on closest Monday.
May 31, Memorial Day, celebrated on closest Monday.
July 4, Independence Day.
September, Labor Day, first Monday after first Tuesday.
October 12, Christopher Columbus Day, celebrated on closest Monday.
November 11, Veterans Day.
November, fourth Thursday, Thanksgiving Day.
December 25, Christmas Day.

Telephone and Telegrams

Most public pay phones require a 25¢ coin deposit, but read the instructions before inserting your coin. When calling long distance, dial 1, the area code, and the number. Telephone numbers preceded by an (800) number are toll-free in the United States; you dial 1-800 and number.

To send a mailgram (guaranteed next-day delivery by mail and less expensive than a telegram), telegram, international message, or charge-card money order, call Western Union, 922-0844.

Tipping and Taxes

Tipping is your way of rating and rewarding service. These several guidelines will help you adjust the size of the tip you wish to give. A 15% tip is customarily considered for restaurant service, hotel laundry and valet service, room service, bar bills, and taxi fares. Bellhops and porters generally receive 50¢ per bag. Pennsylvania levies a 6% sales tax on some merchandise and food; there is no tax on clothes, except for bathing suits (and umbrellas). There is a 3% tax on hotel and motel rooms in Philadelphia.

Translators

The American Language Academy, 572-2900, provides English for international students.

Berlitz Translation and Interpreting Service, 735-8500, provides translations by international language experts.

Council for International Visitors Emergency Language Bank, TRY-5-CIV, offers telephone translations in more than 60 languages 24 hours a day, seven days a week.

Inlingua Translation Service, 735-7646, offers translation service in any language.

Radio Stations Broadcasting in Foreign Languages

WCAM 1310 (AM) Greek, Italian, Polish, and Spanish.
WIBF 103.9 (FM) German, Greek, Jewish, and Korean.
WRTI 90.2 (FM) African, French, and Indian.
WTEL 860 (AM) Hungarian, Italian, Lithuanian, Polish, and Spanish.
WTTM 92 (AM) German, Hungarian, and Polish.

Visa Requirements

Be sure to obtain your visa from the United States Embassy in your country several weeks prior to departure.

METRIC CONVERSIONS

Length

1 millimeter	=	.039 inch (in.)	1 inch	=	2.54 cm.
1 centimeter	=	.39 in.	1 foot	=	0.30 m.
1 meter	=	3.28 feet (ft.)	1 yard	=	.91 m.
1 kilometer	=	.62 mile (mi.)	1 mile	=	1.61 km.

To convert miles to kilometers, multiply the number of miles by 8 and divide by 5.

Weight

1 gram	=	.04 ounce (oz.)	1 oz.	=	28.35 g.
1 kilogram	=	2.2 pounds (lbs.)	1 lb.	=	.45 kg.
			1 ton	=	.91 metric ton

Liquid

		2.11 pints (pt.)	1 pt.	=	.47 liter
1 liter	=	1.06 quarts (qt.)	1 qt.	=	.95 liter
		.26 gallon (gal.)	1 gal.	=	3.79 liters

Temperature

To convert Fahrenheit temperatures to Centigrade (Celsius): Take the Fahrenheit temperature, minus 32 and divide by 1.8 equals the Centigrade temperature.

CONVERSION CHARTS FOR CLOTHING

Dresses, coats, suits and blouses (Women)

British	10	12	14	16	18	20
American	8	10	12	14	16	18
Continental	40	42	44	46	48	50

Suits and overcoats (Men)

American/British	34	36	38	40	42	44
Continental	44	46	48	50	52	54

Shirts (Men)

American/British	14	14½	15	15½	16	16½	17	17½
Continental	36	37	38	39	40	41	42	43

Shoes (Men) for ½ sizes add ½ to preceding number

British	6	7	8	9	10	11
American	7	8	9	10	11	12
Continental	39½	40½	41½	42½	43½	44½

Shoes (Women) for ½ sizes add ½ to preceding number

British	3	4	5	6	7	8	9
American	4½	5½	6½	7½	8½	9½	10½
Continental	35	36	37	38	39	40	41

SPECIAL PEOPLE

SENIOR CITIZENS

The older traveler is recognized as an integral part of the large traveling population in the United States and abroad. Travel agencies nationwide focus many of their travel promotions and group trips on the interests of the mature traveler, interests that range from fixed-income capabilities to comfortable transportation and accommodations, from available medical facilities to theme tours and social life. These are the same concerns of the older person who is visiting Philadelphia.

Most major airlines in Philadelphia offer special rates for senior citizens, but be sure to check with your respective airline for its discounts and when they apply. **AMTRAK** offers a 25% reduction on all trips for persons 65 years and over, and **Greyhound** and **Trailways** bus companies offer 10% off. Greyhound also has a special "two for·one" program for senior citizens.

Public transportation on **SEPTA** discounts its fares for senior citizens as follows: Off-peak hours free (9 am–3:30 pm, 6:30 pm–6 am, all day Saturdays, Sundays, and holidays). Peak hours 35¢, transfers 15¢ (6 am–9 am, 3:30 pm–6:30 pm). **SEPTA Red Arrow and Frontier** divisions: off-peak hours free (9 am–3 pm, 6:30 pm–6 am, all day Saturdays, Sundays, and holidays). Peak hours full fare.

Note: SEPTA's free and reduced rates apply only to persons 65 years and over. Proof of age must be presented to operator when boarding transit vehicle, such as Medicare card or special SEPTA I.D. card. Card can be obtained at SEPTA Building, 200 W. Wyoming Ave., Philadelphia, 19140; 456-4000; or SEPTA General Office, 841 Chestnut St., Ground Floor, Philadelphia, 19107; 574-7365. Be sure to bring proof of age.

SEPTA's Regional Commuter Rail Program offers free transportation during off-peak hours. Trip must terminate prior to the start of peak hours. Full fare during peak hours. The senior commuter must present a "SEPTA Senior Citizen Coupon" along with I.D. when on board. This I.D. can be a Medicare card, Pennsylvania Transit or Railroad Retirement card. Only one coupon can be used per ride and this is valid only in Pennsylvania. It is not valid on AMTRAK trains. Ten-trip coupon books may be obtained free (with proper identification) at SEPTA General Office, all railroad stations, and the

Mayor's Commission on Services to the Aging, Suite 1000-1003, 1317 Filbert St., Philadelphia, 19107. Again, be sure to bring proof of age.

Although hotels and motels in the Philadelphia area do not discount rooms for senior citizens as a rule, it is recommended to inquire when making your reservations or checking in. Also check Bed-and-Breakfast under LODGING.

Two organizations stand ready to assist senior citizens visiting or traveling through Philadelphia. They are excellent places to obtain referrals for specific needs.

The **American Association of Retired Persons** is a non-governmental, non-partisan, non-profit national organization for men and women 55 and older, whether employed or unemployed. Among the benefits of the $4 annual membership are 10% to 25% discounts at major hotel and motel chains which include Holiday Inn, Howard Johnson's, Quality Inn, Ramada Inn, Rodeway Inn, Treadway Inn, and Sheraton. Members should always call in advance to confirm the discounts available. AARP members are entitled to discounts of up to 30% on car rentals from Hertz, Avis, and National; but once again, call in advance for reservations and information. For further information regarding the AARP, write or call the Assistant State Director (AARP) for Philadelphia, 7600 Stenton Ave., Philadelphia, 19118; 248-4979.

Also available is the **Traveler's Aid Society,** which provides emergency service to travelers of all ages and background. This organization is headquartered at 310 S. Juniper St., Philadelphia, 19107; 546-0571; branch offices are located at the Greyhound Bus Terminal (569-3222), the Trailways Bus Terminal (972-3334), and Philadelphia International Airport (365-6525).

HANDICAPPED PERSONS

Thousands of handicapped persons pursue active, fruitful lives, and Philadelphia has made admirable strides in making itself accessible to the disabled in all aspects of urban living. The Mayor's Office for the Handicapped offers a **Guide to Philadelphia for the Handicapped,** which provides detailed information about the accessibility of specific theaters, museums, shops, restaurants, hotels, motels, and special services. It is a must for the handicapped traveler visiting Philadelphia, and is available free of charge by writing the **Mayor's Office for the Handicapped,** City Hall, Philadelphia, 19102; 686-2798.

The expansion and remodeling of **Philadelphia International Airport** has made it much more accessible and convenient for the handicapped person. Specially designed areas in the parking garage provide direct and level access to the terminals and wheelchairs will be made available with prior notification. Specially equipped restrooms are located throughout the airport. Most terminals are equipped with jetways, enabling direct and level access to planes. Elevators operate between the departure/arrival and baggage areas. For information or assistance, call the Public Transportation Director at 686-1776.

Regarding rental cars, **Hertz** provides automobiles with hand controls if notified at least one week in advance. **Avis** provides hand controls on intermediate-sized cars only, and also must be notified at least one week in advance. For information call 492-2902 (Hertz) or 492-3350 (Avis).

At the **30th Street Station,** a level entrance provides access from the sidewalk. If previously arranged by telephone, a porter will meet the disabled traveler and assist him or her to the track level via elevator. For AMTRAK service, the person in a wheelchair must transfer to a regular seat, unless traveling in a special car. For information call: 824-1600.

At **Suburban Station,** 16th and Market Streets, the main entrance on 16th Street is level. Elevators and escalators are available to all levels. For information call: 387-6600.

At **Reading Terminal,** 12th and Market Streets, level access is available at the 12th Street entrance. Elevators are available to all train levels. For information call: 922-6530.

SEPTA buses operating on fixed routes are accessible by wheelchair lifts at the center door, as are many buses on regular routes. On both fixed and regular routes, SEPTA enables handicapped persons to ride half-fare during off-peak hours, provided they have obtained the required card through SEPTA. For information on routes served by special buses and discount fares, call SEPTA at 574-2780.

For information regarding the **PATCO** high speed line, call 922-4600.

Many hotels and motels in the Philadelphia area provide rooms and facilities tailored to the needs of the handicapped person. Among them are the Holiday Inn, Marriott, Hilton, and Best Western chains, as well as the Franklin Plaza, and the Philadelphia Centre Hotel. For specific information call your hotel in advance.

When planning to attend a theater, concert, or sporting event, the handicapped person should telephone in advance for information and any special arrangements where available.

Library for the Blind & Physically Handicapped, Free Library of Philadelphia, 919 Walnut St.; 925-3213. Books and magazines are available for adults and children in braille, large print, and recorded form, including *The New York Times.*

Radio Information Center for the Blind, 919 Walnut St.; 922-5450. Special radio programs are provided that include the reading of local newspapers, books, and popular magazines. Special receivers are necessary, but are available for $15 and some are donated to the needy. Daily 10 am–11 pm.

Easter Seal Society for Handicapped Children and Adults, Philadelphia Rehabilitation Center, 3975 Conshohocken Ave.; 879-1000. The Society offers a wide variety of services to all handicapped people.

Travel Service for the Handicapped, Moss Rehabilitation Hospital, Travel Information Center, 12th and Tabor Rd.; 329-5715. Information is available regarding the needs of handicapped travelers in Philadelphia, as well as those traveling in the United States and abroad.

STUDENTS

Students visiting Philadelphia will find camaraderie at the many colleges and universities in the area. Your most important document is your student identification card, which certifies your student status and helps stretch the travel budget. Always ask if a student discount is applicable for accommodations or travel systems, at restaurants, theaters, cultural programs, museums, and at places of entertainment.

Lodging —————————————————————————————

American Youth Hostels, 35 S. 3rd St.; 925-6004. This organization offers 18 youth hostels in Pennsylvania. An AYH membership card allows you to use these hostels and all others in the United States. The card costs $20 for ages 18 through 54 and $10 for those under 17 and over 60. **Chamounix Mansion,** for example, is one such hostel. Located on Chamounix Drive in West Fairmount Park, it charges $4 per night for AYH members, as well as for those with International Youth Hostel membership. Fee is $5 per night for non-members. Kitchen facilities are available. Closed from December 15–June 15. Call 878-3676.

International House, 3701 Chestnut St.; 387-5125. This is a high-rise dormitory on the University of Pennsylvania campus with housing for foreign students and transients.

Philadelphia Colleges and Universities ———

Philadelphia and its surrounding counties are graced by more than 40 colleges and universities, which offer degrees and advanced degrees in every conceivable course of study. Among them are:

Art Institute of Philadelphia, 1622 Chestnut St.; 567-7080.

Community College of Philadelphia, 1700 Spring Garden St.; 751-8000.

Drexel University, 32nd and Chestnut Sts.; 895-2000.

Hahnemann Medical College, 230 N. Broad St.; 448-7600.

LaSalle College, 1240 N. Broad St.; 951-1000.

The Medical College of Pennsylvania, 3300 Henry Ave.; 842-6000.

Moore College of Art, 20th and Race Sts.; 568-4514.

Pennsylvania College of Optometry, 1200 W. Godfrey Ave.; 424-5900.

Philadelphia College of Art, Broad and Spruce Sts.; 893-3100.

Philadelphia College of Pharmacy & Science, 43rd St. and Kingsessing Mall; 596-8800.

Philadelphia College of Podiatric Medicine, 8th and Race Sts.; 629-0300.

The Philadelphia College of Textiles and Science, School House Lane and Henry Ave.; 951-2700.

St. Joseph's University, 5600 City Ave.; 879-7300.

Temple University, Broad St. and Montgomery Ave.; 787-7000.

University of Pennsylvania, 34th and Market Sts.; 243-5000.

Colleges and Universities in Suburban Philadelphia

Bryn Mawr College, Bryn Mawr; 525-1000.

Haverford College, Haverford; 642-7644.

Rosemont College, Rosemont; 527-0200.

Swarthmore College, Swarthmore; 544-7900.

Villanova University, Villanova; 527-2100.

Popular Student Hangouts

Carney's, 36th and Chestnut St; 382-7400. Students love to mingle here and enjoy the good food and the neat music system.

Cavanaugh's, 3132 Market St.; 386-4889. The Jailhouse is a favorite gathering spot in this 50-year-old Philadelphia saloon and restaurant.

Chestnut Cabaret, 38th and Chestnut Sts.; 382-1201. Students love this club for its large stage and dance floor. Dress code; drinks served until 3 am.

Chestnut Street Bar & Grill, 3942 Chestnut St.; 222-4250. This place has the longest sit-down bar on the Penn campus and the largest selection of imported beers in town. DJ on Thursday nights, guitarist on Saturday.

Khyber Pass, 56 S. 2nd St.; 922-0763. This funky, earthy pub features local music every night of the week.

La Terrasse, 3432 Sansom St.; 387-3778. This is a very special restaurant in which to romance that very special person. The menu is French and outstanding. Penn and Drexel students mingle with faculty members at this bar.

Margarita's, 4002 Chestnut St.; 387-4477. A casual Cantina restaurant has good Mexican food available at good prices.

O'Hara's Dining Saloon, 3925 Walnut St.; 382-5195. Sassy Irish atmosphere and unusual munchies.

O'Hara's Fish House, 39th and Chestnut Sts.; 349-9000. You can drink and eat on a shoestring here. Pop and rock by local bands Saturday nights in the lounge.

Smart Alex, 36th and Chestnut Sts.; 386-5556. This multilevel bar and restaurant in the Sheraton University City is especially fun when the six-foot TV screen comes alive with a major sporting event. There's dancing nightly, too. Steaks, hamburgers, and omelettes highlight the menu.

Smokey Joe's. 40th and Walnut Sts.; 222-0770. The carved booths in the rathskeller of this super-popular watering hole date back to the Prohibition years. Food from hamburgers to prime rib.

CHILDREN

Children will enjoy many of the sights listed in this book. Try to accent their visits with some of the fascinating places to eat in Philadelphia, among them, **The Bourse** and **The Gallery,** both of which feature international fast-food and dining. The **Reading Terminal** is another interesting spot to catch a bite to eat; here you will find authentic Pennsylvania Dutch cooking, as well as many more over-the-counter delights.

Remember that Philadelphia is the ice cream capital of the nation, and Reading Terminal offers **Bassett's** ice cream, one of Philly's favorites. Other spots to try the city's ice cream delights are **More Than Just Ice Cream** on Pine Street, **Once Upon a Porch** in Head House Square, and throughout Center City and suburban counties, **Hillary's** and **Baskin-Robbins.**

Undoubtedly at the top of any child's list of places to visit will be the **Philadelphia Zoo** (including the Daniel W. Dietrich Memorial Children's Zoo), and the **Elmwood Park Zoo,** where children can pet animals in their natural habitat. Then there's the **Academy of Natural Science's** mini-museum, **Outside-In.** The **Please Touch Museum,** designed for children seven years or younger, is most unusual, and the only one of its kind. The **Franklin Institute's** many exhibits always fascinate children, especially the **Fels Planetarium's** special programs.

Children love toys, so don't forget to visit the **Perelman Antique Toy Museum.** In Bucks County, there's Big Bird, Bert, and Ernie at **Sesame Place;** in Lancaster County, in addition to Hershey Park, the younger set never misses **Dutch Wonderland.** And after enjoying the spectacular train display at the **Choo Choo Barn** there, they must take a ride on the **Strasburg Railroad** (see ONE-DAY EXCURSIONS).

Throughout the year, many of Philadelphia's theaters and museums offer special programs for children. The **Philadelphia Orchestra** even holds special concerts (see PERFORMING ARTS and SIGHTS).

The **Free Library of Philadelphia** presents 12 popular book concerts, free of charge, for ages 6 through 13 from September through April on Sundays at 2 pm. Call 686-5372.

The **Children's Repertory Company,** an adult professional touring company dedicated to bringing quality theater to children and families in the tri-state area, delights with shows that both entertain and educate. Call 284-1319.

Then there's the **Philadelphia Marionette Theater,** which features Hal Taylor and his 25 marionettes, wood-carved in traditional European style. All virtually come alive in performances of Punch and Judy and Pinocchio. In addition, a museum is available. Admission is $3 per person; a $2 group rate is available, but reservations are a must. Call 879-1213.

FOR RESIDENTS

Philadelphia is your new home. Welcome to the City of Brotherly Love. This is both an exciting time, and, sometimes, a confusing one: locating housing, opening bank accounts, relocating your family, moving furniture, and the adjustment of living in a new area. Here we offer some important facts to help ease this transition period. You will find that Philadelphia and its surrounding counties have a lot to offer. It is a wonderfully exciting place in which to live.

Welcome Services

Welcome Wagon, regional office: 674-5105. This is a nationally-recognized organization that offers friendly assistance, introducing you to local merchants and offering coupons to be used in local stores.

AN INTRODUCTION TO PHILADELPHIA LIVING

Philadelphia is the birthplace of the United States. Both the Declaration of Independence and the Constitution were adopted in Philadelphia's Independence Hall. Very few other cities can match the many historic attractions here.

In addition to the historical attributes, this city takes pride in its world-famous orchestra; the excellent schools of higher education; its many scenic parks, and museums of art, history, and science. Philadelphians also have an enormous pride in their championship sports teams—the football Eagles, hockey Flyers, baseball Phillies, and basketball 76ers.

This city swells with opportunities. It ranks as one of the greatest industrial and commercial centers of the United States.

What often makes a city interesting are the people who reside there. Philadelphia is populated with many European ethnic groups. Virtually every national and racial group in the U.S. lives within this city. Many of these nationalities enjoy sharing their customs through organized programs such as street parties, parades, and information centers. William Penn very appropriately named this city Philadelphia, Greek for "brotherly love."

GEOGRAPHICAL PROFILE

Philadelphia is, by population, the fifth largest city in the United States, with its 45,330 square miles surrounded generously by bounties of nature that include many lakes and rivers, parks, lush woodlands, the rolling green hills of countryside. This rich combination provides us with a vast diversification of industrial endeavors and human pleasures. You may enjoy a visit with a farming family in the Pennsylvania Dutch country or a day rafting down the Delaware River; camping in one of the many state parks or skiing the challenging slopes of the Pocono Mountains. Wherever you go, you will find adventure and warm, hospitable people.

PHILADELPHIA INSIGHT

Automobiles

Auto Insurance

As a new resident, Pennsylvania law requires every driver to carry no-fault insurance; you are required to have a Pennsylvania Insurance Identification card in your possession at all times. These cards are issued at the time of the purchase of insurance. Check with your local insurance agency.

Driver's Licenses

A new resident must obtain a Pennsylvania driver's license within 30 days of establishing residency. The driver's license is good for four years, and the fee is $21.50.

The legal driving age is 16. If you have a driver's license from another state or an international one, you are expected to visit a State Police Examination Point to apply for a Pennsylvania license. Take with you:

1. A valid out-of-state license
2. Your vehicle registration
3. Proof of insurance
4. Proof of birth date

To obtain a license, you must pass an eye test, demonstrate your knowledge of the traffic laws, and pass a driving test. This is done at a State Police Examination point nearest you (refer to the telephone book, under "Government, State").

If you are a new driver, you must obtain a learner's permit before you may drive. To drive with a permit, you must be accompanied by a person who has a valid Pennsylvania license. This person is expected to occupy the seat next to you while you are driving. You may apply for a permit 60 days prior to your 16th birthday, but you will not receive the permit until you are 16.

Before applying for a learner's permit, you need to pass an eye test, a traffic law test, and a physical examination. Consent from a parent or a person over 18 years of age is necessary if you are between 16 and 18 years old. To apply, you also must present proof of your age.

Car inspections are due on a yearly basis. Check your local phone book for the inspection center (almost without exception, a gas station) nearest you.

Emission Control Inspection

State law requires that all owners of passenger cars and/or small trucks in the five-county Philadelphia area are required to have their vehicles inspected for emission control annually.

Inspection stations are located throughout the five-county region. For more information, call 215-698-8100 or toll-free, 800-932-4600.

Reporting of Auto Accidents

If you are involved in an accident, stop your car at or near the scene of the accident. When possible, move your car off the road so that you don't block traffic.

Notify police if the accident involves death or injury, or if the car requires towing. Obtain names and addresses of all people involved in the accident, as well as those of witnesses and of any injured persons.

If the accident involves a parked car and you are unable to locate the owner, leave a note on the car and notify the police. The note should contain your name and address, driver's license number, date and time of accident, and your insurance company's name and policy number.

If the police do not investigate the accident and if it involves death, injury, or a vehicle which requires towing, then forward a written report within five days to the bureau of Safety Programming and Analysis, Department of Transportation, Transportation and Safety Building, Harrisburg, PA 17120. To report such an accident by phone, call 717-787- 2855.

Banking

The first United States financial institution was established in Philadelphia, where today there are 20 major commercial banks, trust companies, and savings and loan companies. There are many others, however, mostly branches in the surrounding counties.

Philadelphia banks continue to move forward with the changing times. With the upcoming changes in federal laws, we will soon see the development of interstate banking with neighboring states, in particular. Electronic banking is prevalent throughout the area, and in the not-too-distant future, we will do our banking from home through computerized communication.

Banks vary with the services they provide, so shop around and choose the one which serves your needs best. For information, call the Pennsylvania Department of Financial Institutions at 717-787-1854, or the Federal Reserve Bank of Philadelphia at 574-6000.

Chambers of Commerce ─────────────

Chambers of Commerce are ideal sources of general information for newcomers and prospective home buyers. They are vital to the development of business, and most companies subscribe to their many services to the community.

Available through the Philadelphia Chamber of Commerce is a newcomers' kit which includes maps, transportation information, a guide to city services, and brochures on activities and historical sights. The fee for this kit is nominal.

Below is a list of chambers in principal areas of metropolitan Philadelphia and the outlying regions:

Philadelphia: **Greater Philadelphia Chamber of Commerce;** 545-1234.

Montgomery County: **Greater Jenkintown Chamber of Commerce;** 887-5122.

Delaware County: **Delaware County Chamber of Commerce;** 565-3677.

Chester County: **Greater Downtown Chamber of Commerce;** 269-2145.

Bucks County: **Central Bucks Chamber of Commerce:** 345-7051.

Churches, Synagogues, and Temples ─────────

Sometimes Philadelphia is referred to as the "Quaker City" because it was the Quakers—the first settlers of Pennsylvania—who laid the foundation of religious thought and custom here. Today, there is the widest possible variety of religious and ethnic groups in the area. The largest denomination is Roman Catholicism. Other denominations include Baptist, Episcopalian, Lutheran, Methodist, Jewish, and many others. The principle established 300 years ago still prevails today: "Religious freedom to all."

Churches in Philadelphia are actively involved with the community. They offer assistance in many areas of social service, including daycare, health care, food programs, and activities for senior citizens and teenagers.

For more information regarding your religious organization, call one of the major denominational and ecumenical organizations listed below:

Pennsylvania Baptist Association,
711 S. 12th St.; 922-6691.
The Religious Society of Friends,
1501 Cherry St.; 241-7210.
United Presbyterian Church in the
U.S.A., 453 State St., Lancaster;
732-1842.
Lutheran Church of America, 2900
Queen Lane; 438-0600.

Reformed Church in America, 1300
Bristol Rd., Churchville; 357-5636.
United Church of Christ, 620 Main
St.; Collegeville; 489-2056.
United Methodist Church, P.O. Box
820, Valley Forge; 666-9090.
Catholic Information Center, 936
Market St.; 587-3520.
Jewish Family Service, 1610 Spruce
St.; 545-3290.

Education

Public Schools, Primary and Secondary

Public education is free in Pennsylvania for children from kindergarten through the 12th grade. There are more than 200 public schools in Philadelphia alone.

As a newcomer, you are certainly concerned with your child's education. It is often a major consideration in choosing where you will live. For information regarding the elementary schools, it is suggested that you contact the Board of Education at 299-7665, or the Superintendent of Parochial Schools in the district you have in mind. Set an appointment with the school principal to inspect the school and discuss the curriculum and special courses for the gifted and handicapped.

The Philadelphia school district works to meet the needs of the handicapped and exceptional students. If there is no appropriate program within your district, it will place your children within state-approved private schools, free of charge.

The Philadelphia school system also offers Magnet schools, which offer studies not available in the regular schools. Students need to apply for admission. Career education, including vocational-technical training and courses, is found within the regular schools or at the four independent vocational high schools. Alternative education programs are offered primarily to juniors and seniors and are designed to increase learning experiences and other diverse career opportunities. Adult education programs are available throughout the city and are free of charge to anyone 18 and older who wishes to earn a high school diploma.

Public school kindergarten is available to 5-year-olds. Children entering the first grade must be at least 6-years-old before September 1 of the entering year. Enrollment requires your child's birth certificate and immunization documents, and for a transfer student, the latest report card.

For phone numbers of the local school board in your district, refer to the yellow pages of your telephone book under "Schools."

In the suburbs, the elementary schools are broken down by county into school districts. Many of these schools are rated among the finest in the United States.

Each school district has its own school board. Once you have determined the county where you may be living, call the school administrative office within your district and make an appointment with the superintendent. He or she will be able to answer any questions you may have.

Private Schools

Philadelphia has a wealth of excellent private schools, many of which are located in the suburbs. In all, there are at least 62 private schools in the area.

For more information on accredited private schools, a booklet may be obtained from the **Middle States Association of Colleges and Secondary Schools,** 3624 Market St., Philadelphia 19104, or call 662-5600. Also, your local library has an invaluable reference book, **The Handbook of Private Schools,** which provides pertinent information as well as the general characteristics of each school.

For Catholic parochial schools, call the **Catholic Archdiocese of Philadelphia** at 587-3500.

Colleges and Universities

Philadelphia boasts of its major impact on higher education and with good reason. There are 89 colleges and universities in the area, many of them offering degrees in medicine, law, music, art, religion, business, and science.

Major Philadelphia and suburban colleges and universities are listed in the Special Traveler chapter.

Government ————————————————

City Government

Philadelphia's is a Mayor-Council form of government. The Mayor is the chief executive office of the city and is responsible for the administrative functions of the city. The elected Mayor appoints a managing director who, with the Mayor's approval, appoints the commissioners heading each department. The legislative branch of the city's government is composed of 17 members of the City Council. Ten councilmembers represent the city districts, and seven of them are elected at large. Elections for mayor and councilmen are held every four years; city representatives are elected every three years.

County Government

The surrounding counties of Philadelphia are, by and large, governed by a Board of Commissioners. Refer to the information below for a synopsis by county.

Montgomery County, Court House, Norristown, PA 19401; 278-3000. A board of county commissioners.

Delaware County, County Court House, Media, PA 19063; 891-4000. Operates under a Home Rule Charter. Five county councilmembers are elected.

Chester County, County Court House, West Chester, PA 19380; 431-6000. Its Board of County Commissioners is comprised of three members.

Bucks County, Court House, Doylestown, PA 18901; 348-2911. Its Board of County Commissioners consists of three members.

Congressional Districts

Philadelphia has five representatives; Montgomery County, three; Chester County, two; Delaware County, two; and Bucks County, one.

U.S. Senators from Philadelphia

Senator John H. Heinz III, Republican, 9456 William Green Federal Building, 6th and Arch Sts.; Philadelphia 19106.

Senator Arlen Specter, Republican, 9400 William Green Federal Building, 6th and Arch Sts.; Philadelphia 19106.

Senatorial elections are held every six years.

Health Care/Philadelphia

Philadelphia is one of the leading medical centers of the world. The city as well as the suburbs have all types of general and specialized hospitals. Wherever you reside, you will find an excellent full-service hospital nearby.

Medical schools, health institutions, and physicians work together to provide the best possible medical care. Good quality and comprehensive services are available at reasonable prices. At most clinics, both specialized and general, you will find services on a par with those found in private practices. Information and listings are available from the Delaware Valley Hospital Council, 1315 Walnut St., Philadelphia 19107.

Hospitals

Of the 52 hospitals in Philadelphia, we have listed some below:

Albert Einstein Medical Center, 1429 S. 5th St. (southern division) or York and Tabor Rds. (northern division); 456-7890.

Booth Maternity Center, 6051 Overbrook Ave.; 878-7800.

Chestnut Hill Hospital, 8835 Germantown Ave.; 248-8200.

Children's Hospital of Philadelphia, 34 Civic Center Blvd.; 596-9100.

The Graduate Hospital, One Graduate Plaza; 893-2000.

Hahnemann Medical College and Hospital, 230 N. Broad St.; 448-7000.

Lankenau Hospital, Haverford and City Aves., Overbrook; 645-2000.

Philadelphia Center for Young Adult Psychiatry, 111 N. 49th St.; 471-2128.

Scheie Eye Institute, 51 N. 39th St.; 662-8100.
St. Christopher's Hospital for Children, 2600 N. Lawrence; 427-5000.
St. Joseph's Hospital, 16th and Girard; 787-9000.
Temple University Hospital, Broad and Ontario Sts.; 221-2000.
Thomas Jefferson University Hospital, 11th and Walnut Sts.; 928-6000.
University of Pennsylvania Hospital, 3400 Spruce St.; 662-4000.
Wills Eye Hospital, 9th and Walnut Sts.; 928-3000.

Medical Facilities for Specialized Treatment and Aid

Alcoholics Anonymous, 545-4023.
Children's Hospital, 596-9100.
Crisis Intervention Service, 686-4420.
Poison Control, 922-5523.
Rape Crisis Center, 922-3434.
Renfrew Center, 475 Spring Lane; 482-5353. Specializes in eating disorders such as bulimia and anorexia nervosa.

Referral Associations

Dental Society of Philadelphia, 925-6050.
Department of Health, 686-1776.
Philadelphia County Medical Society, 563-5343.
Planned Parenthood, 592-4112.

Health Care/Montgomery County ———

Hospitals

Abington Memorial Hospital, 1200 Old York Rd., Abington; 576-2000.
Bryn Mawr Hospital, Bryn Mawr Ave., Bryn Mawr; 896-3000.
Montgomery Hospital, 1300 Powell St., Norristown; 631-3000.
Pottstown Memorial Medical Center, High St. and Firestone Blvd., Pottstown; 327-7000.
Suburban General Hospital, 2701 DeKalb St., Norristown; 278-2000.

Medical Facilities for Specialized Treatment and Aid

Alcoholics Anonymous, 642-9679.
Montgomery County Mental Health Emergency Service, 279-6100.
Montgomery County Emergency, 279-6100.
Poison Control, 648-1043.
Rape Crisis Center, 277-5200.

Referral Associations

Dental Society, 925-6050.
Pennsylvania Department of Health, 631-2280.
Planned Parenthood, 279-6095.

Health Care/Delaware County ——————

Hospitals

Crozier-Chester Medical Center, 15th St. and Upland Ave., Chester; 447-2000.
Delaware County Memorial Hospital, Landsdowne and Keystone Aves., Drexel Hill; 284-8100.
Havertown Community Hospital, 2000 Old West Chester Pike, Havertown; 645-3600.
Riddle Memorial Hospital, Baltimore Pike, Media; 566-9400.
Sacred Heart General Hospital (north division), 248 N. Marple, Haverford; 527-5230.
Tri-County Hospital, Sproul and Thompson Rds.; Springfield; 328-9200.

Medical Facilities for Specialized Treatment and Aid

Alcoholism Council of Delaware County, 566-8143.
Delaware County Medical Society, 559-3833.
Dental Society of Chester and Delaware Counties, 544-4111.
Emergency Crisis Intervention, 565-4300.
Planned Parenthood Association of Southeastern Pennsylvania, 876-2591.
Poison Control Center, 494-0721.

Health Care/Chester County ——————

Hospitals

Chester County Hospital, 701 E. Marshall St., West Chester; 696-7700.
Coatesville Hospital, 300 Strode Ave., Coatesville; 384-9000.
Paoli Memorial Hospital, Lancaster Ave., Paoli; 648-1000.
Phoenixville Hospital, 140 Nutt Rd., Phoenixville; 933-9281.

Medical Facilities for Specialized Treatment and Aid

Alcoholics Anonymous, 323-3450.
Crisis Intervention Service for Mental Health, 873-1000.
Poison Information Service, 648-1043.
Rape Crisis Council, 692-7273.

Referral Associations

Chester County Health Department, 431-6225.
Chester/Delaware Dental Society, 544-4111.
Planned Parenthood of Chester County, 436-8645.

Health Care/Bucks County ─────────

Hospitals

Delaware Valley Hospital, Pond and Wilson Sts., Bristol; 785-1266.
Doylestown Hospital, Belmont Ave. and Spruce St., Doylestown; 345-6500.
Eastern State School and Hospital, 3740 Lincoln Highway, Trevose; 671-3474.
Quakertown Community Hospital, 11th St. and Park Ave., Quakertown; 536-2400.
Warminster General Hospital, 225 Newtown Rd., Warminster; 674-4400.

Medical Facilities for Specialized Treatment and Aid

Alcoholics Anonymous, 788-9920.
Bucks County Department of Health, 343-2800.
Bucks County Department of Health/Mental Retardation, 343-2800.
Bucks County Mental Health Society, 757-5952.
Bucks County Emergency Health Council, 348-2911.
Bucks County Fire and Ambulance Dispatch Center,
    Lower Bucks: 547-5222.
    Central Bucks: 345-1411.
    Upper Bucks: 795-2904.
Planned Parenthood Association of Bucks County, 785-4591.

Referral Associations

Bucks County Community Information and Referral—757-6794, 343-3005, 345-7515, and 249-9311.

Home Decorating ─────────

Decorating your new home is a creative challenge which is a pleasure for some, but a confusing chore for others. For everyone the home is meant to be a tranquil place, a place of comfort, a reflection of you and your family.

John Wanamaker, Strawbridge & Clothier, and Bambergers, are just a few of several department stores which offer a staff of decorators whose services may be complementary to your style.

One exciting concept, a wholesale showroom complex for interior design, is the Market Place at 2400 Market Street. The main function of The Market Place is to display, in 53 showrooms, everything for the home: furniture, carpets, fabrics, wallcoverings, lamps, and accessories. Designers often shop here for their clients. Generally the showrooms are not open to the public, except when specially arranged, usually through a designer.

As a consumer seeking the services of a designer, information may be obtained through the Eastern Pennsylvania chapter, The American Society of International Designers, 568-3884.

Jury Duty

For the state and county courts, jurors are called from the registered voter lists of persons 18 and older. The Petit Jury and the Grand Jury are the two levels of court service in the state federal court. Jurors are called from the ten districts. Exceptions include: convicted felons who have not had their rights restored; doctors, lawyers, teachers, policemen, firemen, elected officials; those with a physical handicap, or those 70 years of age or older, and primary caretakers of children ten years and under.

There are two weeks of duty at $30 a day, plus a mileage allowance for those who serve in federal court.

The above information does not necessarily apply to the county courts. Contact your county courthouse for details.

Legal Services

For references call the Lawyer Referral and Information Service (686-1701) or the Philadelphia Bar Association (238-6300).

County referrals are:

Montgomery County—**Legal Aid Society,** 275-5400.

Delaware County—**Legal Assistance Association, Inc.,** 874-8421.

Chester County—**Legal Aid of Chester County,** 436-9150.

Bucks County—**Legal Aid of Bucks County,** 348-9447.

The Philadelphia Bar Association offers free taped legal information by phone, Dial Law at 238-1131, weekdays between 9 am–4:30 pm. Refer to the phone book in the blue pages for the list of numbers to call for various legal questions.

Libraries

The Free Library of Philadelphia (686-5310) has a central library at Logan Square, 19th and Vine Streets. In addition to the main library, there are 49 neighborhood branches and three regional libraries; refer to the white pages of the phone book under Free Library of Philadelphia for locations and phone numbers. A free Library Borrowers Card may be obtained at any of the libraries.

Major county libraries are:

Abington Free Library, 885-5180.

Chester County Library, 363-0884.

Free Library of Springfield Township, 836-5300.

Lower Merion Library Association, 527-1280.

Pottstown Public Library, 326-2532.

West Chester Public Library, 696-1721.

For the Library for the Blind and Physically Handicapped, call 925-3213.

Local Laws

Curfews

Minors (17 years and under) are forbidden to be in public places from 10:30 pm until 6 am, except on Friday and Saturday nights when the time is extended to midnight. Exceptions are minors accompanied by a parent, minors who have been sent on an errand by a parent, and minors employed during the curfew hours. Parents of violators will be notified by the police. A second violation may bring a fine or imprisonment.

Liquor Laws

State Law requires that you must be 21 to buy and to be served liquor. You are also required to have a liquor I.D. card. An application for an I.D. card may be obtained from a local state store or by writing to the Liquor Control Board. Possession of a photo driver's license is also acceptable I.D for service and purchases.

In Pennsylvania, all alcoholic beverages except beer are sold in State Liquor Stores. Beverage distributors sell beer.

An establishment selling liquor on Sunday must have a Sunday Sales Permit; by law they may serve liquor from 1 pm–2 am.

Property Laws

Philadelphia has established firm zoning laws that require certain procedures for changes in residential districts from one use to another. Variances or minor changes of a structure within the same zoning classification require obtaining a work permit from the Licenses and Inspection Department at City Hall.

In the surrounding counties, the laws differ from one county to the other, or from each borough. Contact your township building for clarification.

Medical

See Health Care in previous section.

Newspapers and Publications

The two major newspapers are The Philadelphia Inquirer (morning paper) 854-2000, and The Philadelphia Daily News (evening paper) 854-2000.

Popular Philadelphia neighborhood papers include 41 weeklies from the Associated Neighborhood Newspapers, 922-3555.

Other small newspapers from the surrounding counties include:

Bucks County Tribune (Horsham) 675-6600.

Chestnut Hill Local (Chestnut Hill) 248-4250.

Daily Local News (West Chester) 696-1775.
King of Prussia Courier (King of Prussia) 265-0775.
Main Line Times (Ardmore) 473-6050.
Suburban and Wayne Times (Wayne) 688-3000.
The most recognized Philadelphia magazine is the *Philadelphia Magazine* (545-3500), which is published monthly.

Pets

Laws require rabies vaccinations for pets by a licensed veterinarian. Pets must be confined to the owner's property except when on a leash. Dogs running at large will be picked up by the Animal Control Unit, and the owner will be fined.

Laws require every dog owner to buy an annual license.

In 1981, the City Council enacted the "Pooper-Scooper" law which places the responsibility on the owners for cleaning up their pet's litter. Violators will be fined.

For additional information call the SPCA (426-6800) or the Women's SPCA (225-4500). There are local SPCA's in the suburban areas.

Public Services

Philadelphia

City of Philadelphia Services are supplied by the following:
Electric: **Philadelphia Electric Co.;** 841-4141.
Natural Gas: **Philadelphia Gas Works;** 235-1212.
Water/Sewage: **Philadelphia Water Co.;** 686-3900.
Garbage collections:
Household pickup for trash and garbage is free for Philadelphia residents. Each is collected separately and must be placed in separate containers: garbage in tightly fastened metal containers; trash into covered containers, or sturdy bags securely tied; and newspaper and magazines tied into bundles. For information regarding pick up days for your area, call 686-5560 (trash) and 686-5564 (garbage).

The suburban counties are supplied by the following:

Montgomery County

Electric: **Pennsylvania Power and Light Co.,** 437-4441. **Philadelphia Electric Co.;** 272-2121.
Natural Gas: **Philadelphia Electric Co.;** 272-2121.
Water: **Philadelphia Suburban Water Co.;** 525-7300.
Sewage: There are many authorities in the county. Call the Montgomery County Sewer Authority. Fee for services.

Delaware County

Electric: **Philadelphia Electric Co.**, 494-5141 or 645-1600.
Natural Gas: **Philadelphia Electric Co.**; 494-1200.
Water: **Philadelphia Suburban Water Co.**; 525-7300. Other water services are privately and municipally operated. Refer to the Pennsylvania Department of Environmental Resource, 717-631-2400.
Sewage: There are 13 sewer authorities in Delaware County. Fee for services.

Chester County

Electric: **Philadelphia Electric Co.**; 384-3000.
Natural Gas: **Philadelphia Electric Co.**; 384-3000. **Oxford Gas Co.**; 932-2000.
Water: Water services are privately and municipally operated. See above for phone number.
Sewage: Refer to the Municipal Authorities. Fee for services.

Bucks County

Electric: **Philadelphia Electric Co.**; 672-8161. **Pennsylvania Power and Light**; 437-4441.
Natural Gas: **Philadelphia Electric Co.**; 672-8161.
Water: Water services are privately and municipally operated. See above for phone number.
Sewage: **Bucks County Water and Sewage Authority.** Fee for services.

Taxes

Individual Income Tax

Philadelphia requires a tax on all sources of income unless they are exempt by statute. Employers are required to withhold state income tax for both the resident and non-resident employees (except New Jersey).

Property Tax

Property taxes are levied by counties, municipalities, schools, and special districts. A 4-mill tax is applied on the market value of intangible personal property (real estate). Philadelphia homeowners should refer to the Property Tax Assessment Committee for questions regarding property taxes.

A state sales and use tax of six percent is added to all retail purchases, rentals, uses, and consumption of tangible goods, personal property, and special services (take-home food and clothing are exempt). For clarification of what is and is not taxable, write for a free booklet to Pennsylvania Department of Revenue, Strawberry Square, Harrisburg, PA, 17105.

City Wage Tax

The city of Philadelphia has a wage tax of 4.96 percent of the gross income for those who work and reside within the boundaries of Philadelphia. For those who work in Philadelphia but do not reside there, the tax is 4.31 percent Real Estate Tax.

This tax is $67.50 per $1000 of assessed value.

TV and Radio ───────────────────────

Television

There are many television stations available to you. The VHF TV stations include Channels 3 (NBC), 6 (ABC), and 12 (PBS). On UHF, there are channels 17, 29, and 48.

Cable television is beginning to make its impact on the Philadelphia area. Some areas are fully serviced by one or more companies. To inquire about the availability of cable television in your area, contact your local Township Office.

Radio

The Philadelphia area offers many excellent radio stations. There are more than 30 radio stations in the eight-county area (see MATTERS OF FACT).

Volunteering ───────────────────────

For those people who wish to volunteer their time and talents, call Volunteer Action Council, 568-6360. Their primary function is to screen you for your interests, and they will then place you accordingly.

Voting ───────────────────────

1. 18-years-old by the day after election.
2. A resident 30 days prior to election.
3. A citizen of the U.S. 30 days prior to registration.

It is required that you register to vote at any courthouse. Take with you proof of age (driver's license, birth certificate, etc.) and proof of residency (rental agreement or home sale agreement). To register by mail, obtain a mail-in registration form from the following places—borough or city office, township office, U.S. Post Office, Pennsylvania State Liquor Store, or free library.

For further information, contact your County Board of Elections:

Philadelphia— 686-3469 or 686-3943.
Montgomery County— 278-3275.
Delaware County— 891-2271.
Chester County— 431-6410.

Bucks County— 348-2911.

The local League of Women Voters (922-4499) is a non-partisan, informed source which may be able to assist you with registration requirements and provide information on elected state and community representatives.

PHILADELPHIA REAL ESTATE

An Overview

Philadelphia is often referred to as the "city of homes." As an incoming resident, you will find that this city has many diverse neighborhoods, with a variety of styles and concepts. The prices for residential real estate are 10 to 25 percent less than prices for comparable homes in most other metropolitan areas.

Each Sunday, *The Philadelphia Inquirer* has a comprehensive Real Estate section. The Chamber of Commerce offers an in-depth briefing on the region in the Relocation Center, as well as Real Estate brochures.

Information and Referral

The Board of Realtors has information on residential property and a list of realtors. Contact the Board of Realtors in the area in which you are interested. Listed below are Boards of Realtors:

Philadelphia 732-5980.
Montgomery County, Eastern 887-7979.
                    Central 272-0667.
Delaware County 543-3620.
Chester County 363-2056.
Bucks County 788-7816.

Other sources include the Apartment Referral Service, 638-9898, the Philadelphia Home Builders, 732-1004, and the Real Estate Commission of Harrisburg, 1-800-822-2113.

Buying and Renting

Consider the many variables that confront you when you are seeking to buy or rent a home. The proximity of your residence to your place of employment is important. For those who are employed in city government jobs, there is the requirement which states that you must reside within the city limits. Be clear on the geographical territory according to the rule before you begin looking. Spend time checking out the neighborhood of your choice. Consider less space, for a better location. Be certain of how much you

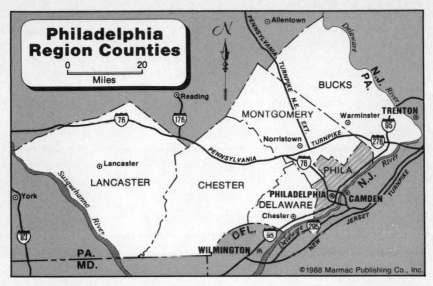

can afford. Inquire about school systems. Many apartment complexes have exquisite landscaping, pools, social centers, racquet sports, and health clubs.

The season from April through October is regarded as the key time when renters select their accommodations for the coming year.

Regional and Neighborhood Profiles

As in many other big cities, Philadelphia's close-in residential areas are experiencing a resurgence of popularity. If you want old-world charm at a reasonable price, consider Old City, University City, or Overbrook Park.

The following is an analysis in brief of some of Greater Philadelphia's most recognized neighborhoods to facilitate your choice and introduce you to the many possibilities for settling in. Most civic associations have newsletters; ask your real estate agent to make these available to you. You can sense the spirit of a neighborhood from these publications, along with your inspection of houses, condominiums, and apartments.

Public transportation, SEPTA, is available to all parts of the city within the perimeter and beyond to the suburbs. SEPTA also operates a network of subway-elevated systems, trolley lines, and bus services. For a street and transit map which shows the scheduled routes, write to Southeast Pennsylvania Transportation Authority, 200 West Wyoming Ave., Philadelphia, PA 19140; there is a small fee.

Intown Neighborhoods

Center City's ability to attract a growing number of home buyers has been linked to the ever-increasing employment market. Developers are concentrating on developing new vacant properties, upgrading existing housing, and converting industrial buildings to residential use. Federal tax incentives have encouraged restoration of old historical properties.

The in-town neighborhoods in brief profile are:

Society Hill. South of Center City lies Society Hill, one of Philadelphia's chief historical neighborhoods. Restoration of this area began in the 1950s, and is now nearly completed. Once a wholesale food center, it is now characterized by restored 18th-century rowhouses and some contemporary structures as well. It is considered to be among the more exclusive residential neighborhoods in the city.

Abbott Square is a condominium complex within Society Hill. These lovely units were completed in 1985.

Rittenhouse Square. This area was developed between 1850 and 1880 as a residential neighborhood. Many of these large 19th-century homes are still maintained as private homes, others have been converted into apartments or condominiums. This affluent area is comprised primarily of single-person and non-family households, and most are rentals. In the warm weather months, this square is a popular site for flower shows, art exhibits, concerts, and a general gathering place.

Old City is located in the northeast corner of Center City. It was the original commercial center of the city. Today, the area is characterized by obsolete industrial loft buildings. These once old, decaying warehouses have been converted into spacious, charming, and architecturally creative spaces. The area attracts mostly young, single professionals and childless married couples. Rentals are moderate to expensive.

Northern Liberties is something of a continuation of the Old City in that it has become the latest habitation of local artists who are often in search of cheap, well-lighted space. Commercial properties are being converted into airy and expensive spaces. This area ia a mixed bag, sociologically and structurally. Developers will undoubtedly be paying close attention to this location. Rentals are moderate to expensive.

Spring Garden/Franklin Town is another neighborhood in the Art Museum area. These large 19th-century rowhouses have seen substantial reinvestment activity through private funding. It recently was designated as a historic district by the Commonwealth of Pennsylvania. The location is popular with young folks and couples with children. There is a wide range of rental prices.

Bella Vista is one of the oldest areas in South Philadelphia. Here you'll find the Italian Market, which is widely known as a mecca for food shoppers. The neighborhood is characterized by two- and three-story rowhouses and is one of the more affordable areas. Significant residential reinvestment activity began in the latter part of the 1970s. Primarily a blue-collar neighborhood with rental from inexpensive to expensive.

Chinatown is located in the north central part of the city. It is best known for its streetscape and many restaurants. An exceptionally large part of this area is rental. Housing values continue to rise quickly each year. In the past few years much attention has been placed on new subsidized housing construction. The residents are predominately foreign born.

Penn's Landing is located on Philadelphia's waterfront. It has exciting plans for real estate development. Residential towers and low-rise condominiums will be incorporated with shops and attractive landscaping. The biggest appeal is having a home with a waterfront view within the city. Construction is still in the planning stages.

Fairmount Park. Just outside of the city in the upper Roxborough area, surrounded on three sides by Fairmount Park, is a semirural resident enclave of single homes. There are trees and open spaces, a wish come true for the city dweller, especially for those who are required to live in the city limits.

Chestnut Hill is a posh suburb within Philadelphia County. For the most part, "The Hill" is a town of stately homes, fine shops, and superb restaurants. Many of the residents have passed their homes down from one generation to the next. Some of the best private schools in the country were founded here. Commuter train services into the city are excellent. Expect rentals to be expensive.

Suburban Neighborhoods

Philadelphia's Main Line is a series of communities located along the "main line" of the old Pennsylvania Railroad from Philadelphia to Paoli. As an area, the Main Line is considered symbolic of wealthy society and gracious suburban living. Here you will find turn-of-the-century estates with glorious gardens and great tall trees. The area boasts of some of the best schools in the country. There are some of the country's most challenging golf courses, as well as some of the best known country clubs, swim clubs, and equestrian centers. The Main Line offers a variety of housing styles. In recent years there has been a surge in townhouse and condominium construction. Many units offer affordable prices, a variety of architectural styles, and recreational facilities. Contact the Main Line Board of Realtors for assistance in getting you acquainted with the area, call 527-0444.

Montgomery County

Montgomery County has a diverse mix of religious, social, and income groups. Generally, it is a community comprised of upper middle class families. There are many small, older communities with garden complexes, new townhouses or condominiums, a few high-rises, and single homes. Rentals and homes run from expensive to very expensive.

Delaware County

In Delaware County, as a rule, the farther north and west you go, the nicer and more expensive the housing becomes. Springfield, Media, Wallingford, and Swarthmore are lovely and expensive; Upper Darby, Drexel Hill, Landsdowne, Havertown, Pilgrim Gardens, and Alden are more reasonably priced. It is predicted that this section will become the housing renaissance area of the 90s. For rent, there are mostly older converted houses, garden apartments, mid-rise buildings, and single family homes. Prices range from moderate to high.

Chester County

Chester County is tucked into rolling hills and meadows. An afternoon drive may take you through historic Valley Forge, through wooded bridges, passing a fox hunt, or stopping at an inn for brunch. There are acres and acres of preserved open spaces wonderful for picnics, walking, bicycling, riding, or for living. You'll find many old stone farmhouses, Cape Cods, and contemporaries with solar details. In recent years developers have put an emphasis on townhouses and condominiums with recreational facilities and beautiful landscapes. Rental prices vary from moderate to expensive.

Bucks County

Bucks County is a rustic artist community. The scenic area abounds with rolling farmlands, charming country inns which offer bed-and-breakfast, elegant dining, or simple country fare. A home may be a converted barn or mill. Many of the village shops have maintained their original style of yesteryear. There is much growth in new housing construction. It is a young family area. Prices are moderate.

HOME AND GARDEN
SHOPPING NEEDS

Air Conditioning Repairs—AAA Appliance Corporation; 455-1100.

Appraisals—Samuel T. Freeman & Co.; 563-9275.

Auto Repairs—Costa's Auto Hospital; 483-7525.

Blinds and Shades—Pemper's; 537-0515.

Building Materials—10th Street Lumber & Millwork, Inc.; 225-4050.

Carpet and Rug Cleaners— A. Adams Rug Cleaners; 423-7979.

Cleaners—Roxy Cleaners; 649-3089.

Doors—Doors Unlimited; 843-7200.

Electrical Repairs—Collier Hastings; 247-7407.

Furniture Rentals—IFR Rental Furniture; 482-8100.

Furniture Repairs and Upholstery—Calico Corners; 563-2814.

Glass (Auto and Home Mirrors)—Jem Auto Glass; 739-2624.

Home Accessories—Urban Outfitters; 569-3131 and 222-3358.

Lamp Repairs—Herbert Kanig Company; 644-0926.

Landscaping Nursery—Waterloo Gardens; 293-0800.

Leather Cleaning—Forest Launders and Cleaning, Inc.; 331-5750.

Locks—Arrow Safe and Lock Service; 535-2345.

Painting, Residential—Joseph A. Davis & Sons; 748-0431.

Paintings Restored—Newman Galleries; 563-1779 and 525-0625.

Pest Control—Orkin; 671-9300.

Picture Frames—Custom Frame Shop; 922-5708.

Plaster Moldings and Character Items—Gargoyle's, Ltd.; 629-1700.

Plumbing—Ace Plumbing & Heating Company; 925-5280.

Pool Services—Abbot Complete Pool Service; 426-3434.

Remodeling—Youngstown Builders & Remodelers, Inc.; 426-6969.

Rentals (tools, machines, cleaning equipment)—E-Z Tool Rental; 329-4400.

Silver Repair—Chelsea Silver Plating; 925-1132.

Stained Glass—Scaffer's; 923-2949.

Wrought Iron—Colonial Metal Arts; 879-5850.

LET'S HAVE A PARTY

It's time to try something different for that special occasion. Let us make a few wild and wonderful suggestions. If you can't afford the time researching sites and services for your wedding, birthday party, or whatever the occasion, the following people are excellent for handling all the details from A to Z: **Lockhart and Lockhart Party Planners** (Pam or Peter of Berwyn, 296-9944); **Huber Associates** (Adele and Joel of Radnor, 525-5675); or **Virginia Bloodgood** (Radnor, 688-6378).

Buy The Bus

Climb aboard a motorized replica of the original trolleys that clanged through Fairmount Park. Ask your friends to come along for a celebration (maximum of 31 adults). You can have food, drink, live music, and have the trolley decorated. The minimum is $100 for two hours. Call **Fairmount Park Trolley-Buses**; 879-4044.

Get Me To The Church On Time

If you are looking for the unusual with a touch of colonial and a romantic flair, then how about a horsedrawn carriage to get you to the church? Call **Philadelphia Carriage Co.**, 922-6840.

Rolling Down The River

Landlubbers will enjoy that special birthday, graduation, or retirement party aboard the cruiseship, *The Spirit of Philadelphia*, with cocktail lounges and dance floors. This boat glides out of Penn's Landing down the Delaware River, rain or shine, from around noon and into the moonlight hours. Call **Cruise International**; 923-4993.

Up, Up, And Away In A Balloon

It's your anniversary and you're looking for something really out of the ordinary. Have you experienced soaring in the sky at sunrise or sunset in a hot-air balloon? Glide for an hour or for the day, enjoying a moment you'll never forget. Champagne will be added for the celebration, and if you choose, a picnic lunch may be included. Call **Sky Signs** in Valley Forge; 933-6952.

A Barge Party

Hans and Spooky could be the names of the mules who draw your barge down the Delaware Canal in New Hope. The **New Hope Mule Barge** offers a private barge party for rent. Call 862-2842. Party packages include flowers, music, food, and a stop at a secluded picnic grove an hour and a half out of town. Sit back and enjoy the view of Bucks County countryside.

A Rafting Adventure

For those who thrive on adventure, a rafting trip is a must. Laugh, scream, get soaked, and enjoy the raw beauties of Mother Nature's own health spa. Bring your party to the Lehigh River in the Poconos. All equipment is provided and trained guides will lead your group. A streamside charcoal barbecue lunch is included and maybe a cake will survive the ride.

Christmas Cheer

Have a family party or bring together your favorite families to spend a day celebrating in the Christmas spirit. Begin by driving out to Chester Springs in Chester County to **Proctor Wetherill's** Christmas tree farm; 469-9472. Once you've cut down the perfect tree, take it back to the shed and they will tie it up while you sip a hot drink and warm your hands.

Continue on over to Chadds Ford to the **Brandywine River Museum** for a show of Christmas decorating and interesting art; 459-1900. For the children and the children-at-heart there are displays of antique dolls and model trains.

Just down the road is **Longwood Gardens,** a holiday wonderland during the Christmas month. Stroll through the Christmas Tree Lane of illuminated trees to the indoor gardens which are transformed into a splendor of poinsettias, decorated wreaths and trees, and many other plantings. Organ concerts are featured daily. Call 388-6741. And now . . . to all a good night.

Let's Party With The Animals

The **Philadelphia Zoological Garden** is available for a party with the gorillas and chimps in the Rare Mammal House, or with the snakes in the Reptile House. Animal shows can even be arranged for additional entertainment. Obviously no decorating is needed here; however, you provide the caterer, tables, chairs, and linens. Call 243-1100, ext. 265.

Kids' Time Out

Please Touch Museum is really the name of the place. It is a delightful place to charm a child's friends at birthday time. Everything here is scaled for the children's enjoyment and nothing is off-limits, as the name implies. Closed on Mondays. The Museum is in Philadelphia; call 963-0667.

BITS AND PIECES

For a city as old and historic as Philadelphia, traditions and interesting facts inevitably arise through the years. Here we offer by no means a history lesson, but rather a collection of intriguing information that may enhance your position in some future trivia contest.

Did you know that:

—Since 1871, when William Penn's statue was mounted on the tower of City Hall, it has been traditional that no other building be taller than this monument (548 feet from the top to bottom).

—Philadelphians buy more tickets to professional sporting events than residents of any other city in the nation, including New York and Los Angeles.

—Two people can fit inside one of the pipes of the huge organ at Longwood Gardens.

—Philadelphia has the smallest and most concentrated center of any major city in America. It doesn't extend much beyond the city of William Penn's original plan of more than 300 years ago.

—It is still against the law to sleep in a barber shop and to take a cow to Logan Circle.

—The Benjamin Franklin Parkway is one of the widest streets (250 feet) in the world.

—In 1816, property developers came close to convincing the city fathers that Independence Hall should be torn down and Independence Square divided into housing lots.

—The vending tradition, which is so popular in Philadelphia, dates back to 1723, when Benjamin Franklin bought a loaf of bread from a street peddler.

—The only statue of Charles Dickens in the world is located in Clark Park at 43rd and Baltimore.

—The intersection of Frankford and Cheltenham Avenues is the only one in the world with a cemetery on each of its four corners.

—A giant strawberry is painted on every telephone pole and light standard on Ridge Avenue in the Strawberry Mansion area.

—The width of the stage at the Academy of Music is half the length of a football field.

—Market Street is the oldest business district in the world.

—Philadelphia Brand Cream Cheese, which has been on the market for 106 years, has always been manufactured in upstate New York.

—In Philadelphia, there are 32 bridges spanning the Schuylkill River.

—A manuscript collection of more than 14 million documents fills seven miles of shelves in the Historical Society of Pennsylvania at 13th and Locust Streets.

—William Penn originally planned to call Pennsylvania "Cambria," the ancient name of Wales.

—According to legend, William Penn unwittingly named Fairmount Park, too. As the story goes, he was standing on the hill where the Art Museum is now, gazing across the expanse of green toward the Schuylkill River, when he remarked what a "Faire mount" it was. In any event, the park was included as "Faire Mount" on Thomas Holmes' plan for Philadelphia that was drawn up in 1862.

—John Wilkes Booth played a one-week engagement at the old Arch Street Theater a few months before he assassinated President Abraham Lincoln. (His acting performances were panned by the reviewers.)

—Thomas U. Walter, who designed the dome of the Capitol building in Washington, also designed the four cantilevered stairways in the corners of City Hall.

—The first steel-bladed ice skates were made in 1850 and were known as "Philadelphia skates."

NOTES

Guidebook Order Form

_____ Marmac Guide to Houston and
     Galveston   @ $ 7.95 _____

_____ Marmac Guide to Atlanta   @ $ 7.95 _____

_____ Marmac Guide to Philadelphia @ $ 7.95 _____

_____ Marmac Guide to Los Angeles @ $ 8.95 _____

_____ Marmac Guide to New Orleans @ $ 7.95 _____

_____ Pelican Guide to the Bahamas @ $11.95 _____

_____ Pelican Guide to New Orleans @ $ 4.95 _____

_____ Pelican Guide to Plantation
     Homes of Louisiana   @ $ 4.95 _____

_____ Pelican Guide to Sacramento @ $ 9.95 _____

_____ Pelican Guide to the Ozarks   @ $ 4.95 _____

_____ Pelican Guide to the
     Shenandoah   @ $ 7.95 _____

_____ Pelican Guide to Maryland   @ $ 9.95 _____

_____ Maverick Guide to Hawaii   @ $11.95 _____

_____ Maverick Guide to Australia   @ $11.95 _____

_____ Maverick Guide to New Zealand @ $11.95 _____

Subtotal _____

*Shipping and handling _____

**Sales tax _____

Total enclosed _____

*Add $1.50 for shipping and handling, plus 25 cents for each additional book ordered. **Jefferson parish residents add 8% sales tax, all other Louisiana residents add 4% sales tax.

Prices subject to change without notice.

To: PELICAN PUBLISHING COMPANY
     P.O. Box 189
     Gretna, Louisiana 70054

Please send me the books indicated above.
Name _____
Address _____
City _____ **State** _____ **Zip** _____

THE LEGEND
OF THE MARMAC

The Legend of the Marmac
is obscure and hard to trace.
This fabled bird was one-of-a-kind,
produced by an unusual brace.
Born of the gentle dove,
fathered by the soaring eagle,
with mother's grace and father's strength,
he grew to a bird quite regal.
In his young breast a calling stirred,
a mad desire to wander,
See sights unseen, to make a mark,
for followers to ponder.
Wherever he lighted, travelers delighted,
Passing the word to all who heard:
"Follow the flight of the Marmac."